IDEAS ABOUT THE FUTURE.

A History of Futurism, 1794-1982

Second Edition, with Bibliography

by

Burnham P. Beckwith, Ph.D.

Published by B.P. Beckwith
656 Lytton Ave., (C430), Palo Alto CA 94301
Price $12.50, postpaid

Copyright by Burnham P. Beckwith
ISBN No. 0-9603262-6-X

PREFACE TO FIRST EDITION

This book is the first history of scientific thought about future social events and trends. It covers almost 200 years, 1794 to 1982. It includes an introduction, critical essays on 25 different writers on the future, and a brief concluding restatement of some of the author's own major predictions. Only the essay on Condorcet has been previously published (<u>World Future Society Bulletin</u>, July, 1981).

One of the best ways to prepare to make scientific predictions about the future is to review the predictions made by the most able and/or stimulating earlier futurists, and their reasons for making them. Unfortunately, these predictions are scattered among hundreds of different books and articles, and no history of them has been available. As a result, most futurists have paid little attention to the brilliant contributions of their predecessors. They rarely explain whether their own ideas are original in part or whole. In other, more firmly established disciplines, writers usually take pains to acknowledge the contributions of their predecessors, and to explain when and why their own ideas are original. Futurists should begin to adopt these customs.

I am well aware that this brief history is very incomplete, that my selection of futurists for review is arbitrary, and that the author is biased. I hope that some other author will soon publish a more complete, more perceptive, and more objective history of futurism.

Burnham P. Beckwith

Palo Alto, CA
April, 1984

PREFACE TO THE SECOND EDITION

The only change in the second edition is the addition of an Annotated Bibliography of some 70 books. It favors authors who made many verifiable long-run predictions concerning major social trends, and notes their most significant or unusual forecasts. It does not include books discussed in the text.

Burnham P. Beckwith

September, 1986

TABLE OF CONTENTS

Preface

1.	INTRODUCTION	1
2.	CONDORCET	10
3.	SAINT-SIMON	21
4.	COMTE	29
5.	ALEXIS de TOCQUEVILLE	39
6.	JOHN STUART MILL	51
7.	MARX AND ENGELS	61
8.	EDWARD BELLAMY	74
9.	H.G. WELLS	85
10.	KEYNES	95
11.	J.B.S. HALDANE	106
12.	C.C. FURNAS	114
13.	JAMES BURNHAM	123
14.	JOSEPH A. SCHUMPETER	135
15.	MORRIS L. ERNST	146
16.	GUNNAR MYRDAL	158
17.	FERDINAND LUNDBERG	172
18.	ARNOLD TOYNBEE	182
19.	STUART CHASE	192
20.	DANIEL BELL	199
21.	R.L. HEILBRONER	210
22.	HERMAN KAHN	221

23.	ALVIN TOFFLER	238
24.	JOHN NAISBITT	255
25.	GERARD O'NEILL	264
26.	ADRIAN BERRY	279
27.	MAJOR U.S. SOCIAL TRENDS, 1984-2100	288
	ANNOTATED BIBLIOGRAPHY	304
	INDEX	323
	ABOUT THE AUTHOR	326

INTRODUCTION

1. The Scope and History of Futurism

In its most general use, the term futurism connotes all forecasts of future events. It covers naive, unscientific prophecies as well as scientific predictions of things to come.

Since at least the dawn of civilization, men have eagerly sought to foretell the future. They have used the cracks in turtle shells, the entrails of birds, the stars, holy books, natural disasters, dice, cards, and innumerable other objects, events and methods to forecast coming events. Even today there are thousands of witch doctors, shamans, mediums, astrologers, palm readers, priests, spiritualists, gurus, etc., who still use such prescientific means of predicting the future. For instance, in the U.S. astrologers are far more numerous than astronomers.

By contrast, scientific futurism, the use of scientific methods to predict or forecast the future, is relatively new. It began in France during the French Enlightenment. The first great scientific futurist was Condorcet, the subject of the first essay in this book.

Scientific futurism developed so late because it depended upon the previous invention of the scientific method of investigation, and because it deals with social events and trends, which are more difficult to study than simple physico-chemical changes. Recently interest in it has soared. Since all modern futurism should be scientific, the term futurism is now commonly used as a synonym for scientific futurism.

The innumerable men who forecast the future prices of individual securities or assets are specialized futurists in the broadest sense of the term, but they are not futurists in the narrow and common sense of the term because their forecasts are relatively unimportant. The same reasoning applies to short-range weather forecasts. Futurists restrict their predictions to social events and trends so important that, if verified, the events and trends will be included in histories of the period covered.

Futurists are generalists. They predict social trends and events in a wide variety of fields of social behavior. Ideally they should, and in time will, cover all such fields, but futurism is so new and undeveloped, and professional futurists still so few and young, that few if any futurists have yet tried to cover most or all major fields of social behavior.

In every field of social science there are scientists who have made one or more important predictions about future behavior which falls within their special field of study. Such scientists are not futurists because they are not generalists, but they have provided many predictions and supporting arguments which futurists can and should use.

It may seem that scientific and technological progress are so important that futurists should devote a great deal of time and space to predicting such progress. But it is far more difficult to predict individual scientific and technological advances than to predict social trends and changes. Most of the major social changes which will occur in the next century or two have already been conceived and discussed, but few if any of the great scientific advances of the future have been conceived and published. The futurist can often predict the future social effects of technological advances which have already been made, and he can safely predict continued general technological progress, but he can rarely predict specific individual technological advances. Moreover, such progress and such advances are important to the futurists and the historian only if and when they can have important social consequences. Few individual technological advances have such consequences.

A scientific futurist does not predict what may or can happen; he predicts what probably will happen. In other words, he does not merely describe possible alternative social policies. Nearly all well-rounded or impartial discussions of social problems suggest alternative solutions or policies, but such discussion is not futurism. The body of literature on social problems and possible solutions is a thousand times as large as the literature of futurism because it is far easier to suggest alternative social policies than to predict which of them will be adopted.

A good scientific futurist does not prescribe what he believes ought to happen. Rather, he predicts what will happen, regardless of his own wishes. Scientific futurism ought to be as free of so-called moral judgements and other personal prejudices as biology or geology. But such ideal objectivity is much more difficult to achieve in social than in natural sciences, and futurists have been even less successful than other social scientists in achieving it, probably because wishful thinking about the future is much more tempting than wishful thinking about the past.

2. Futurism, Utopianism, and Science Fiction

Futurism differs radically from both utopian and science fiction. Utopian (and dystopian) ideas are usually presented in novels about imaginary perfect or vastly altered societies, remote in time or space. Futurist ideas are usually presented in nonfiction works which predict gradual changes continuing over a long time in our own society and in other contemporary societies. Futurist predictions are, or should be, based largely on scientific research on recent technological and social changes and are realistic as well as plausible. Utopian predictions may also use such research results, when available, but are far more imaginative and daring, and include much more wishful thinking. Utopian writers have suggested many hypotheses which futurists have tried to verify, and futurists have suggested many future trends which later utopians have then projected much further into the future. Futurists have devoted far more attention than utopians to the modes and rates of social changes, and to the interrelationships between different social changes.

Utopian thought is much older than futurist thought. It goes back at least to Sir Thomas More's Utopia (1516), and perhaps to Plato. Futurist thought goes back only to Condorcet's Sketch (1794). Moreover, far more utopian than futurist works were written in the 18th and 19th Centuries. Only since about 1950 has the volume of new futurist literature perhaps come to exceed that of new utopian literature. This change in emphasis is a natural result of the growth of knowledge, especially in the social sciences.

The differences between futurism and science fiction are similar to those between futurism and utopianism. The futurist begins with the contemporary world and explains realistically how it will change. Most authors of utopian novels or science fiction stories ignore the long process of change and describe in detail an imagined, radically different, future society. Moreover, they narrate the lives of individual persons. Futurism ignores individuals. It discusses only social events and trends.

3. Futurism Related to History

What was once the future is now the past. What is is the future now will become the past. The past and the future are bound together by unbreakable strands, namely the long-run historical trends which run smoothly and inevitably from the past into the future. The past portends the future, and the future extends the past. Therefore, to understand the structure of the future, we must study that of the past.

Individual historical events which are not a part of some important and continuing long-run social trend are insignificant. Reporting them does little if anything to explain the past and does nothing to help predict the future. The chief function of historians should be to help men predict the future. Therefore, historians should devote far less attention to such anomalous events and far more attention to those which are part of significant, continuing, long-run social trends.

For almost 200 years historians have been giving more and more attention to normal, peace-time economic and social trends, and less and less to abnormal or non-significant political and military events. This trend will continue for many decades, and will facilitate ever more accurate prediction of future social trends.

The best historian is the one who has most fully discovered, and called special attention to, the most significant long-run social trends, i.e., those which are most likely to continue for many years into the future and have the largest future social effects. The historian who has failed to discover and stress such trends is a poor historian because he has failed to learn about and/or properly emphasize the most significiant historical events and trends.

It follows that to be a good modern historian one must be a good futurist. Every history book covering recent history should end with a chapter on the future, a chapter in which the author further reveals the importance of significant recent long-run historical trends by projecting them well into the future. Such a chapter will not only clarify recent history but will also enable future generations of historians to determine how well the author understood the historical events he recorded. An historian who cannot predict major future social trends has failed to discover and understand past social trends. He is a poor historian!

4. Belief in Progress and Futurism

In recent decades several new histories of the belief in progress have been published, but, so far as I am aware, none of them have tried to explain how futurism is related to this belief. Moreover, futurists have virtually ignored the dependance of futurism on belief in progress.

It is possible to believe in progress without being a futurist, but nearly all futurists have believed in progress. Indeed, most futurism is simply a detailed explanation of the paths or trends that future progress will take. A believer in progress may have very nebulous ideas about future progress. He may merely believe that most future social trends and events will be beneficial. A futurist tries to describe these future trends in some detail, and explain how, when, and why they will occur.

5. Social Reformers as Futurists

The roots of modern scientific futurism are to be found in the writings of early general social reformers like Condoret, Bentham, Saint Simon, Place, J. S. Mill, etc. Nearly all important reformers have believed or asserted that the reforms they advocated would be adopted, and in a great many cases their implicit or explicit predictions have been at least partially verified by history.

Many reformers concentrated their efforts on one or a few social reforms. They were, at most, only specialized futurists. But some reformers, like Condorcet, advocated and explicitly predicted the adoption of a wide variety of social reforms. They were the first explicit general futurists.

Moreover, futurism and social reform are still closely related. Most modern futurist publications consist largely of predictions that desired social reforms will be adopted.

6. Conservatism and Futurism

For several reasons it is difficult for conservatives and reactionaries to be successful futurists. First, they disapprove of and oppose most continuing or prospective social changes. Therefore, they rarely enjoy thinking or writing about them.

Reactionaries are eager to believe that well-established contemporary social trends will soon reverse their direction, and often predict such reversals, for instance a reversal in the long decline of religious faith. But it is always very risky to predict such a reversal. At any given moment, nearly all established social trends are likely to continue, most for a long time.

Most conservative social scientists are still bound or limited by absolute religious or ethical dogmas which strongly affect their predictions of social change. Such dogmas tend to support traditional social behavior, not possible new kinds of behavior like divorce, birth control, or abortion. Progressive social scientists are more scientific, i.e., less religious and moralistic. Hence, they find it much easier to accept and predict new forms of social behavior, new immoral mores. On the other hand, progressive thinkers often fall into wishful thinking about the future because they want the future to be different from the present.

It may be objected that the above argument and conclusion is based upon an incorrect definition of <u>conservative</u> as denoting one who opposes all or nearly all social change, and would be invalid if conservatives were defined as people who merely oppose unduly rapid and/or harmful social change. But nearly all progressive or liberal social scientists claim to be conservative in this sense. And those who endorse, and predict the continuance of, most contemporary social trends are rarely called conservatives.

Realizing their handicaps as futurists, conservative and reactionary futurists often state their predictions so that they cannot be disproven by future statistical data. For instance, the common prediction by conservatives that men will become less materialistic, more spiritual, more unselfish, or more moral are unverifiable.

7. Reasons for Growing Interest in Futurism

Public interest in futurism has been growing rapidly in recent decades. <u>The Futurist</u>, the first American journal devoted to futurism, was founded in 1966 and grew to a circulation of over 60,000 in 1982. The World Future Society, publisher of <u>The Futurist</u>, publishes two other journals on futurism and holds large annual conventions of futurists. Other independent futurist journals have been founded recently, and more and more colleges and universities have begun to offer courses in futurism.

Growing interest in scientific futurism is a result of increasing acceptance of the theory of continuous, inevitable social progress. When men did not believe in such progress, they had little reason to try to predict the course of progress.

Another major reason for growing interest in futurism has been the recent rapid growth in knowledge about past, and especially about recent, social trends. Every increase in such knowledge makes it easier to predict the future. It also often makes men wonder about the possible dangers and benefits of the probable continuance of these trends.

8. Ideal Qualifications for Futurists

Since nearly all future social trends will be continuations of recent past social trends, a study of the modern history of advanced countries is the best preparation for the scientific prediction of future social trends. Unfortunately, very few writers on the future have been historians. Only one of the futurists reviewed in this book, Toynbee, was an historian, and he did not specialize in modern history. A knowledge of ancient history is of relatively little value to a futurist.

Since nearly all trends in social behavior are preceded by long gradual changes in public opinion, study of recent changes in public opinion, especially among experts and intellectuals, is very useful in predicting the future.

After the study of recent history, the study of political economy is probably most useful to a would-be scientific futurist because many major social trends are wholly or partly economic trends, or the natural results of such trends. But only five of my futurists were economists. And one of them, Karl Marx, was trained in philosophy, not political economy, in his university years, a serious handicap for any scientist.

Among modern general historians and political economists, those best suited to become successful futurists are those who believe in and favor social progress and reform in many different fields. History is largely a record of past attempts at social reform. However, many, perhaps most, proposed new reforms are unsound and/or are never adopted, so a successful futurist must be able to distinguish between sound and unsound reform proposals. That is one reason why professional training in social science, especially political economy, can be of great help to a scientific futurist.

The science of futurism is so new and so controversial that it has probably not yet attracted the lifelong, full-time attention of any writer on the future. Few if any of the futurists covered in this book devoted as much as 10% of their career to deliberate preparation for, or practice of, the study of the future. I am confident that a profession of well-trained, full-time, professional scientific futurists will be created during the next century. As this occurs, scientific prediction of the future will become more and more accurate, detailed, and respectable.

9. Methods of Prediction

Futurists have successfully used at least twelve different methods of predicting the future.

1. They have obtained statistical and verbal data on continuing past social trends and projected them into the future.
2. They have obtained such data on continuing trends in public opinion and used them to predict when proposed new reforms will be adopted.
3. They have observed current differences in opinion between social scientists and laymen about such reforms, and have predicted the eventual acceptance of expert opinion.
4. They have studied differences in social policy between backward and advanced countries, and have predicted that the backward countries will adopt the policies of the more advanced.
5. They have studied the differences in organization and operation between more and less efficient similar social units within an advanced country, and have predicted that the less efficient will adopt the policies of the more efficient.
6. They have studied the differences in the consumption habits of the rich and the poor in a single country, and have predicted that, as real incomes rise, more and more people will adopt the habits of the rich.
7. They have observed the differences in consumption habits between the more and less educated in a single economic class, and have predicted that the less educated will adopt the habits of the more educated.
8. They have observed successful pioneer social reforms in one advanced country, and have predicted its adoption by other countries.
9. They have observed distinctive customs peculiar to a single region, and have predicted that they will be abandoned because of strong forces favoring cultural homogenization.
10. They have studied recent technological advances and predicted the continuing social effects of such advances.
11. They have predicted some technological advances and the probable social effects of these advances.
12. They have studied the predictions and supporting arguments of other futurists, and have accepted and/or revised the more plausible ones.

Although all of these methods are available, few futurists have explicitly endorsed and/or used more than half of them. Fortunately, the first method noted above, projection, is so useful that it can be used alone to make a very large number of sound predictions.

The value of a prediction depends largely upon how well it is supported by reference to past trends, public opinion polls, expert opinion, possible social benefits, technological progress, and other reasons for future social trends. A purely dogmatic assertion that some social changes will occur is of relatively little value.

Any important social change or trend is likely to cause, or be related to, one or more other significant social changes. Therefore, the best futurists are those who explain most fully the major causal relationships between the different social events and trends they predict.

CONDORCET, THE FIRST SCIENTIFIC FUTURIST

Marie Jean Antoine Nicolas Caritat, Marquis de Condorcet (1743-94), was not only the first great scientific futurist, but probably the greatest of all to date. He successfully predicted most of the major social and political trends which have made up the framework or outline of history in advanced countries during the almost 200 years since his death, and which are likely to be equally important in the history of most less advanced countries during the next 200 years. Moreover, he developed or used methods of scientific prediction which remain today the most fruitful and the most widely used of all such methods. Yet his major futurist work, Sketch for a Historical Picture of the Progress of the Human Mind (1795), is available in few American public libraries, and is rarely mentioned in modern American books and articles on futurism.

Condorcet was a mathematician who became Secretary of the French Academie des Sciences, and, as Secretary, wrote a long series of eloges of the most famous scientists of his time. He was also an active reformer and politician who in 1791 became a member, and later President, of the Legislative Assembly in Paris. When the Jacobins came to power in 1793, he went into hiding for many months, and hastily wrote his masterpiece, The Progress of the Human Mind. He was arrested in March, 1794, and was found dead in his cell the next day. His masterpiece was published by a new French government about a year after his death. A poor English translation was published in England in 1795 and in the U. S. in 1796. In 1955 a new, improved translation, with an Introduction by Stuart Hampshire, was published in London by Weidenfeld and Nicholson, Ltd. This was reprinted by the Greenwood Press, Inc., Westport, Conn., in 1979. My page citations refer to this edition. In their recent magisterial book, Utopian Thought in the Western World (1979), Frank E. and Fritzie P. Manuel devote over 30 pages to a review of Condorcet's work, a review which covers some of his unpublished manuscripts on the future.

The Progress of the Human Mind covers the entire period of intellectual evolution from "the first stage of civilization...that of a small society whose members live by hunting and fishing," down to the French

Revolution. Only the last 30 of its 202 pages are devoted to "the future progress of the human mind." In them Condorcet created a new science, futurism, which has flowered only in recent decades.

Condorcet's Methods of Scientific Prediction

The first and most urgent problem facing those who wish to create a new science like sociology or futurism is that of developing new scientific methods useful in the new science. Condorcet suggested several new or neglected methods of scientific prediction.

He believed that scientific method is as applicable to social change as to physical phenomena. "If man can...predict phenomena when he knows their laws ...if, even when he does not, he can still...forecast the future on the basis of his experience of the past, why, then, should it be regarded as a fantastic undertaking to sketch...the future destiny of man on the basis of his history?...the general laws directing the phenomena of the universe...are necessary and constant. Why should this principle be any less true for the development of the intellectual and moral faculties of man...?" (p. 173).

This pioneer claim that futurism should be based on scientific reasoning is marred by a remnant of metaphysics, the belief that scientific laws determine, rather than merely report, events. In fact, events determine laws.

It should be noted that, although Condorcet repeatedly referred to himself, and to anyone who wrote on social theory, as a "philosopher," he did so only because both the natural and the social sciences were still considered to be divisions of philosophy. Actually, he was both a positivist, one who rejects as senseless or irrelevant most of what we now call formal philosophy or theology, and a consistent utilitarian, like most modern political economists.

During Condorcet's life the idea of inevitable social progress was increasingly accepted by advanced social thinkers, and he used it as a basic method of predicting the future. The idea of social progress originated at this time largely because there had been more obvious and continuous social progress in recent centuries in Europe than ever before, and because the philosophers were rebelling against orthodox Christian views of society and religion.

Condorcet stressed his claim that, to predict the future, we must know and understand the past, and by the past he meant major social trends, not the individual acts of rulers and generals. "What happens at any particular moment is the result of what has happened at all previous moments, and itself has an influence on what will happen in the future" (p. 4). Here we have an explicit acceptance of scientific causation, and an implicit rejection of religious dogmas concerning history.

The above quotations clearly suggest the most effective and widely used scientific method of predicting the future, namely the projection or extrapolation of past historical trends into the future. Condorcet was prudent enough to explain that predictions based on "past experiences" cannot possess "a certainty superior to that warranted by the number, the constancy, and the accuracy of...observatrions" of past experience (p. 173), but he clearly relied heavily on the extrapolation of past social trends.

When he wrote The Progress of the Human Mind, Condorcet had long been an advocate of a variety of social and political reforms. In this essay he apparently restated some of his hopes for social reform as firm predictions of future reform. The Manuels accuse him of ingenuously gliding from mere hopes to scientific predictions (pp. 493-94). But if Condorcet's hopes were so incredibly realistic and soundly based that they were nearly all justified by subsequent history, what can we gain by distinguishing them from explicit scientific predictions? A social scientist bases his hopes for social reform on the same bases used by scientific futurists to predict social changes. That is why most social scientists and reformers are optimists. They have good reason to expect that their hopes will be realized, and therefore are not naive or ingenuous when they restate their realistic hopes as predictions.

Condorcet suggested that another good way to predict the future is to study the opinions of "enlightened men" because the continued growth of education is certain to spread their enlightened views among ever larger numbers of people, until they are accepted and applied by rulers or by other men (p. 175). He may have been the first to suggest this method, which, I believe, is still one of the most useful.

He explained that "there is always a large interval between the point to which philosophers have carried the progress of enlightenment and the degree of enlightenment attained by the average man of education" who in turn is far more enlightened than "those who direct public affairs" (p. 127). This implies that, by studying the views of enlighted men or experts, we can see quite a long way into the future. I agree.

Condorcet believed that all men have common basic needs, and therefore tend to arrive at similar utilitarian solutions. Therefore, when a new technology has proven itself in one country, its use will gradually but surely spread to other countries. Moreover, the progress of less advanced peoples "is likely to be more rapid and certain than our own because they can receive from us everything that we have had to find out for ourselves..." (p. 178). This clearly suggests an easy method of predicting major social trends in backward countries, namely to predict that these countries will soon do what advanced countries have already done. Since over 90% of the world's people live in less developed countries, this is a very important method of scientific prediction.

For Condorcet the growth of knowledge, due to scientific discovery and education, was the chief cause of social progress in advanced countries. The invention of printing had been especially influential because it had speeded up the progress of research and education, and would long continue to have this effect. He elaborated this thesis in some detail. For instance, he claimed that printing had "freed the education of the people from all political and religious shackles" (p. 102). As an historical claim, this was a gross exaggeration, but, as a statement of a long-run trend which will continue far into the future, it is an important futurist principle.

II. Condorcet's Predictions

1. On Education

Although he considered education to be a major cause of social progress, Condorcet said little about its future in The Progress of the Human Mind. He predicted "greater equality...in wealth" (pp. 183-84), and "a more universal system of education" (p. 186). He anticipated that education would "be extended to women as well as to men," and that the education of future mothers would greatly benefit their children and society (pp. 193-94). He also foresaw great progress in the sciences, and noted that such progress "ensures the progress of the art of education..." (p. 196).

The reason Condorcet said so little about education in this book may be that he had discussed it in great detail in earlier writings. For instance, in a 1792 report on education to the new French Legislative Assembly he had recommended that education should become a function of government, that elementary education should be universal and free, both sexes should be educated, coeducation should be adopted, scholarships should be granted to poor students, extension classes for adults should be created, classical courses should be largely replaced by scientific and vocational courses, the teaching of religious dogma in state schools should cease, teachers should be given tenure, and all state schools should be supported by local governments, aided by the national government. Nearly all of these recommendations have been adopted in most advanced countries since 1792.

2. On the Growth of Knowledge

Knowledge precedes education, and the growth of knowledge is therefore the most basic cause of social progress. Condorcet stressed such growth as a fundamental cause of social change. After a discussion of the alleged limits to the growth of knowledge, he rejected such limits, and asserted that, "If we apply these general reflections to the various sciences, we can find in each of them examples of progressive improvement that will remove any doubts about what we may expect for the future...in particular the progress that is both likely and imminent in those sciences which prejudice regards as all but exhausted" (p. 186). As a mathematician he especially stressed the beneficial future "result of a more general and philosophical application of the sciences of calculation to the various branches of knowledge."

He foresaw certain specific kinds of medical research. "The knowledge of physical man, medicine and public economy are bound to benefit from the researches about the duration of human life and the way this is influenced by differences in sex, temperature, climate, profession, government and ordinary habits; about the dependance of the death-rate on various illnesses..." (p. 161).

The Manuels report a variety of other detailed suggestions for scientific research not repeated in The Progress of the Human Mind (pp. 505-10).

Condorcet predicted that "a more universal system of education would both increase interest in the sciences and greatly increase the number of able scientists, "for at present, even in the most enlightened countries, scarcely one in fifty of the people who have natural talents receives the necessary education to develop them; and...if this were done there would be a proportionate increase in the number of men destined by their discoveries to extend the boundaries of science" (p. 186).

3. On Technological Progress

Condorcet explained that this reasoning also applies to the growth of knowledge in the arts," i.e., technology, because "the procedures of the different arts can be perfected and simplified in the same way as the methods of the sciences; new instruments, machines and looms can add to man's strength and can improve at once the quality and the accuracy of his productions, and can diminish the time and labour that has to be expended upon them. The obstacles still in the way of this progress will disappear" (p. 187).

He applied this prediction of unlimited technological progress to agriculture as well as to industry. "A very small amount of ground will be able to produce a great quantity of supplies of greater utility or higher value; more goods will be obtained for a smaller outlay; the manufacture of articles wll be achieved with less wastage in raw materials...Every type of soil will produce those things which satisfy the greatest number of needs;...and so on" (p. 187). Here we have a summary of both the coming agricultural revolution and the coming industrial revolution.

4. On Wealth and Population

"With all this progress...each successive generation wll have larger possessions, either as a result of this progress or through the preservation of the products of industry, and so, as a consequence of the physical constitution of the human race, the number of people will increase" (p. 188).

Condorcet even anticipated and refuted in advance the Malthusian objection to this line of reasoning. He predicted that men would recognize and reduce or prevent the evils of overpopulation by adopting suitable methods of birth control: "...the absurd prejudices of superstition will have ceased to corrupt and degrade the moral code" and "The progress of reason" will have taught men "that they have a duty towards those who are not yet born, that duty is not to give them existence but to give them happiness;..." (p. 189). Unfortunately, "the absurd prejudices of superstition" were still so strong that Condorcet was afraid to predict the precise methods of birth control which he foresaw would be used. But in writings still unpublished he advocated and predicted the use of contraception, which he believed would both increase sexual gratification and reduce infidelity and perversion (<u>Manuel</u>, p. 515). In other words, he foresaw the sexual revolution of the Twentieth Century.

5. On Length of Life

Condorcet confidently predicted a continuous and indefinite increase in the average length of human life. "No-one can doubt that, as preventive medicine improves and food and housing become healthier, as a way of life is established that develops our physical powers by exercise without ruining them by excess, as the two most virulent causes of deterioration, misery and excessive wealth, are eliminated, the average length of human life will be increased and a better health and a stronger physical constitution will be ensured" (p. 199). Here we have seven major long-run predictions in a single sentence.

6. On Human Heredity

Condorcet foresaw continuous improvement in hereditary human "physical...intellectual and moral faculties," but he mistakenly based this expectation on improved education and the inheritance of acquired characteristics, not on sound eugenic measures (p. 201).

Elsewhere he discussed artifical insemination and "hinted at the improvement of the species through eugenic measures" (<u>Manuel</u>, p. 516). He probably thought it dangerous to be more explicit.

7. On the Decline of Religion

He repeatedly predicted that the growth of knowledge and education would result in a long and continuous decline in religious faith or superstition, ending in the universal acceptance of reason and science. "The time will therefore come when the sun will shine only on free men who know no other master but their reason; when...priests...will exist only in works of history and on the stage..." (p. 179). This time has not yet arrived, and may never arrive, but the long decline of religious faith since 1794 is recognized by nearly all historians.

8. On Feminism

Condorcet anticipated the growth of the feminist movement which has occurred since his time. He advocated and expected "the complete annihilation of the prejudices that have brought about an inequality of rights between the sexes." He explained that "this inequality has its origin solely in an abuse of strength, and all the later sophistical attempts that have been made to excuse it are vain" (p. 193). He further predicted that "the abolition of customs...

[and] laws dictated by this prejudice would add to
the happiness of family life...[and] would favour
the progress of education" because educated mothers
would desire the education of their children, both
boys and girls.

9. On Political Democracy

He wrote that in Europe "the principles of the
new French constitution are already those of all
enlightened men," and would therefore guide the
future political evolution of all countries, first
in Europe and then elsewhere (p. 175). He did not
restate these principles—political democracy, freedom of the press, religious toleration, equality
before the law, etc.—because he assumed that they
were very well known, but he was explicit about their
increasing application throughout the world.

10. On Colonial Progress and Freedom

Condorcet predicted that nearly all European
colonies in the Americas would become independant
nations. "Can we doubt that either common sense or
the senseless discords of European nations will add
to the effects of the slow but inexorable progress
of their colonies, and will soon bring about the
independance of the New World? And then will not
the European population of these colonies, spreading
rapidly over that enormous land, either civilize or
peacefully remove the savage nations who still in-
habit vast tracts of its land?" (p. 175). In 1794
this was surely an extraordinarily perceptive outline
of the future history of the New World!

He also foresaw a great improvement in the
management of European colonies in Africa and Asia,
and eventual political freedom for them. He explained that "our trade monopolies, our treachery, our
murderous contempt for men of another colour or
creed...have destroyed the respect and goodwill that
the superiority of our knowledge...first won for
us.... But doubtless the moment approaches when...we
shall become the beneficent instruments of their
freedom" (p. 176). "We shall see the monks who
brought only shameful superstition...replaced by men
occupied in propagating amongst them the truths that
wil promote their happiness..." (p. 177).

11. On Individual and Social Insurance

One of the most important social trends in advanced countries since 1794 has been the great and
continuous expansion of insurance. Condorcet

noted the recent growth of private insurance, and foretold a great expansion in it, and also the creation and growth of social insurance, unknown in his day. An expert on probability theory, he explained that the "misery which ceaselessly threatens the most numerous and most active class...can be in great part eradicated by guaranteeing people in old age a means of livelihood produced partly by their own savings and partly by the savings of others who make the same outlay, but who die before they need to reap the reward; or again, on the same principle of compensation, by securing for widows and orphans" similar insurance benefits. This system would be applied "not merely to a few individuals, but to society as a whole...organized in the name of the social authority" (p. 181).

12. On International Peace

Condorcet foresaw the creation of international peace-keeping organizations, like the United Nations, and predicted eventual success in their mission, "organizations more intelligently conceived than those projects of eternal peace which have filled the leisure and consoled the hearts of certain philosophers will hasten the progress of the brotherhood of nations, and wars between countries will rank with assassinations as freakish atrocities..." (pp. 194-95). Unfortunately, this prediction on decline in warfare is one of his least verified predictions. But it may yet be fully verified.

13. On Wealth and Income Distribution

Condorcet predicted that the distribution of personal wealth and income would become more equal in all advanced countries for several reasons. Some of these reasons—freer trade and industry, tax reforms, more equal credit, marriage reform, etc.—were merely mentioned (p. 180). Others—the reform of education and the expansion of insurance—were discussed in some detail, as recorded above. He noted that, "These various causes of [the growth of] equality do not act in isolation; they unite, combine, and support each other, and so their cumulative effects are stronger and more constant. With greater equality of education there will be greater equality in industry, and so in wealth; equality in wealth necessarily leads to equality in education..." (pp. 183-84). These predictions have been partially verified by the course of history, especially in communist countries.

III. Comments

In hiding from the police and facing death in prison, Condorcet solaced himself by contemplating the future progress of mankind. In the last paragraph of his famous essay he wrote, "How consoling for the philosopher who laments the errors, the crimes, the injustices which still pollute the earth, and of which he is often the victim, is this view of the human race, emancipated from its shackles, released from the empire of fate and from that of the enemies of its progress, advancing with a firm and sure step along the path of truth, virtue and happiness!" (p. 201). Here we have a satisfying scientific substitute for belief in a personal reward in heaven.

I have noted or discussed about fifty different predictions made by Condorcet in a wide variety of fields, but mostly about long-run social trends. It is amost incredible that nearly all of these predictions were more or less verified by the course of history since his time. Few of them have been completely verified. For instance, there are still a few small European colonies in the Americas. But he set no time limits, and nearly all of his incompletely verified forecasts are likely to be more fully verified in the future. The striking fact is that none of his numerous predictions have been clearly disproven by history. There have been no social trends running in the opposite direction from those he predicted, except temporarily in individual countries, as in Germany from 1933 to 1945.

There are several reasons why Condorcet was so remarkably successful as a pioneer scientific futurist. First, he largely restricted himself to predicting long-run social trends. It is much easier to predict such trends than to predict short-run trends or individual historical events. Abnormal or chance events distort short-run trends much more than they distort long-run trends. One of the chief reasons recent American futurists have made so many dubious or disproven predictions is that they have concentrated on short-run trends and indidivual events.

Secondly, he did not predict dates, or set time limits. It is much easier to predict the direction of a trend than to predict the date of any event in the trend. And most futurists who have predicted such dates have grossly overestimated the speed of social change.

Thirdly, he was highly successful as a futurist because he was a well-rounded, sensible social reformer. As a result, he had many sound ideas about the future. History consists chiefly of a long series of social reforms. Only a minority of reform proposals are ever adopted, but social scientists who advocate numerous social reforms are in a far better position to predict the future than are conservatives who oppose or ignore nearly all sound reform proposals. And the rare reformer who, like Condorcet, is able to distinguish between sound and unsound reform proposals is especially qualified to become a successful scientific futurist.

Some futurists claim that the function of futurists is to suggest and discuss alternative future events, trends, or scenarios. It is noteworthy that Condorcet rarely suggested such alternatives. He nearly always predicted a single social trend or event, thereby submitting to the test of verification by history, an essential requirement for any scientific theory. It requires much more knowledge and courage to predict a single trend or event than it does to suggest two or more possible alternatives.

Finally, by far the most important conclusion to be drawn from this review of Condorcet's predictions is that it is possible to successfuly predict most long-run social trends for at least two hundred years into the future. This should greatly encourage contemporary and coming futurists.

SAINT-SIMON AS A FUTURIST

Count Claude Henri de Saint-Simon (1760-1825) was born in a chateau in Picardy, became an army officer at age 17, fought with Washington at Yorktown, participated as a Girondist in the French Revolution, acquired temporary wealth as a post-revolutionary speculator, and spent the last 35 years of his life as a student and advocate of social progress. Ignored or ridiculed by most contemporary thinkers and politicians, he strongly influenced disciples and followers who were to play prominent roles in French government, industry, and social reform.

Saint-Simon was a great admirer of Condorcet, his senior by 17 years, and a strong influence on Comte, who served as his secretary from 1917 to 1824. He restated and endorsed some of Condorcet's predictions, and he briefly suggested some of the major ideas elaborated later by Comte.

This essay is largely based on the selection of writings of Saint-Simon collected by Keith Taylor in his book, Henry Saint-Simon (1760-1825), Writings on Science, Industry and Social Organization, published by Croom Helm, London, 1975. I have also used Frank Manuel's, The Prophets of Paris (1962), and his The New World of Henri Saint-Simon (1956), both published by the Harvard University Press. All page references are to these books (T, MPP, and MNW).

1. Ideas on Futurism

Like Condorcet, Saint-Simon was a firm believer in both past and future social progress. For him too the golden age was in the future, not in the past (T, 136). Moreover, he confidently predicted the creation of a science of social evolution which would permit men to predict the shape of the historical future (T, 31,74). He believed that all science makes possible verifiable predictions. He claimed that, "A scientist...is a man who predicts" (T, 74).

Saint-Simon believed that social progress had been, and would continue to be, based largely on intellectual progress (T, 33). To predict the future, therefore, one needs to understand the past evolution of human ideas, especially the evolution of the basic methods of thought.

2. The Rise of Scientific Thought

Saint-Simon's most basic theory was that religious and metaphysical methods of reasoning had been declining among educated Europeans because scientific methods of reasoning had been spreading and improving. He forecast that these trends would continue indefinitely until all fields of human thought had become positive, i.e., scientific, by which he meant based solely on scientific observation.

He restated Turgot's law of the three stages of thought (T, 228n) but he wrote mostly about the decline of theology and the rise of science, largely ignoring the metaphysical stage in intellectual evolution.

3. The Creation of Sociology

Saint-Simon did not use the term sociology, which was coined later by Comte, but he clearly and repeatedly predicted the creation of a full-fledged positive science of man in society, which he called physiology. For instance, he asserted that, "The science of social organization will become a positive science. Its theory will be based on the general observations of Condorcet" (T, 84). Furthermore, he predicted that, "Morals...Politics...[and] Philosophy will [each] become a positive science," the first two presumably as divisions of the coming positive science of man in society (MNW, 135).

Saint-Simon predicted the rise of a science of politics consisting of verified and generally accepted principles (T, 21). He thought that the rise of such a science would justify some restriction of unscientific political dissent. He explained that, "when politics has risen to the ranks of the sciences of observation, which must be before too long,...the cultivation of politics will be entrusted exclusively to a special class of scientists who will impose silence on all twaddle" (T, 230). This was a pioneer adumbration of the idea of government by experts, i.e., by social scientists, but later he favored rule by business leaders.

He was aware that most political problems were becoming economic problems,and predicted that "In future...it [political economy] will itself comprise the whole of politics" (T, 167n). This was an exaggeration, but it called attention to a major long-run political trend.

He predicted that "celestial morality" will be replaced by "terrestrial morality" (T, 33). He explained that, "Morals will become a positive science," and a part of sociology, because, "The

physiologist [i.e., the sociologist] is the only
scientist who is in a position to demonstrate that in
every case the path of virtue is at the same time the
road to happiness" (MNW, 135). Since he wrote these
words, sociologists have increasingly applied scientific methods to the solution of problems once considered
purely moral problems—divorce, birth control, crime,
euthanasia, etc., so that his prediction has been
significantly verified, but many old moral problems
now fall within the scope of other sciences. For instance, today the doctor of medicine, not the sociologist, tells us that the use of tobacco and narcotics
is not "the road to happiness." However, regardless
of which science is relevant, the trend from celestial
to terrestrial morality has continued ever since
Saint-Simon noted and predicted it.

Saint-Simon also claimed that, "Morals certainly
improve as industry develops" (T, 167n). Since he
forecast continued industrial development, this was an
implicit prediction that human behavior will improve
morally and thereby increase human welfare, as indeed
it has.

He was unduly confident that the application of
scientific methods to the study of social, political,
and moral problems would soon result in full agreement
among social scientists and most educated laymen on
the proper solution of such problems (T, 144). That
is why he suggested that dissenters would deserve
little consideration and freedom of expression in the
coming scientific industrial societies. Some critics
have called him a protofascist because of his attitude
towards dissent. I believe it is more reasonable to
criticize him for grossly overestimating the future
rate of progress in sociology and political science.
Nearly all futurists have overestimated the rate of
future social progress.

4. Decline of the Clergy and Nobility

Saint-Simon repeatedly predicted that the long
domination of European society and government by the
clergy and the landowning nobility would be gradually
replaced by domination by scientists, artists and/or
business leaders (T, 26, 36, 48, 104). He clearly
foresaw that scientists and writers would increasingly
replace priests and theologians as intellectual leaders, and that business men would increasingly replace
nobles as political leaders. I believe that these
very important forecasts have been more and more fully
verified in every European state in the over 160 years
since they were made. Moreover, they are likely to be
ever more fully verified in coming centuries in all
countries. Saint-Simon correctly forecast that

European civilization and ideas would gradually spread throughout the world (T, 6).

5. Parliamentary Government

Saint-Simon did not advocate or predict the rise of democratic government because he believed most citizens were incompetent to participate in politics, but he did welcome and predict the further growth of parliamentary government under a constitutional monarchy and a very limited suffrage. He expected such government, then very new and rare on the continent, to spread throughout Europe (T, 141-43), but he predicted that it would be transitional and would be followed by non-parliamentary rule by business leaders (T, 44).

He learned to admire the new American system of government when he served as a French officer in the American Revolution, but he explicitly predicted that "civilization would not follow the same course in the two hemispheres" (T, 162). This was one of his worst forecasts. Nearly all of the major long-run social trends of the last 200 years have appeared in both of "the two hemispheres."

6. The Political Role of Business Leaders

Saint-Simon changed his mind several times about the future political role of scientists, artists, and business men. At one time he predicted that all three groups would play major roles in national government (T, 36, 104). Later, he suggested rule by scientists (T, 236). In the end, he forecast rule by successful business leaders elected by substantial property owners and advised by scientists (T, 44, 254). He argued that only successful business leaders had proven themselves to be successful managers and budget balancers. He also claimed that, "In future...it [political economy] will itself comprise the whole of politics" (T, 167n). This was a brilliant anticipation of the growing role of economists in government, but it ignored the future importance of non-economic government activities like war, scientific research, education, etc.

Saint-Simon forecast that domination of the French government by "industriels," i.e., business men, "cannot be very far away now" (T, 254). He predicted that business men would achieve political rule in France before they achieved it in Britain, because the nobility were more powerful in England than in post-revolutionary France. I believe these forecasts were substantially verified. As late as 1914, English peers played key roles in British government.

At another point he explained or qualified his estimate of not "very far away" by asserting that, "it will not be until the end of the century that the establishment of a truly positive, industrial, and liberal regime will be practicable" in France (T, 170).

7. The Integration of Government and Industry

Saint-Simon predicted an eventual integration of industry and government in a single national economic organization. He forecast that this integration would radically reduce the size and importance of most functions of government because it would radically reduce conflicts between units of society (MPP, 134,36). For instance, units of a single giant organization rarely compete with and sue each other. In a fully integrated national economy managed by business leaders these leaders and their subordinate executives would perform nearly all of the necessary functions now performed by governments, and many unnecessary, parasitic activities of business and government could be eliminated.

This predicted complete integration of business and government has not been achieved in any capitalist country, but it has been closely approached in some communist countries.

Saint-Simon asserted that the best government is the one which governs least and most economically (MPP, 135), but he predicted that this goal would be achieved by combining government and industry, which may be regarded by some as a vast expansion of government.

8. Meritocracy

Saint-Simon predicted the ultimate creation of a completely meritocratic society. In the coming industrial society, he explained, "All privileges will be abolished...The men who show the greatest capacity in the positive sciences, in the fine arts, and in industry, will be called by the new system to enter the top echelon of social prestige and will be placed in charge of public affairs—a fundamental disposition which destines all men possessing a transcendant talent to rise to the first rank, no matter what position the chance of birth may have placed them" (MPP, 128, 135). As I have explained, he later assigned the function of political rule to business leaders, but he never reversed his forecast of the eventual full adoption of meritocracy within each field of human activity. And he never advocated revolution. Thus he implicitly predicted a long gradual trend towards meritocracy. I believe that this prediction has been partially verified by history since he made it, and will be increasingly verified in the future. Some later writers called this trend in business the managerial revolution.

9. Industrial and Technological Progress

Saint-Simon repeatedly assumed, implied, or asserted that the trend towards industrial or economic progress would continue indefinitely in Europe and spread throughout the world (T, 46), but he had very little to say about individual technological advances as a basis for such progress. For instance, he did not even mention the steam engine. But he believed that the general growth of knowledge and education, especially in the sciences, would assure continued economic progress (T, 43).

However, he had read Adam Smith and had become aware of the importance of the division of labor and specialization. He repeatedly predicted that these measures would spread. For instance, he explained that, "as civilization progresses, the division of labour—both spiritual and temporal—...increase at the same rate" (T, 229). By "spiritual and temporal" he probably meant "mental and physical." The division of labor has certainly increased steadily since he made this prediction, and this trend has helped to insure industrial progress.

Saint-Simon also predicted that scientists would devote more and more of their time to the solution of the practical problems of producers, with ever-increasing social benefits. He asserted that "the general application of mechanics and of all the other sciences" will enable "the most numerous class of producers...to increase its comforts and diminish its physical exertions, with the result that the price of human muscular labor will rise in direct relationships with the perfection of scientific processes. In a word, scientists will undertake a series of works directly intended to perfect industrial arts" (MPP, 123). This important prediction has been continuously verified since he made it in 1825.

10. Education

Saint-Simon predicted the provision of both primary and secondary education for all youth (T, 42), but he did not predict that such education would be largely provided by state agencies. He foresaw that secondary and higher education would pay much more attention to the sciences, including new social sciences (T, 143), but he failed to foresee the coming radical increase in emphasis on vocational and professional education.

However, he foresaw the coming long decline of the influence of orthodox priests on education.

11. Religious Evolution

In the last years of his life Saint-Simon became convinced that the best way to weaken the influence of the orthodox Catholic Church was to found a new religion which would retain most of the customs and ceremonies of the old church, or adopt similar ones, but which would substitute secular scientific thinking for obsolete theological dogmas. He called his new religion, the New Christianity, but it was much closer to modern scientific humanism than to any religion.

He optimistically but mistakenly predicted the rapid general adoption of his new religion (MPP, 141). However, the subsequent steady growth of scientific humanism, naturalism, positivism, and the social gospel, may be treated as a partial verification of this prediction.

According to Frank Manuel, the leading authority on Saint-Simon, "The gulf between Saint-Simon and traditional faiths is so unbridgeable that it seems presumpuous to embrace his humanitarian creed and the Judeo-Christian revelations under the same rubric of religion, were it not for the fact that the actual practices of many Jewish and Christian modernists is far closer to Saint-Simon's morality religion than to orthodox belief" (MPP, 143).

12. Comments

Saint-Simon's chief contributions to futurism were: (1) his elaboration of the prediction that business men would continue to displace the nobility as political rulers in advanced countries due to the rise of an industrial society, (2) his forecast concerning the creation of a new social science or sciences, including futurism, and (3) his foresight as to the rise of a new, more liberal form of Christianity.

He was also perceptive enough to repeat or endorse Condorcet's predictions on social progress, the decline of theological and metaphysical thinking, and the rise of science. Unlike most modern futurists, he noted and praised the chief contributions of his most important predecessor as a futurist.

On the other hand, he failed to foresee several already apparent major social trends—the growth of feminism, the rise of democratic government, the growth of public education, the rise and fall of colonialism, the industrial revolution, the agricultural revolution, etc.—some of which had already been forecast by Condorcet and/or other writers. For these reasons, he ranks well below Condorcet as a futurist.

COMTE AS A FUTURIST

Auguste Comte (1798-1857), the founder of positivism and sociology, was an alumnus of the Ecole Polytechnique. He spent seven years as an assistant to Saint Simon, from whom he acquired the seeds of some of his most important ideas. He sought, but never achieved, a university professorship, and spent his life in near poverty, working incessantly on his life task, the creation of new basic theories of science, sociology, ethics, and politics.

In this essay I shall concentrate on Comte's most significant and verifiable predictions, ignoring both his trivial forecasts concerning positivist (i.e., humanist) ceremonials and his unverifiable predictions concerning the spread of love and sympathy.

This essay is based primarily on L. Levy-Bruhl's book, The Philosophy of August Comte (1903), a summary of the six volumes of Comte's Cours de Philosophie Positive (1830-42), and on the Burt Franklin 1968 reprint of Comte's four volume System of Positive Policy (1852-54). All page references are to these sources (LB and PP).

For modern readers, Comte's arguments are often obscured by the use of old terms to denote new and often radically different ideas. For instance, he used the term philosophy to denote the general principles of science, the term morals to denote the principles of applied social science, the term spiritual to mean intellectual, and the term religion to denote scientific humanism. In most cases, I have translated such terms into their more accurate modern equivalents. Thus any critic could easily question my conclusions by citing quotations from Comte which use his misleading terminology.

1. On the Need for Futurism

Comte was probably the first to call for scientific study of future social evolution. After discussing the age-old conflict between the human need for social order and that for social progress, he concluded that "what is needed is a true picture of the future of Humanity" (PP, IV, 10).

He highly praised his "spiritual father," Condorcet for his pioneer effort to predict the future. He claimed that Condorcet had failed in this effort because he had misunderstood the past, but asserted that "the determination of the future, through the philosophic [i.e., scientific] observation of the past, would ...strike us as perfectly natural.... All sciences aim at prevision...all men...make predictions, based on the same principle, the forecast of the future from the past" (PP. IV, 576). He also argued that we must know in order to foresee, and we must foresee in order to control.

The title page of the fourth volume of Comte's System of Positive Polity (1854) describes it as "containing the synthetical presentation of the future of man."

2. Methods of Prediction

Comte was a profound student of history. He believed that history revealed a recent general breakdown of social, political, and religious theories and practices, culminating in the French Revolution (1889-94). This breakdown called for the creation of new basic principles of social, political, ethical, and religious evolution. In his opinion, this breakdown suggested why and how certain new trends would arise. However, he based some of his predictions on the mere projection of old social trends.

Comte forecast that the study of well-established social trends in order to predict the future, i.e., futurism, would become the major division of scientific sociology. He rejected both social experimentation (LB, 241) and mathematical analysis (LB, 239) as methods of social research, and emphasized the use of the historical method. In his opinion sociologists should, and increasingly would, rely largely on the discovery of major past social trends in order to discover both the basic laws of sociology and their effects upon future social evolution. For him, the most important part of sociology was the study of social evolution, not the analysis of an existing society (LB, 244-9, 259-65).

Like Saint Simon, Comte claimed that intellectual evolution is the basis for social, political, and economic evolution (LB, 38-39). This claim conflicts with the later Marxism theory that material economic evolution determines social, political, and intellectual evolution.

John Morley, who wrote a biography of Comte, summarized his views as follows: "The history of intellectual development...is the key to social evolution, and the key to the history of intellectual development is the Law of the Three Stages."

Although Comte claimed that intellectual evolution is fundamental, he also anticipated Marx and Engels by asserting that economic evolution necessarily precedes and provides a basis for aesthetic and scientific evolution. He added that economic evolution plays a more significant role now than in ancient times because it is more rapid today (LB, 287). His claim that economic evolution precedes some scientific evolution seems inconsistent with his claim that intellectual change is basic.

Comte's chief contribution to futurist methodology was his elaboration and wide application of the theory of the three stages of intellectual evolution. He used it both to explain the past and to predict the future.

3. The Law of the Three Stages

As early as 1822, in his *Plan des travaux*...Comte stated his law as follows: "According to the very nature of the human intellect every branch of our knowledge must necessarily pass successively...through three different states: the theological or fictitious state, the metaphysical or abstract state, [and] finally the scientific or positive state" (LB, 36). In the theological stage, phenomena are thought to be caused by the will of the gods. In the metaphysical stage, they are explained by abstract, a priori, invariable laws. In the scientific stage they are explained by inductive, verifiable scientific laws (LB, 37-39).

This fundamental theory of intellectual evolution asserted or implied that dogmatic theological (religious) thinking would become less and less common in every field of thought until it vanished, at least among educated men. It also asserted that metaphysical (philosophic) reasoning, the second normal stage in intellectual evolution, would experience the same fate, to be followed by the adoption of positive (scientific) reasoning. This theory of future intellectual evolution was for him both a major general scientific prediction and a useful basis for making other, more specific, predictions, to be discussed later.

4. The Future of Religion and Philosophy

Comte's law of the three stages clearly implied many more specific predictions, including: (1) the decline of beliefs in a vast number of religious myths such as those of a universal flood, Noah and his ark, creationism, the resurrection of Christ, etc., (2) the decline of belief in all metaphysical theories—including materialism, spiritualism, and absolute ethical and aesthetic principles, (3) the growing application of scientific methods to problems of personal and social behavior, and, as a result, (4) the creation of new sciences such as behaviorist psychology and sociology.

Following Descartes, Comte claimed that logic is the only field of traditional philosophy to prove useful in the coming scientific age, and he rejected all a priori principles of logic. He asserted that the study of mathematics is more useful in training the mind to reason correctly than is the study of traditional logic, and implicitly predicted the rise of mathematical logic (LB, 103-4).

He also condemned the philosophic doctrine of final causes and forecast that the growth of scientific reasoning would lead to its growing rejection (LB, 85).

All of these predictions, and many others implicit in Comte's theory of the three stages, have been increasingly verified by the course of history since 1822. No other theory of future intellectual evolution has ever been so widely useful.

5. Biological Trends

Comte correctly forecast that the application of the positive or scientific method in biology would eliminate several theoretical and/or metaphysical concepts and theories. Thus he called the theory of spontaneous generation a metaphysical idea, and implicitly predicted its rejection (LB, 184). It was abandoned before 1900.

He also criticized the theory of vitalism, and correctly foresaw its rejection by orthodox biologists (LB, 186). On the other hand, he failed to foresee the general acceptance of the Darwinian theory of biological evolution. He mistakenly assumed, tentatively, that species are fixed and unchangeable (LB, 181).

6. Behaviorist Psychology

Comte clearly foresaw that the application of the scientific method to psychology would result in the creation of a behaviorist psychology. He condemned contemporary emphasis upon study of the soul and the ego (LB, 71). He rejected the then popular method of internal observation or introspection, and insisted that psychologists should study both human and animal behavior. "We cannot divide our mind, that is to say, our brain, into two parts, of which one acts while the other looks on, to see how it goes to work.... What will it tell us of the child, of the mentally deranged, of the animal?" Instead, he claimed, we must study the organic conditions of mental behavior and/or human and animal physical behavior. He forecast that this would be done increasingly in the future (LB,189-95, 205). In fact there has been a great development of behaviorist psychology since he wrote.

7. The Creation of Sociology

The theory of the three stages of intellectual evolution clearly implied that scientific methods of research and reasoning would be increasingly applied to all social problems. Comte repeatedly predicted that this would lead to the creation and perfection of a new science, sociology, which he defined so as to cover all social problems (LB, 344-45, 359, 361). He did not expect this perfection to be quickly achieved.

Comte's prediction that sociology would be recognized as a new social science has been largely verified by events. Most western universities now include chairs or departments of sociology and other social sciences. But, as he explained, the elaboration of these sciences can continue for centuries.

Comte rejected the claim that social phenomena can be measured and the claim that we can estimate the probability of future social events. He implicitly predicted that mathematical analyses and probability theory would be of little if any use in the creation of the science of sociology and politics (LB, 239). These turned out to be bad predictions. Since he wrote, social scientists have made steadily growing use of mathematical and probability theory, as Condorcet had foreseen.

Comte was so confident concerning the future growth of scientific sociology and positivist education that he predicted that these trends would in time create a concensus, a uniform or homogeneous public opinion, on all social issues. He claimed that, once scientific principles of social science have been discovered, it will be as unreasonable and rare to dispute them as it now is to dispute the accepted principles of astronomy and physics (LB, 343).

Unfortunately, these predictions have not been verified by events. Comte failed to realize that political opinions will long continue to be determined more by conflicting economic interests than by scientific research. Of course, in the very long run his predictions may be partially verified, but to date there is little if any evidence to support them.

8. Education and Research

Although public class-room education had been growing in the most advanced countries for well over a century, Comte urged and predicted a reversal of this well-established trend, including a return of all elementary education to the home (PP, I, 139). Secondary education should be free only for wage workers. Moreover, all state support for universities and colleges should end. "So far...from inviting government to organise education, we ought rather to exhort it to abdicate the educational powers which it already has" (PP, I, 145-46).

In his opinion, "The official reestablishment of the University [of France] was the worst mistake of Bonaparte." He urged and forecast its suppression. "The whole of modern history teaches us to see in the [coming] abolition of the University the consequence... of the [future] abolition of the Parliamentary regime, for the latter drew its recruits, as did journalism, from the colleges, the constant nursery of our philosophical and political agitators" (PP, IV, 337).

He also urged the elimination of all government subsidies for scientific research (PP, IV, 338). His forecasts on both education and state support of research have been completely disproven.

9. The Spread of Scientific Humanism

Although less than 0.01% of men were scientific or secular humanists in Comte's time, he confidently predicted that nearly all men would abandon orthodox religion and adopt his new positivist religion, i.e., scientific humanism (LB, 279-80, 320). This forecast was supported by his theory of the three stages of intellectual evolution and by his further belief that men naturally want to use science to benefit themselves and society. Since men have ample strong natural needs and acquired wants, they need no unscientific ethical rules to urge them to use science and technology to help them satisfy their needs and wants. Moreover, social science will increasingly make clear that social organization and action can increase such want satisfaction.

Comte rejected the theories of natural religion and deism, popular among the philosophes, on the ground that in the coming conflict between religious philosophy and scientific humanism, the partisans of natural religion and deism would side with religion, and even with Catholicism (LB, 290-94).

He also forecast that in the very long run the inevitable course of cosmic evolution would result in the destruction of the earth and all life on it by the mass of the sun (LB, 153).

Comte predicted that the growing acceptance of scientific thinking would cause men to increasingly abandon belief in objective, physical life after death. He described this belief as chimerical and vulgar. In its place, he forecast, there will arise a belief that men live after death in their influence on their descendants and on subsequent generations. Such immortality can last as long as mankind itself (LB,340-41).

This prediction has been slowly but increasingly confirmed by history. Reliable public opinion polls have revealed both that belief in physical immortality has long been declining and that acceptance of this belief varies inversely with the amount of one's education.

10. Economic Progress

In spite of his emphasis on intellectual progress, Comte once claimed that "material progress is the source of all progress" (PP, II, 147). He was aware of the long previous history of both social and economic progress, and predicted that such progress would continue indefinitely. He specifically mentioned the accumulation of capital as a vital part of material progress (ib., 141), and expected it to continue as indeed it has.

He correctly predicted that continued economic progress would gradually reduce the hours of labor and thus enable men to devote more and more of their time to intellectual, artistic, and political activities, and to promoting the welfare of mankind, which he called moral behavior (ib., 142-43).

He asserted that, "The natural tendency of industrial life is...towards concentration" of capital (PP, IV, 69) because concentration increases efficiency. There has been an ever-growing concentration of capital in advanced countries since his time.

Comte claimed that advanced countries had long been in transition from a military form to an industrial form (LB, 244), but he meant by this the transition from feudalism to individualism, not to industrialization and the factory system. Unlike Saint Simon, he disapproved of the intensified division of labor created by the rise of the factory system, and mistakenly predicted that the English system of division of labor would never be accepted in France (PP, I, 103). He even condemned specialization among scientists (PP, I, 152). In fact, France has increasingly accepted both the division of labor in factories and specialization among scientists. However, it has also moved more and more beyond feudalism and towards a business culture, as he foresaw.

As a result of his failure to predict continued industrialization, he failed to foresee the rise of industrial capitalism. But he did predict a continued trend towards concentration of capital, as noted above.

Comte correctly forecast the abolition of human slavery throughout the world (PP, IV, 453). He also foresaw that one result of such abolition would be the rise of negro governments in most West Indian islands.

11. On Socialism

Comte was well aware of the contemporary growth of the socialist movement, and predicted its ultimate failure. He conceded that the prevailing economic system had serious defects, but argued that they should be cured by improving moral ideas, i.e., applied social science and public opinion, not by socializing private firms. "We [will] substitute moral agencies for political," he wrote (PP, I, 125). He mistakenly predicted that there would be no violent social revolutions, but later changed his mind.

He charged that socialism would tend to suppress individuality, weaken management, and eliminate the benefits of inheritance (PP, I, 126-28). In spite of such charges, the socialist movement has grown stronger in all countries ever since he wrote, and socialists now rule a third of mankind.

He predicted that, "The tendency of modern civilization, far from impeding private industry, is to entrust it more and more with functions, especially those of a material kind, which were originally left to government" (PP, I, 133). It is true that private firms have accepted new functions—the payment of pensions and accident compensation, the provision of workers' housing and recreational facilities, etc.—but few of these were previously performed by governments. And innumerable new laws "impeding private industry" have been adopted in all advanced countries.

He correctly predicted that trade unions would be legalized (PP, I, 134), and that the influence and prestige of workers would rise (PP, IV, 364). He also foresaw that all needy unemployable persons would be given pensions or welfare (PP, IV, 308).

12. The Growth of Government

According to Comte, the social division of labor will become greater and greater, and therefore each society will become more and more complex indefinitely. This, in turn, will cause governments to grow and assume additional functions, including the function of minimizing differences of opinion on social and political issues. In order to reduce the risk of violent internal conflict, all governments will increasingly indoctrinate their citizens with the basic principles of positive or scientific thinking in all fields of thought. He specifically forecast state support of the positivist religion, now called secular humanism (LB, 255-58).

These predictions have been increasingly verified by history. All societies have become ever more complex. The relative size and the functions of all governments have increased. And all communist governments have assumed the function of political indoctrination, including the teaching of secular humanism.

While Comte did not try to predict individual wars and revolutions, he clearly foresaw great internal civil struggles due to continuing ideological conflicts (LB, 273). This easy prediction was confirmed by subsequent civil wars and revolutions in many lands, most of which increased the size and scope of government.

He also predicted that future advances in the new science of sociology would provide governments with more and more sound principles and methods of government control over business and society. He explicitly rejected the nonintervention, laissez faire doctrines of contemporary orthodox economists (LB, 322). However, he also rejected socialist pleas for the nationalization of most private property.

13. The Form of Government

Although the number and power of national legislatures had been growing for centuries among advanced countries, Comte confidently predicted a reversal of this trend and the rise of dictatorship. He urged and predicted "emancipation from parliamentary form" and creation of a strong, independent executive (PP, IV, 341-42). At one point he forecast a triumvirate of bankers (ib., 301-02); at another, rule by workers (PP, I, 161); and at still another, rule by business leaders. "Ultimately...political power will fall into the hands of the great leaders of industry" because they will have learned how to manage in their own large firms (PP, I, 160).

He explicitly rejected the idea of "sovereignty of the people" and all direct participation of the people in government (PP, I, 106). However, he predicted they would exercise strong moral influence over the nation's rulers.

14. Feminism

Comte not only failed to predict the great coming improvement in the legal, political, and economic status of women but predicted that nearly all women would continue to be "confined...to domestic life" (PP, IV, 56). He described the female sex as living in "a kind of state of continuous childhood" and as being inferior to men in intellect and reasoning power. He explicitly disagreed with his benefactor, John Stuart Mill on these vital points (LB, 252).

He also condemned divorce, and failed to predict the great increase in divorce rates in all advanced countries (LB, 253). He even claimed that "hospitals are...destined to disappear utterly" (PP, IV, 372) and be replaced by home care, presumably because loving wives and mothers make the best nurses.

15. Comments

Although Comte expressed great admiration for Condorcet, whom he called "my spiritual father," he failed to endorse, or explicitly rejected, some of Condorcet's most important and perceptive forecasts, notably those on the continued rise of political democracy, free public education, feminism, divorce, birth control, and social insurance. Moreover, all of Condorcet's major predictions have been at least partially verified by history, while several of Comte's have been flatly disproven, for instance his forecast that nearly all women would remain dependent, voteless, full-time housewives. For these reasons, Comte rankes well below Condorcet as a pioneer futurist.

Comte's chief contribution to futurism was his restatement, elaboration and widespread application of the fundamental theory of the three stages of intellectual evolution, a theory which the future history of man will long continue to verify. No social trend is more fundamental or widely influential than the rise of scientific thinking and its growing application to personal and social behavior, and Comte stressed this trend more than any previous or subsequent futurist.

Most of Comte's important ideas about the future were elaborations of ideas previously stated by his early employer and mentor, Saint Simon, to whom Comte failed to give due credit.

ALEXIS DE TOCQUEVILLE AS A FUTURIST

Alexis de Tocqueville (1805-59), a French lawyer and liberal aristocrat, never wrote a book, chapter, or essay entirely or largely devoted to predicting the future, but his two-volume masterpiece, Democracy in America (1835, 1840), contains sufficient sound predictions to justify treating him as a pioneer scientific futurist.

He came to the United States in 1831 and spent nine months traveling through most parts of the young republic, which then had a population of some thirteen million. His nominal chief purpose was to study the American prison system, but in fact he carefully studied the entire society and government of the U.S.

Tocqueville came to study the U.S. and wrote Democracy in America primarily because he believed that the entire Western World had been moving toward political equality and democratic government for some 800 years, and would long continue to do so. He foresaw that the aristocratic and monarchical governments of Europe soon would be overthrown or would peacefully evolve into democratic governments, and he wanted to help Europeans benefit from the pioneer American experience with democracy. Thus his book was motivated by his most significant prediction concerning social evolution. And he was very explicit about his great interest in the future. "I have not undertaken to see differently from others, but to look further, and while they are busied for the morrow only, I have turned by thoughts to the whole future" (I, 17).

This essay is based on the two-volume 1945 Vintage Book edition of Democracy in America, which contains an historical essay, editorial notes, and bibiliographies by Phillips Bradley. All page references are to these two volumes.

1. Methodology

From his basic major prediction that all advanced nations would continue to move towards democracy and equality, Tocqueville derived many more specific predictions, such as the inevitable coming popularization or vulgarization of literature, poetry, art, music, and drama. By so doing, he created a new and fruitful method of predicting the future, namely the use of the most obvious fundamental social trends to predict numerous derivable subsidiary or secondary trends.

Since Tocqueville was firmly convinced that all advanced nations would long continue to become more democratic, his account of the behavior of people in the first great democracy, the U.S., usually implied the forecast that other nations would eventually behave as the Americans were behaving in 1831. "I confess that in America I saw more than America; I sought there the image of democracy itself, with its inclinations, its character, its prejudices, and its passions, in order to learn what we have to fear or to hope from its progress" (I, 15).

Tocqueville defended his use of trend projections as follows: "It is not necessary that God himself should speak in order that we may discover the unquestionable signs of his will. It is enough to ascertain what is the habitual course of nature and the constant tendency of events" (I, 7). This defense of scientific trend projection seems theological and archaic today, but the method defended is sound, and Tocqueville was one of the first futurists to explain and defend it.

2. The Trend Toward Equality and Democracy

In the Preface to the twelfth edition (1848) of Democracy in America, the author explained that, "His work was written...with a mind constantly occupied by a single thought—that the advent of democracy as a governing power in the world's affairs, universal and irresistible, was at hand" (I, ix). And in his Introduction he asserted that his book had "been written under the influence of a kind of religious awe produced in the author's mind by the view of that irresistible revolution which has advanced for centuries...and which is still advancing," namely the trend towards political equality (I, 7). He traced this trend in Europe back to the eleventh century, which suggests that he was merely projecting into the future a trend which he considered old and well-established.

In his opinion the desire for equality was very strong in democratic countries, and was certain to be satisfied. He claimed that it is "ardent, insatiable, incessant, invincible..." Therefore, "All men and all powers seeking to cope with this irresistible passion will be overthrown and destroyed by it. In our age freedom cannot be established without it, and despotism itself cannot reign without its support" (II, 102-03).

Tocqueville concluded his introductory discussion of the trend towards equality and democracy by predicting that all European countries would become more like

America. "It appears to me beyond a doubt that, sooner or later, we shall arrive, like the Americans, at an almost complete equality of condition" (I, 14). I think he really meant equality of political condition, for he was well aware that some Americans were rich, and others poor. If we interpret his forecast in this way, it has been verified in most European nations.

Tocqueville never clearly explained what he meant by the trend towards equality. Apparently it included, or was almost identical with, the trend towards democracy. In his index the numerous page references for equality are almost the same as those for democracy, and he often treated them as synonyms. He used the term democracy to include both social democracy and political democracy. He also used the term equality to include political equality as well as social equality. And he used both democracy and equality to mean all of these four things.

3. Centralization of Government

Tocqueville repeatedly forecast or implied that the inevitable continuance of the trend towards equality and/or democracy would result in steadily increasing centralization of government. He also predicted that growing centralization would result in growing uniformity of legislation. "These ideas take root and spread in proportion as social conditions become more equal and men more alike. They are produced by equality, and in turn they hasten the progress of equality" (II, 308).

He offered several more specific reasons for the continuance of these trends. First, he noted that aristocrats had favored the preservation of regional and local governments because they had controlled them. The trend towards equality weakened this support of local government in Europe (II, 315-16). Secondly, "in politics...the intellect of democratic nations is peculiarly open to simple and general notions" like centralization and uniformity" (II, 306). Thirdly, decentralization makes laws differ from place to place, and "The very next notion to that of a single and central power which presents itself to the minds of men in the ages of equality is the notion of uniformity of legislation. As every man sees that he differs but little from those about him, he cannot understand why a rule that is applicable to one man should not be equally applicable to all others" (II, 310). He concluded that, "I am of the opinion that, in the democratic ages which are opening upon us...centralization will be the natural government" (II, 313).

The course of history since 1930 has certainly verified the general prediction that government would become more centralized and laws more uniform.

4. Collectivization

Tocqueville marveled at the intensive and growing use of private associations to carry on collective activities in the U.S. "Americans of all ages, all conditions and all dispositions constantly form associations. They have not only commercial and manufacturing companies, but associations of a thousand other kinds, religious, moral, serious..." (II, 114). He explained this as due chiefly to the growth of equality, and predicted that the growth of associations would long continue. "Among the laws that rule human societies there is one which seems to be more precise and clear than all the others. If men are to remain civilized or become so, the art of associating together must grow and improve in the same ratio in which the equality of conditions is increased" (II, 118). He clearly implied that all or most other countries would follow the American example in this respect, as in many others.

He noted that, "A government might perform the part of some of the largest American companies" and that, "It is easy to foresee that the time is drawing near when a man will be less and less able to produce, by himself alone, the commonest necessities of life. The task of the governing power will therefore perpetually increase, and its very efforts will extend it every day. The more it stands in the place of associations, the more will individuals, losing the notion of combining together, require its assistance;... Will the administration of the country ultimately assume the management of all the manufacturers which no single citizen is able to carry on?" He expressed his hope that such radical socialization would not occur completely. In any case, he was one of the first to foresee the coming continuous growth of the functions of government (II, 116-17).

Tocqueville predicted that the inevitable further "progress of social equality" would continue to cause "the growth of manufactures," which in turn, would be a "great cause" of the continuing growth of government power and activity. He noted that, "the manufacturing classes require more regulation, superintendence, and restraint than the other classes...and it is natural that the powers of government should increase in the same proportion as those classes" (II, 327). "As the nation becomes more engaged in manufactures, the lack of roads, canals, harbors and other works of a semi-public nature...is more strongly felt; and, as a nation becomes more democratic, private individuals are less able, and the state more able, to execute works of such magnitude" (II, 392).

5. The Welfare State and Socialism

Tocqueville predicted the main features of what we now call the welfare state or socialism—centralization, uniformity, regimentation, social security, and welfare. I have already noted his forecasts concerning centralization and uniformity. Now I shall cite his forecasts on regimentation to promote social security and welfare in the coming more democratic society.

In this future society, "Above...men stands an immense and tutelary power, which takes upon itself alone to secure their gratifications and to watch over their fate. That power is absolute, minute, regular, provident and mild [because it is democratic]. It would be like the authority of a parent.... For their happiness such a government willingly labors...it provides for their security, foresees and supplies their necessities, facilitates their pleasure, manages their principal concerns, directs their industry, regulates the descent of property, and subdivides their inheritances; what remains, but to spare them all the care of thinking and all the trouble of living?" (II, 336).

So far as I am aware, he was the first writer to predict so fully the main features of the welfare states and socialist governments of our day.

6. On Political Revolutions

In 1830 the governments and societies of all countries except the U.S. were still strongly aristocratic. Tocqueville believed that all were moving slowly but steadily towards both social and political equality and that this process would involve numerous violent democratic revolutions. "A people that has existed for centuries under a system of castes and classes can arrive at a democratic state of society only by passing through a long series of more or less critical transformations, accomplished by violent efforts..." (II, 265). However, he predicted that they would become less frequent, as explained below.

Since he made these predictions several Anglo-saxon and Scandinavian nations have evolved from aristocracy to democracy without experiencing violent democratic revolutions, but the great majority of nations have remained aristocratic or have experienced one or more violent democratic revolutions. Therefore, I believe that Tocqueville was largely right in predicting many such revolutions.

He also predicted that the rise of democracy would gradually diminish the chief causes of revolution, namely social and political inequality. "Almost all the revolutions that have changed the aspect of nations have been made to consolidate or to destroy social inequality.... If, then, a state of society can ever be founded in which every man shall have something to keep and little to take from others, much will have been done for the peace of the world" (II, 266).

He claimed that the U.S. had already done so much to reduce social, economic, and political inequality that it would probably never experience a violent revolution, except possibly one caused by the persistence of slavery. "Although the Americans are constantly modifying...their laws, they by no means display revolutionary passions," and "They have changed, but they dread revolutions." Therefore, "If ever America undergoes great revolutions, they will be brought about by the presence of the black race...that is to say, they will owe their origin...to the inequality of condition" (II, 270). This was a remarkably prescient forecast!

7. On the Frequency of War

Tocqueville predicted that the continued growth of democracy would weaken the military passion and reduce the number of wars. "The same interests, the same fears, the same passions that deter democratic nations from revolution deter them also from war.... The ever-increasing numbers of men of property...the growth of personal wealth...the mildness of manners...produced by the equality of conditions...all these causes concur to quench the military spirit...[therefore] among civilized nations the warlike passions will become more rare and less intense in proportion as social conditions are more equal" (II, 279).

Although it is doubtful that wars conducted by civilized nations have become less frequent since 1840, I believe that his reasoning here is sound, and that such wars will become less frequent in coming centuries.

It is noteworthy that Tocqueville was perhaps the first to assert that, "There are two things that a democratic people will always find very difficult, to begin a war and to end it" (II, 283).

He also noted a paradox. Since democratic nations can enroll "the whole male population" in their armies, "in democratic ages armies seem to grow larger in proportion as the love of war declines" (II, 299).

8. U.S. Economic Development

Although American factories were few and small in 1831, Tocqueville predicted that, "The Americans will no doubt ultimately succeed in producing or manufacturing at home most of the articles that they require ..." (I, 439). He also implied that, "The U.S....must become one of the foremost maritime powers of the world" (I, 440). Later he was more explicit and confident. "I cannot help believing that they [the Anglo-Americans] will one day become the foremost maritime power of the globe. They are born to rule the seas, as the Romans were to conquer the world" (I, 447). If the latter forecast refers to naval military power, it has clearly been verified by history.

9. Wages and Inequality

Tocqueville predicted both that wages would continue to rise and that income differences would diminish. He asserted that "a slow and gradual rise of wages is one of the general laws of democratic communities. In proportion as social conditions become more equal" (II, 200).

However, he claimed that there was a counter-trend in manufacturing, in which a new economic aristocracy was arising.

10. Applied and Pure Science

Tocqueville claimed that aristocracy favored pure over applied science and that democracy favors the development of applied science. "You may be sure that the more democratic, enlightened, and free a nation is, the greater will be the number of...discoveries immediately applicable to productive industry" because, in democratic societies, "every new method that leads by a shorter road to wealth, every machine that spares labor, every instrument that diminishes the cost of production...seems to be the grandest effort of the human intellect." Moreover, "the working class takes part in public affairs; and public honors as well as pecuniary remuneration may be awarded to those who deserve them" (II, 46). Since the author predicted the further growth of democracy in all Christian nations, he implied that applied science would long continue to grow there.

Tocqueville feared that the desire for political stability was, or would become, so strong in democratic countries "that men may...regard every new theory as a peril...every social improvement as a stepping stone to revolution..." (II, 277). He therefore predicted that, "if ever social equality is generally and permanently established in the world, great intellectual and political revolutions will become more difficult and less frequent..."

He was right on political revolutions, but certainly wrong on intellectual revolutions. The continuous world wide advance towards democracy since 1835 has been accompanied by even more rapid intellectual progress in nearly all fields of knowledge. And intellectual progress has been more rapid in democratic than in aristocratic countries.

11. Literature and Art

Tocqueville implied that the inevitable further growth of equality and democracy would continue to lower the artistic levels of works of literature and art. "In aristocracies readers are fastidious and few in number; in democracies they are far more numerous and far less difficult to please" (II, 64) because in democracies "the interest of individuals as well as the security of the commonwealth demands that the education of the greater number should be scientific, commercial, and industrial rather than literary" (II, 66).

Moreover, "Democratic nations...will habitually prefer the useful to the beautiful..." (II, 50), and "the democratic principle not only acts to direct the human mind to the useful arts, but it induces the artisans to produce with great rapidity many imperfect commodities, and the consumer to content himself with these commodities" (II, 52).

However, he implied that democracy would also promote pure science because "it enormously increases the number of those who do cultivate it [science]" and some of these additional scientists would be pure scientists (II, 47). In these remarks he seems to have confused the effects of economic progress with those of progress towards equality and democracy.

12. Newspapers

Tocqueville observed that newspapers were more numerous and influential in the U.S. than in any other country because it was more democratic, and its government was more decentralized, and because private associations were more numerous and important (II, 119-22). In his opinion, "The power of the newspaper press must ...increase as the social conditions of men become more equal" (II, 122). Since he had forecast that men will become more equal, this implied that the power of newspapers would increase in all civilized countries. He had also predicted that associations will become more numerous, which has the same implication here. However, he had forecast that government will become more centralized, which implies the contrary.

13. Religion

Tocqueville made several predictions on the future effects of the inevitable continued growth of equality and democracy on religion. He was a devout Christian, and feared that the growing importance of public opinion in countries moving towards democracy would weaken belief in religious dogmas, which he believed necessarily rests upon authority. "The more the conditions of men are equalized...the more important is it for religion...not needlessly to run counter to the ideas that generally prevail...For as public opinion grows to be more and more...the religious principle has no external support strong enough to enable it long to resist its attacks" (II, 28). He seems to have anticipated the Catholic Church's future problems on divorce and birth control.

Since the Koran prescribes far more numerous and detailed rules of personal and social behavior, Tocqueville considered Mohammedanism less suitable than Christianity for the coming, more democratic world. "This alone...would suffice to prove that the former of these two religions will never long predominate in a cultivated and democratic age, while the latter is destined to retain its sway at these as at all other periods" (II, 24).

However, he later undermined the second part of this forecast by predicting that the growth of equality would favor the growth of pantheism. "I believe pantheism to be one of those [ideas] most fitted to seduce the human mind in democratic times" because "it fosters the pride [of men] while it soothes the indolence of their minds" (p. 33).

Tocqueville reported that Americans were more religious than the French, but he expected that the continued struggle between reason and religious authority, due in part to the growth of democracy, would weaken the Protestant Churches in America. "I am inclined to believe that...our posterity will tend more and more to a division into only two parts, some relinquishing Christianity entirely and others returning to the Church of Rome" (II, 31). On the other hand, he confidently asserted that "religions ought to have fewer external obsevances in democratic periods" (II, 26), which suggests the growing future acceptance of one basic Protestant belief.

14. Manners

Tocqueville claimed that manners had long been growing less harsh, and implied that this trend would long continue. "We perceive that for several centuries social conditions have tended to equality, and we discover that at the same time the customs of society have been softened." He asserted that the former trend was the chief cause of the latter, which implies that it will long continue and spread (II, 172).

He explained this causation as follows: "...real sympathies can exist only between those who are alike" and the growth of equality makes men more alike (II, 173).

He asserted that the Americans "are extremely open to compassion" and "in no country is criminal justice administered with more mildness than in the U.S." (II, 176). He clearly implied that most or all other countries would gradually become more Americanized in these respects.

In his opinion, "Democracy does not attach men strongly to one another, but it places their habitual intercourse on an easier footing." He supported the latter claim by comparing the easy social intercourse among Americans with the more formal intercourse among Englishmen (II, 178-79).

He also noted that, "In democracies servants are not only equal among themselves, but...in some sort, the equals of their masters" (II, 191), and clearly implied that this democratic social relationship would spread as all civilized nations became more and more democratic.

He reported several other differences between manners in the U.S. and in Europe, and implied that Europe would become more like the U.S. in these respects also (II, 196-303). For instance, intrafamily relationships will become more democratic (II, 202-08), young unmarried women will become more independent (II, 209-11), behavior will become more moral (II, 215-21), women will become more nearly equal to men (II, 222-25), and social manners will become less dignified and refined (II, 228-31).

15. Negroes and Indians

Tocqueville devoted a long chapter to the past and current harsh and unjust treatment of the negroes and indians in the U.S., and made several predictions concerning the future of these minorities. He quoted with approval Jefferson's forecast: "Nothing is more clearly written in the pages of destiny than the emancipation of the blacks; and it is equally certain that the two races will never live in a state of equal freedom under the same government, so insurmountable are the barriers which nature, habit, and opinion have established between them" (I, 388n). Tocqueville added his own prediction that "the abolition of slavery...will...increase the repugnance of the white population for the blacks" (I, 390), and even forecast a general race war after abolition (I, 391, 394). He expected that, "in the West Indies islands the white race is destined to be subdued, and upon the continent the blacks:" (I, 391). He also correctly forecast that "The negro race will never leave...the American continent..." (I, 393).

After noting the long retreat of the American Indians before white aggression, Tocqueville concluded, "I believe that the Indian nations of North America are doomed to perish, and that whenever the Europeans shall be established on the shores of the Pacific Ocean, that race of men will have ceased to exist" (I, 354). He quoted a similar forecast by Lewis Cass, and claimed that "almost all American statesmen" agreed on this. One of the chief reasons for his unduly dire prediction was his belief that "the Indians will never civilize themselves, or that it will be too late when they may be inclined to make the experiment" (I, 355).

16. On Preservation of the Union

Tocqueville discussed the political struggle between the North and the South, and predicted that the U.S. federal government would fail to preserve the Union. He explained that, "Single governments have... a natural tendency to centralization; and confederations to dismemberment" (I, 400). Moreover, in America, "Patriotism...is still directed to the state and has not passed over to the Union." Therefore, "If...the Union were to engage in a struggle with...the states at the present day, its defeat may be confidently predicted; and it is not probable that such a struggle would be seriously undertaken" (I, 402-03). Fortunately, the Civil War, which began less than 20 years later, proved both of these predictions to have been questionable.

17. U.S. Population Expansion

Although he asserted that the preservation of the Union "can only be a fortunate accident" (I, 414), he predicted in 1835 that the Anglo-Americans would continue to multiply rapidly, and would eventually occupy "the immense space contained between the polar regions and the tropics, extending from the coasts of the Atlantic to those of the Pacific Ocean" (I, 450). Therefore, "The time will...come when 150 million men will be living in North America, equal in condition...and preserving the same civilization, the same language, the same religion, the same habits, the same manners, and...the same opinions..." (I, 452). When he wrote, the U.S. population was only about 14 million, and the European population was about 205 million.

In 1832 Texas had not yet been annexed to the U.S., but Tocqueville implied that it would soon be annexed (I, 363n), and that Americans would also occupy large additional regions of Northern Mexico (I, 448-49).

Perhaps the most famous prediction made by Tocqueville is that in which he compared the future roles of the U.S. and Russia. "There are at present two great nations in the world, which started from different points, but seem to tend towards the same end... their courses are not the same, yet each of them seems marked out...to sway the destinies of half the globe" (I, 452).

Comments

Alexis de Tocqueville was a great pioneer futurist. He made many significant predictions which have been largely verified by history. Among the most significant of these were his forecasts of the continued growth of social democracy, political democracy, centralization, collectivization, and abolition. He made few bad predictions.

His principal fault was his relative neglect of the basic economic factors, especially the industrial revolution. He repeatedly confused the effects of this revolution with the effects of the trend toward democracy, and he largely failed to explain past and future economic evolution, including that from individualism to capitalism.

He also failed to clearly define some of his basic terms—such as equality, democracy, and liberty—which makes some of his predictions obscure or ambiguous.

JOHN STUART MILL AS A FUTURIST

John Stuart Mill (1806-73) was one of the greatest English social scientists and reformers of the 19th Century. He wrote influential books and articles on logic, philosophy, political science, feminism, and economics. His <u>Principles of Political Economy</u> was the most widely used economic text for over thirty years.

He was the son of James Mill, a close friend and leading follower of Jeremy Bentham, the founder of utilitarianism. John Stuart Mill never attended school or college. He was educated at home by his brilliant father, who taught him to read widely in Greek and Latin by age 12. At sixteen he went to work as a clerk in the East India Company, which then governed all of India, and was employed there continuously for 36 years, rising eventually to a senior position. Thus he achieved great success in business as well as in social science. Most of his serious writing was done while employed full time by the East India Company. After he retired he served one term as a member of Parliament. Throughout his adult life he was active as a speaker, writer, and contributor in many reform movements.

I have not read all of the numerous magazine articles he published, but, so far as I am aware, he never collected his many explicit predictions in a single article, chapter, or book. He was a firm believer in social progress, which justifies the assumption that he anticipated eventual adoption of most of the social reforms he advocated, even when he did not explicitly predict their adoption.

2. Methodology and Theory of Progress

J.S. Mill (hereafter referred to as Mill) was well-read in the early literature of futurism—that written by Turgot, Condorcet, St. Simon, and Malthus—and was personally well-acquainted with Bentham, Comte, and Tocqueville. He endorsed or related some of their most plausible predictions.

He was also well-read in recent European and American history, and often projected well-established progressive social trends into the future because he believed that the factors responsible for them would long continue to operate.

Finally, he repeatedly asserted or implied that backward countries would eventually follow the path of social progress pioneered by advanced countries.

Mill recognized the role of both economic and intellectual factors in social progress. "Economic and social changes, though among the greatest, are not the only forces which shape the course of our species; ideas are not alway the mere signs and effects of social circumstances, they are themselves a power in history" (Essays on Politics, 1963 ed., pp. 259-60). However, he claimed that intellectual progress was the chief and basic cause of social progress. "The evidence of history and ... of human nature combine ... to show that there is really one social element which is thus predominent, and almost paramount, among the agents of the social progression. This is the state of the speculative faculties of mankind; including speculative beliefs ..." (Logic, p.585).

He endorsed Comte's law of the three stages of intellectual progress: theology, metaphysics, and positive science. He believed that new positive sciences of ethics, sociology, and political science were in process of creation, and implied that this process would continue indefinitely. This in turn would result in the adoption of more and more beneficial social reforms as education spreads knowledge of these new sciences ever more widely (Logic, 575-8).

3. Religion

Like his father, Mill rejected Christian theology and anticipated the continual decline of orthodox religious faith in advanced countries. In his lucid and revealing Autobiography he condemned the concept of a being "who would make a Hell—who would create the human race with the infallible foreknowledge...that the great majority of them were to be consigned to horrible and lasting torment. The time...is drawing near when this dreadful conception of an object of worship will be no longer identified with Christianity..." (Columbia Un. Press ed., p. 29). Since he made this prediction, the proportion of Europeans who believe in Hell and such a being has been steadily declining, so his prediction has already been partially verified.

Mill went much further than predicting the reformation of Christianity. He explicitly rejected all supernatural religion. "I am thus one of the very few examples in this country, of one who has, not thrown off religious belief, but never had it..." (ibid, p.30). And he often argued against basic religious ideas. For instance he wrote, "I agreed with him [Comte] that the moral and intellectual ascendancy, once exercised by priests, must in time pass into the hands of philosophers... (ibid, p. 148). By "philosophers" he meant scientists.

Mill forecast that the continued decline of religious faith would occur simultaneously with an indefinite further public acceptance of both utilitarianism and positivism, first among educated people in advanced countries, and eventually among all persons in all countries

He explained that "the old opinions in religion, morals, and politics are so much discredited in...intellectual minds as to have lost the greater part of their efficacy for good..." Hence, "a transitional period commences, of weak conviction...which cannot terminate until a renovation has been effected in the basis of...belief leading to the elevation of some faith ...which they can really believe..." Fortunately, "a spirit of free speculation has sprung up, giving a more encouraging prospect of the gradual mental emancipation of England..." (Auto, 167-68). Like Comte, he forecast that Christianity would eventually be replaced by a religion of humanity which would urge men to work for the welfare of mankind, not for a place in heaven (Works, X, 488-9). I believe this prediction misuses the term religion, which ought to be restricted to certain kinds of faith in the supernatural.

Mill expected that the spread of utilitarianism and positivism would eventually result in a long decline of belief in intuitive ethics. "The notion that truths external to the mind may be known by intuition or consciousness, independently of observation and experience, is...the great intellectual support of false doctrines and bad institutions..." As a firm prophet of intellectual progress, Mill must have anticipated the decline of this unsound philosophic doctrine, though he predicted that it "is likely for some time longer...to predominate" among philosophers.

In spite of the fact that he endorsed the main features of Comtean positivism, Mill, like Comte, called himself a philosopher. Since positivism asserts that all purely philosophic truth claims are invalid, irrelevant, and unverifiable, and that the philosophic method of arriving at basic premises, intuition, is unsound, the claim that positivism is a philosophy is illogical. Positivism is a defense of science against all theology and philosophy, not a new or revised philosophy. Mill's use of the term philosophy often obscures the meaning of his reasoning, and has misled many readers.

4. Economic Progress

Mill was a firm believer is social progress, and repeatedly predicted the indefinite future continuance of such progress, based partly on continued economic progress. In his <u>Principles of Political Economy</u>, he wrote that "We have...to consider the economical condition of mankind as liable to change, and...as at all times undergoing progressive changes." Such changes occur first in the most advanced nations, but "there is no reason to doubt that not only these nations will for some time continue so to increase [their production] but that most of the other nations...will successively enter on the same career." One of the chief features of this progress "is the perpetual, and so far as human foresight can extend, the unlimited growth of man's power over nature, " due to the growth of scientific knowledge, which is still "almost in its infancy." Indeed, "it is impossible not to look forward to a vast multiplication and long succession of contrivances for economizing labor and increasing its produce; and to an ever wider diffusion of the use and benefit of those contrivances" (<u>PPE</u>, Hadley ed., II, 210-2).

He also noted other reasons for continued economic progress. "The progress which is to be expected in the physical sciences and arts, combined with the greater security of property, and greater freedom of disposing of it...and with the more extensive and more skillful employment of the joint-stock principle, afford space and scope for an indefinite increase of capital and production, and for the increase of population which is its ordinary accompaniment. That the growth of population will overpass the increase of production, there is not much reason to apprehend..." This implies that real per person incomes will rise (<u>PPE</u>, II, 214). Here we have six correct major predictions in a single long sentence.

Mill wrote that "mechanical inventions...have enabled a greater population of workers to live the same life of drudgery and imprisonment "and have increased the comforts of the middle classes. But they have not begun to effect those great changes in human destiny, which it is in their nature and in their futurity to accomplish." These "great changers" will be achieved as population growth is restricted and wealth becomes "the common property of the species." (<u>PPE</u>, II, 264-5).

5. The Growth of Security

Mill believed that the security of person and property had long been increasing in advanced nations, and predicted that such progress "will assuredly continue." He explained that such progress would be partly due to the creation of "a more efficient judicature and police, ...the limitation of feudal privileges, ...the reform of taxation, ...the decline of warfare," and "the continual extension of the salutary practice of insurance" (PPE, II, 212). All of these predictions, except perhaps the decline of warfare, have been verified by history.

6. Corporations and Large-Scale Production

Corporations played a very minor role in economic life in Mill's day, but he repeatedly predicted a vast increase in their use. "As wealth increases and business capacity improves, we may look forward to a great extension of establishments, both for industrial and other purposes, formed by the collective contributions of large numbers, ...like those called...joint stock companies, or ...co-operative societies" (PPE, I, 214).

One major reason why he predicted such a large growth in the use of corporate or collective organization was that he believed that almost every increase in the scale of production and/or organization reduces production costs (PPE, I, 131). He therefore predicted a long further increase in the scale of production. "In the countries in which there are the largest markets...the greatest annual increase of capital, and the greatest number of large capitals...there is a perpetual growth not only of large manufacturing estalishments, but also...of shops and warehouses...on a large scale" (PPE, I, 140). Clearly, he expected this "perpetual growth" to continue indefinitely, as in fact it did, and will continue to, do so.

7. International Trade and War

Mill confidently predicted that social progress would continue in backward, as well as in advanced countries. "As civilization spreads, and security of person and property become established, in parts of the world which have not hitherto had that advantage, the productive capabilities of those places are called into fuller activity, for the benefit both of their own inhabitants and of foreigners." However, it will be "many generations before those countries will be raised even to the present level of the most civilized parts of Europe" (PPE, II, 216). Here we have a brilliant early anticipation of the long process of Westernization which has since occurred in non-European countries, and will probably continue indefinitely.

9. Birth Control, Population Growth, and Real Wages

Mill was one of the pioneer advocates of artificial birth control (Auto, 74). As a youth he was arrested for distributing one of Place's birth control pamphlets. And in later years he repeatedly stressed the need for, and predicted the adoption of, effective methods of population limitation. For instance, he wrote that, "It appears to me impossible but that the increase of intelligence, of education, and of the love of independence...must be attended with a corresponding growth of the good sense which manifests itself in provident habits of conduct, and that population, therefore, will not grow as fast as "capital and employment" (PPE, II, 271). Implicit in this forecast is the prediction that real personal incomes will rise.

Mill explained that the coming emancipation of women would reduce the birth rate, presumably because it would enable more women to practice birth control. He foresaw, "among the probable consequences of the industrial and social independence of women, a great diminution of the evil of over-population" (PPE, II, 272). He was surely one of the first, if not the first, to make this brilliant prediction. But he did not dare to use terms like contraception, birth control, abortion, and sterilization.

In his book, Socialism and Utilitarianism (1892) he criticized Malthus and Louis Blanc, the French socialist, for predicting a decline or stagnation in real wages due to the growth of population. He claimed that "experience shows that...the pressure of population on subsistence...is not an increasing evil; on the contrary, the progress of...civilization has a tendency to diminish it" by the accumulation of capital, by the development of new countries, and by other means (pp. 68-70).

10. Aristocracy vs. Political Democracy

Like Comte, Mill was firmly convinced that the political, economic, and intellectual influence of the European aristocracy had long been declining, and would long continue to decline. In a series of articles published in The Examiner in London in 1831, under the title, "The Spirit of the Age," he made clear that the abolition of hereditary distinctions is one of the major historical trends which will continue until it is fully achieved. And he harshly condemned the European aristocratic classes in his Autobiography (pp. 120-2).

Like Toqueville, Mill was well aware of the strong trend towards political democracy in Europe and America, and he predicted its long continuance. "We do not maintain that the time is drawing near when there will be no distinction of classes; but we do contend that the power of the higher classes, both in government and society, is diminishing, while that of the middle and even lower classes is increasing,,and likely to increase." He added that "the Newspapers and the Railroads are solving the problem of bringing the democracy of England, like that of Athens, simultaneously in one agora" (Essays on Politics, 224, 226, 228).

Mill predicted that the intelligence of the "mass of the people" would be gradually and indefinitely increased by the growth of education and newspaper reading. "From this increase of intelligence, several effects may be confidently predicted. First, that they will become even less willing than at present to be led and governed...by the mere authority and prestige of superiors...still less will they have hereafter any deferential awe, or religious principle of obedience... they will require that their conduct and condition shall be essentially self-governed" (PPE, II, 271).

He correctly foresaw that the broadening of the franchise would result in a gradual shift of political power to the left, and the adoption of more and more liberal social reforms (A. Ryan, J. S. Mill, 196-8).

Mill was an ardent advocate of proportional representation in democratic states, and favored the Hare system. He asserted that this great discovery had made him much more hopeful concerning the results of the adoption of political democracy, "the form of political institutions towards which the whole civilized world is manifestly and irresistibly tending" (Auto., 181-2).

11. Socialism

In his later years, Mill passed on from advocating and predicting the continued growth of political democracy to advocating and predicting the adoption of a conservative form of socialism, consisting initially of municipal socialism and numerous consumers' and producers' cooperatives. He called himself a socialist because "we...looked forward to a time when society will no longer be divided into the idle and the industrious; when the rule that they who do not work shall not eat, will be applied not to paupers only, but impartially to all; when the division of the produce of labour, instead of depending...on the accident of birth, will be made...on an acknowledged principle of justice..." He anticipated "common ownership in the raw material of the globe, and an equal participation of all in the benefits of combined labour" (Auto., 162). This implies the eventual elimination of private ownership and inheritance of the means of production.

In his Principles of Political Economy he explained that, "in the present stage of human progress, when the ideas of equality are daily spreading more widely... it is not to be expected that the division of the human race into two hereditary classes, employers and employed can be permanently maintained" (II, 273). When Mill made these predictions he was unacquainted

with Marx or Engels, whose writings were little known
in England and America until much later. In sharp
contrast, Mill's Principles was the most widely used
text on economics for some thirty years.

In Chapter VII, "On the Probable Futurity of the
Laboring Classes," he forecast that, "The form of
association...which if man continues to improve, must
be expected in the end to predominate, is not that
which can exist between a capitalist as a chief, and
workpeople without a voice in the management, but the
association of the laborers themselves on terms of
equality, collectively owning the capital...and working
under managers elected and removable by themselves"
(PPE, II, 280-1).

He described in detail the recent growth of the
cooperative movement and profit sharing (II, 275-97),
and predicted that "the relation of masters and workpeople
will be gradually superseded by partnerships in one of
[these] two forms...perhaps finally in all [cases] by
associations of laborers among themselves" (II,275).
He was much more confident in predicting the final
result, socialism, than in predicting the means by
which it would be achieved.

Mill failed to explicitly forecast the vast growth
of government ownership and operation of industry which
occurred between 1830 and 1980, but he explicitly
defended, and implicitly predicted, government ownership
of many public utilities as a means of preventing the
private appropriation of monopoly profits (PPE, II, 463).
And such public ownership has grown steadily since he
wrote.

Mill never urged or predicted a socialist revolution
He always recommended peaceful democratic reform. He
was the first great Fabian socialist.

12. Free Public Education

Although Mill "looked forward to a time when"
socialism will be achieved, he anticipated that this
achievement would occur only after the working class
had become literate. This process of preparation for
socialism will be "prolonged through successive
generations" but, in time, "education, habit and
cultivation of the sentiments will make a common man
dig or weave for his country, as readily as fight for
his country" (Auto., 163).

Mill was an able early advocate of public financing
of elementary education. In his Principles he discussed
the arguments for and against this violation of laissez
faire, and concluded, "I hold it therefore the duty of
the government to supply...pecuniary support to elementary
schools, such as to render them accessible to all the
children of the poor..." (II, 457).

Mill forecast that workers would increasingly educate themselves by reading newspapers and magazines. Thus, "it cannot be doubted that they will increase in intelligence, even by their own unaided efforts," but, in addition, "there is reason to hope that great improvements both in the quality and quantity of school education will be effected by the exertions either of government or of individuals..." (PPE, II, 271). This prediction has been largely fulfilled.

13. Freedom of Speech and Press

Mill was a frequent and powerful advocate of freedom of speech and press, including freedom from social as well as legal inhibition. In his Autobiography he reported that his father had warned him against open avowal of his agnostic beliefs, but he asserted that the cases in which such reticence was prudent were "becoming fewer every day" (p. 31), which was an implicit prediction that they would continue to become fewer. This prediction was verified. Social and legal limitation of free speech has certainly decreased greatly in most countries since his day.

14. Feminism

In an early (c1832) essay on marriage and divorce, unpublished during his lifetime, Mill wrote that, "Every step in the progress of civilization has been marked by a nearer approach to equality in the condition of the sexes; and, if they are still far from being equal, the hindrance is not now in the difference of physical strength, but in artificial feelings and prejudices" (Midway, Autumn, 1963, p. 110).
In confidently predicted that, "The ideas and institutions by which...sex is made the groundwork of an inequality of legal rights and a forced dissimilarity of social function must ere long be recognized as the greatest hindrance to moral, social, and even intellectual improvement" (PPE, II, 272).
When serving as a member of parliament, he introduced a bill giving votes to women. It received 70 votes in its favor. Unfortunately, he was not re-elected.
According to Mill, "The first and indispensible step...towards the [economic] enfranchisement of woman, is that she be so educated as not to be dependant on her father or her father or her husband for subsistence... It does not follow that a woman should actually support herself because she would be capable of doing so..." He failed to anticipate the great coming increase in the proportion of women who work outside the home, but he clearly anticipated the coming great and long increase

in the proportion of women who become educated and capable of earning a good living (<u>Midway</u>, p.111).

In the same early essay, Mill argued strongly for liberalization of divorce laws (pp. 114-22) and obviously anticipated such liberalization. He even predicted that, when divorce became easy, more and more "wise" couples would postpone having children until they had lived together "for a considerable length of time" and found themselves compatible (p.118). There has in fact been a steady trend in this direction in advanced countries ever since he made this forecast.

15. Comments

John Stuart Mill predicted the long further continuance of most of the major social trends which occurred in advanced countries during the succeeding 130 years—including the rise of political democracy, free public education, technological progress, industrialization, affluence, birth control, utilitarian positivism, feminism, international trade, large corporations, cooperatives, and socialism.

Moreover, he did not make any important prediction, except on international peace, which has been disproven by subsequent events. He was therefore one of the most successful of all futurists. His record, like that of Condorcet's, proves that it has long been possible to predict major social trends with a high degree of success.

In his essay on J.S. Mill, historian Bernard Wishy asserted that "Few other Victorians so skillfully read the future." I agree.

MARX AND ENGELS AS FUTURISTS

Karl Marx (1818-83) and Friedrich Engels (1820-95) were not primarily futurists, nor did they write any books or articles devoted chiefly to predicting the future. Primarily, they were ardent social reformers. But they believed that social reform proposals should be based on a comprehensive scientific analysis of history, and that their analysis yielded a new theory of inevitable social evolution which enabled them to predict some major social trends many years into the future. Both their theory of social evolution and their predictions have had enormous influence, indeed almost as much as the Darwinian theory of biological evolution.

Marx and Engels collaborated so closely and so long, and agreed so fully, that it is difficult and pointless here to try to distinguish between their ideas on the future. Therefore, I shall deal with them as a single person.

They advocated some important social reforms without explicitly predicting their adoption. However, since they were self-confident and optimistic, and since they believed that social progress is inevitable, I shall occasionally treat such advocacy as implicit prediction of the future. In most cases they did not hesitate to make explicit predictions.

1. Methods of Prediction

Marx and Engels created and applied a major new method of scientific prediction of social trends, namely, their famous economic interpretation of history, future as well as past history, the theory that major changes in the methods of production precede and largely cause major subsequent social changes. For instance, they observed recent technological advances which had made factory production more efficient than domestic handicraft production in many industries, and therefore predicted that factory production would increase steadily and indefinitely in all advanced countries at the expense of handicraft production. This trend, they foresaw, would in turn, directly or indirectly, cause other major social trends.

The creation of this scientific method of predicting social change was their greatest contribution to the science of futurism. Since the process of industrialization is still very incomplete in the most advanced countries, and has barely begun in many other countries, this particular application of their general economic interpretation of history can still be used to make many highly probable predictions about future social trends in every country in the world.

In addition to using their novel economic interpretation of history as a means of predicting the future, Marx and Engels repeatedly stated and used another method. They explained that what has already happened in advanced countries is very likely to happen later in less advanced countries. They often used England as the most advanced state, and claimed that its recent economic history "shows to the less developed the image of its own future" (<u>Capital</u>, Kerr ed., I, 13). Since the nations of the world are in many different stages of development, this method of forecasting the future can be used to make a great number of scientific predictions about future social trends in all countries except the most advanced.

Finally, like most modern futurists, Marx and Engels frequently referred to recent statistical trends and projected them into the future.

I turn now to a discussion of their major predictions.

2. On Technological Progress

Marx and Engels repeatedly emphasized their conviction that technological progress had been, and would long continue to be, a fundamental cause of major social change. In the <u>Communist Manifesto</u> (1848) they explained that, "Modern industry has converted the little workshop of the patriarchal master into the great factory of the industrial capitalist" by means of "the extensive use of new machinery and...division of labor." And they wrote of "the increasing improvement of machinery," which clearly implies a prediction of long-continuing future technological progress. This progress is so rapid and irresistible that it "is like the sorcerer who is no longer able to control the powers of the nether world," another clear implication that such progress will continue.

In a long-unpublished 1848 manuscript (<u>Outlines of a Critique of Political Economy</u>) Marx even foresaw that the introduction of machinery would eventually be followed by more and more automation, a foresight which David McLellan has called "extraordinary" (<u>Karl Marx</u>, 295).

Marx and Engels did not try to predict individual technological advances, but their firm belief in the indefinite continuance of technological progress is evident in many parts of their writings. And this important expectation has been fully justified by history. However, it was not a new or rare expectation. By 1848 most social scientists expected such progress. But only Marx and Engels foresaw the major social effects of such progress.

3. On Industrialization

Marx and Engels predicted a long-continuing growth of factory production and other forms of collective mechanical production at the expense of handicraft production. They noted that the industrial revolution had begun, and had achieved its greatest development, in England, and they predicted continuing industrialization in England. They also predicted the initiation or continuance of industrialization in all other countries. These predictions have been largely verified by the source of history since they were made. Moreover, they are likely to be more and more fully verified in nearly all the countries of the world.

4. On Concentration of Capital

Marx and Engels forecast that free competition among capitalist firms would drive more and more small firms out of business because large firms can use newer and more costly machinery. As a result, "One capitalist kills many..." which results in a "constantly diminishing number of the magnates of capital." Eventually, "centralization of the means of production and socialization of labor...become incompatible with their capitalist integument" (Capital, I, 836-37).

This prediction has been partially verified by history. There has been a long-continuing, but slow and very incomplete, concentration of productive capital in ever larger firms in all advanced countries. However, Marx and Engels failed to anticipate how active and vigorous capitalist governments would become in their efforts to slow down this trend.

5. The Rise of the Managers

In his book, The Coming of Post-Industrial Society (p. 60), Daniel Bell noted that Marx had predicted the managerial revolution. Bell quoted Marx as follows: "That not the industrial capitalists, but the industrial managers are 'the soul of our industrial system' has already been remarked by Mr. Ure.... The capitalist mode of production itself has brought matters to such a point that the labor of superintendance, entirely separated from ownership of capital, walks the streets....

The cooperative factories furnish the proof that the capitalist has become...superfluous..." (*Capital*, III, 454-55).

Marx also explained that this managerial trend would help to bring about socialism because managers would eventually realize that they would be even more numerous and powerful under socialism.

6. The Increase of White-Collar Workers

According to Bell, Marx also predicted that continuing growth in the number and size of capitalist firms would continue to expand the relative size and influence of white-collar workers. Bell quoted from Marx' *Capital*: "...commercial operations increase... the scale of production is enlarged.... This necessitates the employment of commercial wage workers who form the office staff" (III, 352). He noted a more explicit prediction of Marx' *Theorien uber den Mehrwert*: "The size of the middle class increases and the [blue-collar?] proletariat will always form a comparatively small part of the populace (although it is still growing)."

However, Marx forecast that the growth of capitalism would lead to the proletarianization of the white-collar workers because the spread of free public education would lower the relative wage rates of literate white-collar workers (*Capital*, III, 354). I believe that history has verified this forecast.

7. On Proletarianization

Proletarianization is the relative growth of the working class, i.e., the proletariat. In the *Communist Manifesto* Marx and Engels explained that, "with the development of industry the proletariat...increases in number" at the expense of other classes, especially of independent artisans, peasants, and small business men. They predicted that the proletarianization trend would soon begin and/or continue in all countries in the world until the great majority of the population consisted of wage workers or employees. This prediction has been largely verified by history in all advanced countries. The continuous relative growth of factories, department stores, chain stores, chain banks, large law firms, government agencies, etc., has steadily increased the proportion of paid employees in the population of every advanced country since 1848, and will probably continue to do so for many more decades.

8. On the Growth of Trade Unions

Marx and Engels observed that the growth in the numbers of wage workers in advanced countries had already encouraged and enabled them to organize more and more trade unions. In the Communist Manifesto they explained that, as proletarianization proceeds, "the workers begin to form combinations against the bourgeois; they club together...they found permanent associations..." Marx and Engels projected this major social trend into the future and predicted a long-continuing growth in the number and economic power of labor unions in capitalist states. This forecast has been largely and increasingly verified by the course of events since 1848.

9. On the Growth of Democracy

The success of the French Revolution, which led to the first democratic elections in Europe, the growth of public support for such elections in most advanced European nations between 1790 and 1848, the success of democratic government in the northern states of the U.S., and the growing power of European trade unions led Marx and Engels to predict the near-future adoption of democratic government in the most advanced European countries, and its eventual adoption in most or all other countries.

For instance, even before 1848 Marx wrote that political democracy will be a great step forward and "the final form of human emancipation inside the present world order" (Early Texts, 95). Later, in the final pages of the Communist Manifesto, Marx and Engels proclaimed that, "In France the Communists ally themselves with the Social Democrats," who advocated democratic government, that Communists "labor everywhere for the union and agreement of the democratic parties of all countries," and that "the first step in the revolution by the working class is...to win the battles of democracy."

Moreover, during the German revolution of 1848, they founded and edited a Cologne newspaper, The New Rhenish Gazette, An Organ of Democracy, in which they repeatedly called for the creation of a united democratic German state. And in 1871 they advised the Paris workers not to rebel against the new democratic French government.

When the first Marxist political party was founded in Germany in 1869, with the blessings of Marx and Engels, it was named the Social Democratic Workers' Party in order to stress the fact that it advocated political democracy, as well as socialism. In 1975 it adopted the Gotha program, which demanded "universal, equal, and direct suffrage; direct legislation;...freedom of speech," and other reforms. Marx commented on this program in detail in his <u>Critique of the Gotha Program</u> (1875), and noted its restatement of the "old familiar democratic litany," which he approved but wanted to go beyond.

In addition to predicting the general adoption of political democracy, Marx and Engels predicted that democracy would be achieved by means of revolution in many or most undemocratic countries. They eventually conceded that full democracy and socialist electoral victories might be achieved in a few of the most advanced countries—England, Holland, America, etc.—without a revolution, but they clearly considered such cases to be exceptional. Their prediction of democratic revolutions was proven correct by the 1848 revolutions in various European nations, and by the subsequent successful democratic revolutions in France (1870), Mexico (1910), Russia (1917), Germany (1918), Austria (1918), and other countries.

Many critics have assumed that, when Marx and Engels advocated or predicted social revolution, they were usually or always talking about socialist revolution. In fact, their theory of economic evolution asserted that a bourgeois revolution, like the French Revolution, must normally precede a socialist revolution and permit a ruling capitlist class to create full-blown democratic capitalism, thereby creating the necessary conditions for the growth of the urban working class and their political party. Many loyal Marxists opposed the Bolshevik Revolution in Russia because they believed that Russia needed a period of democratic bourgeois rule to develop capitalism and a proletariat in Russia.

It may be objected that Marx and Engels predicted a "revolutionary dictatorship of the proletariat" in their <u>Critique of the Gotha Program</u>, which implies a rejection of political democracy. But they were speaking of a "political transition period" between capitalism and socialism, a period which might be very short, and which would occur only after the overthrow of an undemocratic government. The fact that they never elaborated the idea of such a dictatorship, and mentioned it only once in many publications, suggests that they attached little importance to this vague idea. In his 1895 Introduction to a new edition of Marx' book, <u>The Class Struggle in France, 1848-50</u>, Engels noted that the recent adoption of universal suffrage in some countries had transformed elections "from a means of deception...into an instrument of emancipation" without revolution (Marx, <u>Selected Works</u>, II, 1982).

10. On the Rise of Socialist Parties

Marx and Engels believed that the mere growth in the numbers, education, and class consciousness of the proletariat, combined with the growth of political democracy, would soon result in the organization of socialist political parties which would continue to grow until they controlled the governments of all democratic countries. In the Communist Manifesto they foresaw "this organization of the proletariat into a class, and consequently into a political party" as inevitable. This foresight was especially remarkable because in 1848 there was not a single democratic government or socialist party in Europe, and human slavery still prevailed in North and South America. Nevertheless their prediction on the creation and growth of socialist parties in advanced countries has been largely verified.

11. On Free Public Education

The growth of free public education was one of the most significant social trends of the Nineteenth Century, but was still in a very early stage when Marx and Engels began writing. They repeatedly predicted that this trend would continue until all advanced countries provided such education for all children. When workers obtain the vote, they explained, "The proletariat will use its political supremacy" to make available "free education for all children in public schools." Since they first made this prediction, the proportion of children in free public schools has probably increased more than tenfold in Europe, the U.S., and Japan, largely due to pressure from newly enfranchised workers and/or socialist parties.

12. On Other Reforms under Capitalism

Their prediction of the continued growth of free public education is included in a numbered list of ten demands, implicit predictions, some including more than one idea, near the end of Section II of the Communist Manifesto:
"1. Abolition of property in land and application of all rents to public purposes." This implicit prediction has been largely fulfilled in nearly all communist countries, but not in any other countries.
"2. Adoption of 'a heavy progressive or graduated income tax.'" This implicit prediction has come true in nearly all advanced capitalist countries. Communist countries have directly controlled personal incomes in such a way as to make such a tax largely or completely unnecessary.

"3. Abolition of all rights of inheritance." This implicit prediction has been largely verified in all communist countries, but only to a minor degree in advanced capitalist countries.

"4. Confiscation of the property of all emigrants and rebels." Most communist, and a few capitalist, states have adopted this bad practice.

"5. Centralization of credit in the hands of the State, by means of a national bank with State capital and an exclusive monopoly." This implicit prediction has come true in most countries.

"6. Centralization of the means of communication and transport in the hands of the state." This has occurred in many countries.

"7. Extension of factories and instruments of production owned by the state;..." This too has been a common trend.

"8. Equal liability of all to labor. Establishment of industrial armies,..." The prediction of "equal liability of all to labor" has proven valid only in communist states. That as to industrial armies has proven valid nowhere.

"9. Combination of agriculture with manufacturing industries; gradual abolition of the distinction between town and country by a more equitable distribution of the population over the country." There has been little such combination in any advanced country, but agriculture has been highly mechanized in some countries.

"10. Free education...Abolition of children's factory labor...Combination of education with industrial production..." The implicit prediction concerning child labor has been very largely realized in all advanced states. That on the combination of education with industry has been largely realized only in some communist countries."

Taken as a whole, this 1848 list of implicitly predicted social reforms has proven to have been remarkably prescient.

Marx and Engels made a careful study of the pioneer English factory legislation on child labor, hours of labor, etc. They approved of this legislation and predicted its elaboration and extension in England, and its imitation in other countries. In his preface to <u>Capital</u> (1867) Marx explained that, "I have given so large a space in this volume to the history, the details, and the results of English factory legislation" partly because "one nation can and should learn from others," in this case from England, the first locus of the industrial revolution.

They also approved, and predicted the continued growth of, the cooperative movement. In his 1964 <u>Inaugural Address to the First International</u> Marx praised this movement and asserted that, "It ought to be developed to national dimensions, and, consequently, to be fostered by national means" (p. 10). This implicit forecast was largely verified by history in most advanced countries.

13. Demands of the German Communist Party

In the same year, 1848, that the <u>Communist Manifesto</u>, containing the above list of ten demands, was published, the five-member Central Committee of the German Communist Party approved a list of seventeen demands, which included some reforms not included in the <u>Manifesto</u> list (Marx, <u>Selected Works</u>, II, 17-18). Since Marx and Engels were members of this committee and signed the platform, the additional reforms demanded may be added to their implicit predictions. they include:

"1. The whole of Germany shall be declared a single indivisible republic." This came to pass in 1918.

"2. Every German, on reaching 21 years of age, is eligible to vote and can be a candidate." This reform too was adopted in 1918.

"3. Representatives of the people shall be paid, so that workers also can sit in the parliament..." Such a reform has been adopted in nearly all advanced countries.

"4. Universal arming of the people." This reform has not been adopted in any advanced country, except perhaps Switzerland. The progress of military technology has made this reform proposal obsolete.

"5. Administration of justice to be gratis." Great progress toward the achievement of this goal has occurred in all advanced countries.

"6. All feudal burdens...will be abolished without compensation." Feudal burdens have been abolished in all advanced, and many less advanced, countries, but some compensation has been paid in some countries."

"7. The royal and other feudal estates...shall be declared state property." This demand has been fully satisfied in all communist countries, and partially satisfied in some capitalist countries.

"16. Establishment of national workshops. The state guarantees a living for all workers and provides for those unable to work." These demands have been largely or entirely satisfied in advanced communist states, and have been partly satisfied by the vast new social insurance and welfare programs of advanced capitalist states.

It may be objected that such demands are not explicit scientific predictions, but the fact that nearly all of these demands have been largely or completely granted in most advanced countries proves that they were based on careful scientific study.

14. On the Rise of Service Industries

Many modern futurists have noted the relative growth of service industries, and predicted its continuance. Marx anticipated them by a hundred years. In a long-unpublished book, Results of the Immediate Process of Production (1933), he discussed the tendency of capitalism to "reduce as much as possible the number of those working" in the production sphere and to increase the number of workers in purely service industries (McLellan, Karl Marx, 350). He foresaw that wasteful competition among capitalist producers in advanced countries would result in relatively larger and larger expenditures on personal selling, advertising, retailing, cross transport of goods, etc.

15. On Increasing Misery

Perhaps the worst single major prediction made by Marx and Engels was their repeated prediction that the misery of the workers would increase as long as capitalism lasted. In the Communist Manifesto, for instance, they wrote of "ever-decreasing wages" and the "ever-increasing burden of toil." In Volume I of Capital Marx elaborated this forecast by predicting that: (1) the length of the working day will increase (pp. 291, 334-46), (2) money wages will fall and/or remain at an irreducible minimum, as David Ricardo had predicted (pp. 657-58), (3) unemployment will increase (pp. 690-93), (4) work tempos will be speeded up (pp. 450, 462), (5) the physical conditions of labor will worsen (pp. 466, 528), (6) the quality of workers' food will decline (pp. 277, 659), and, therefore, (7) the average length of life of workers will decrease (pp. 291, 295). All of these forecasts, except that on work tempos, have been clearly disproven by history.

Some defenders of Marx and Engels have claimed that they were predicting an increase in relative poverty, but a careful study of the references cited above does not support this defense.

The prediction of increasing misery for workers in capitalist countries was seriously qualified and weakened, if not implicitly contradicted, by other important Marx-Engels predictions, for instance, the prediction that technological progress would continue, the prediction that labor unions would grow and become more powerful, the prediction that the cooperative movement would grow, the prediction that advanced countries would become more democratic, and the prediction that socialist political parties would arise and become more and more powerful in democratic states. All of these major predictions were verified by history, and all helped to reduce the misery and increase the real wages of workers in capitalist countries.

16. On Declining Profit Rates

Another bad prediction was that average profit rates would fall continuously in capitalist countries:" ...it is the nature of the capitalist mode of production, and a logical necessity of its development, to give expression to the average rate of surplus value by a falling rate of average profit...this rate must fall continuously" (Capital, III, 210). This prediction was based on unsound Marxian value theory, not on recent profit trends or the Marxian theory of economic evolution. So far as I am aware, there is no statistical evidence that profit rates have declined significantly since this prediction was made. I believe they have risen.

17. On Business Depressions

In the Communist Manifesto and in later writings Marx and Engels forecast that business depressions would continue to occur in capitalist lands, and would become more and more severe. "It is enough to mention the commercial crises that, by their periodical return, put on its trial, each time more threateningly, the existence of the entire bourgeois society." In the ninety years following this 1848 prediction, business depressions did become more and more severe, culminating in the Great Depression of 1929-39, which brought Hitler to power and thereby became the major indirect cause of World War II. Since 1945 advanced capitalist countries have increased state control over their economies enough to make depressions much less severe. Marx and Engels did not anticipate the success of this kind of capitalist reform. But the stagflation now afflicting nearly all advanced capitalist states may eventually bring about another, more severe, great depression. In any case, the 1848 prediction of worsening business depressions has proven valid throughout 70% of the period since 1848.

18. On the Adoption of Socialism

The most original and important of all the predictions made by Marx and Engels was the prediction that the socialist movement would spread and grow until all advanced countries were governed by socialists and had been reorganized as socialist economies. This prediction was based upon the expected growth of the proletariat, of democracy, and of socialist parties.

It was extraordinarily prescient because, when it was first made, no country had ever been ruled by socialists, and the socialist movement was small, weak, and persecuted in all advanced countries. Yet, if either Marx or Engels had lived to be 100 years old, he would have enjoyed the intense pleasure of seeing the first socialist governments come to power in Russia, Hungary, Austria, and Germany, and of seeing strong socialist parties in several other European states.

19. On the Adoption of Communism

Marx and Engels predicted that socialism would be followed by communism because socialist governments would continuously improve technology, and would eventually increase real economic output enough to create optimum abundance. Thus, in 1875 Marx forecast that, "after the productive forces have...increased...and all the springs of cooperative wealth flow more abundantly—only then can...society inscribe on its banners: from each according to his ability, to each according to his needs" (Critique of the Gotha Program, 24).

This definition of communism implies the elimination of both money wages and prices for consumers' goods. Such communism is still the explicitly professed goal of most communist governments. It is much too early to determine whether this remote goal will ever be realized, but such realization seems very unlikely for several reasons, including: (1) no economy will ever be able to provide costly luxuries for everyone, (2) free distribution of tangible goods would permit gross private extravagance and waste, (3) workers need economic stimuli to induce them to produce ideal outputs, and (4) free distribution would require extreme standardization of consumers' goods because no one would choose inferior goods. For these and other reasons (see my book Free Goods), I believe that Marx and Engels' prediction of the eventual adoption of communism was one of their few bad predictions. But it has not yet been disproven, and personal incomes are very likely to become far more equal in the future.

20. On Wars, Revolution, and Independence

Marx and Engels predicted that growing competition among advanced capitalist countries for foreign markets and sources of raw materials would lead to wars between these countries, and that these wars would create conditions favoring the success of violent democratic social revolutions. These predictions were confirmed by later wars and revolutions. Russia,

Finland, Hungary, France, Czechoslovakia, Austria, Germany, Japan, and other states became temporarily or permanently democratic only after democratic revolutions caused by defeat in war.

Before 1848 Marx and Engels forecast the unification of Germany, which did not occur until 1870. In an 1847 letter to Engels Marx foresaw self-government for Ireland, which did not come until 1920 (McLellan, 380). In articles in the Rheinische Zeitung in 1848 Marx predicted that a war between a united Germany and Czarist Russia would result in the liberation of Poland (McLellan, 203). He also predicted national independence for India (Berlin, 188). On the other hand, in 1852 Marx and Engels explicitly rejected the idea that the Czechs and the Jugoslavs would ever achieve such independence (Marx, Selected Works, II, 91). History proved them wrong.

When Germany annexed Alsace-Lorraine in 1871, Marx predicted that this would sow the seeds of fresh wars, including a German "war with the combined Slavonian and Roman races." He further foresaw that this war "will bring to birth the inevitable social revolution in Russia" (McLellan, 390-91). These forecasts were largely verified within fifty years.

21. Comments

I have noted and/or discussed about three dozen predictions made by Marx and Engels, the great majority of which have been substantially or largely verified by history. Only two major predictions, those on increasing misery and declining profit rates, have been definitely proven mistaken.

Moreover, Marx and Engels created a method of predicting the future, namely, the economic interpretation of history, which has so far proven to be extremely useful.

For these reasons, Marx and Engels should be recognized as among the greatest and most successful of all scientific futurists.

EDWARD BELLAMY AS A FUTURIST

Edward Bellamy's book, Looking Backward, 2000-1887 (1887), is the best and most popular utopian novel ever written by an American. Over one million copies of it were sold. A supplement, Equality, was published in 1897, but it was far less popular and influential. He died in 1898, at age 48.

Most readers of utopian novels regard them as pure fiction, not as serious, scientific efforts to predict the future, but the chief value of such novels is that they do help men to predict the future. And Bellamy explained that "Looking Backward...is intended, in all seriousness, as a forecast, in accordance with the principles of evolution, of the next stage in the industrial and social development of humanity, especially in this country;..." (LB, Mod. Lib. ed., 273). In other words, Bellamy was trying to be a pioneer scientific futurist. Moreover, he predicted social trends in a wide variety of fields. And, as I shall show, he was one of the most original and successful futurists who ever lived.

The following survey of Bellamy's predictions is incomplete. I have ignored many minor predictions, but have tried to cover all of his major predictions.

1. On Socialism

The most significant prediction in Looking Backward is the forecast that all advanced countries will evolve peacefully from competitive capitalism to monopolistic socialism (pp. 42-43, 111-12). When Bellamy was writing this book, there was not a single socialist city, province, or country in the world. Today, over one-third of mankind lives in largely socialist countries, and all other advanced nations have made almost continuous progress towards socialism since 1887.

Like nearly all futurists, Bellamy greatly overestimated the speed of normal social progress. He predicted that all advanced countries would become fully socialist well before 1000 A.D. This process may require another century or more. But it is far more important to predict the direction and limit of major social trends than to predict the rate at which they will move.

Bellamy also erred when he predicted that the transition to socialism would be universally peaceful. Nearly all communist governments have been established by revolution or by external military intervention, mostly in the immediate aftermath of World War I or II. Bellamy did not forecast such events because he did not want them to happen. All futurists make some bad predictions based on wishful, not on scientific, thinking.

Bellamy based his prediction of the rise of state socialism on observable economic and political trends. He described the past trend toward "the concentration of capital in greater masses" (LB, 38), and explained that "All that society had to do was to recognize and cooperate with that evolution..." (LB, 35). He also noted that "the widespread industrial and social troubles, and the underlying dissatisfaction of all classes with the inequalities of society, and the general misery of mankind, were portents of great changes of some sort" (LB, 36).

The trends and portents on which Bellamy based his forecast of the rise of socialism were discussed more fully in Equality (1897) than in Looking Backward. In Equality he also stressed "the growth of intelligence and diffusion of knowledge among the masses" (E, 305) as additional trends responsible for the past and future growth of the socialist movement.

2. On Communism

His second most important long-run prediction was his forecast that personal incomes would be equal in all advanced countries well before 2000 A.D. (LB, 72-74, 111). This prediction has not been verified by history. Incomes have become much less unequal in communist countries, and a little less unequal in England, Sweden, and a few other countries, but there are very persuasive reasons for doubting that personal incomes will ever be equal, or based on needs, in any country (see my Liberal Socialism, 374-376).

3. On Feminism

Perhaps his third most important general prediction was his forecast that the social, political, and economic status of women would become equal to that of men by the year 2000 (LB, 208-17). He developed this prediction in some detail. He expected that women would normally be employed outside the home (LB, 209), would enter all trades and professions (E, 43-44), would engage in all sports (E, 144-45), would receive incomes equal to those of men (LB, 213-14), would be equally well educated (LB, 176), would dress more sensibly (E, 46-47), would be freed from most housekeeping duties (LB, 94), and would even learn to declare their love as freely as men can (LB, 217).

Bellamy predicted that the double-standard sexual code for men and women would be replaced by a single-standard code for both sexes, one nearer the old code for men than that for women (E, 140-42). "The common ...code for men and women...would first become possible...when men and women...in the sexual relation, as in all others...[had] absolute equality and mutual independence" (E, 142). While these feminist goals are still far from complete achievement, great progress towards their achievement has been made, and is continuing, in all advanced countries.

Bellamy was especially interested in the health and physical measurements of women. He predicted that, as a result of more exercise, more freedom, and more healthy clothing, American women would, by 2000 A.D., become two inches taller, two inches wider at the shoulder than at the hips (also widened), and one and one half inches deeper in the chest. Overall, they would become stronger and more healthy. "Womens' invalidism was one of the great tragedies of your civilization, and her physical rehabilitation is one of the greatest single elements in the total increment of happiness which economic equality has brought to the human race" (E, 147-49).

Apparently he based these predictions on expert opinion and on the previous growth in the propaganda for female liberation by writers like John Stuart Mill (E, 132), for there was little if any reliable statistical data to support such predictions in 1887. In any case, Bellamy proved himself to be more prescient in the field of female liberation than in any other major field. Nearly all of his specific feminist forecasts have been significantly or largely fulfilled, and all the trends he predicted are still moving as he foresaw they would.

It is noteworthy, however, that he failed to foresee the coming decline in the number of children per female, a decline which has been a major cause of female liberation since 1887. This was one of his most serious failures as a futurist.

On the other hand, he did foresee the greatly increased use of commercial housekeeping professionals, ready-made clothing, electric heaters, and restaurants as means of reducing housekeeping chores for women (LB, 93-95).

4. On Education

Another very important prediction was his forecast that nearly all youth would continue in school to the age of 21. He predicted that such prolonged education would become free and compulsory because it is needed to make workers more productive, better neighbors, and wiser parents (LB, 176-81).

Bellamy's predictions on education have been largely verified by the course of events. There has been a vast expansion in secondary and higher education in all advanced countries since 1887, and this expansion is almost certain to continue. But no country is likely to adopt compulsory education to age 21 by 2000 A.D.

Moreover, he failed to foresee the great expansion in preschool education which has occurred since 1887. Already 50 to 90% of children age 3 to 5 are in schools or kindergartens in the most advanced countries, and this expansion is certain to continue for many decades.

On the other hand, he forecast a vast expansion of adult education. He explained that his utopia "maintains a vast system of what you would call elective post-graduate courses of study in every branch of science, and these are open freely to every one to the end of his life..." (E, 249). This forecast has been substantially verified in the most progressive regions of the U.S., and further progress in this direction is almost certain.

5. An International Language

Bellamy predicted the adoption of a single universal supplemental international language. In his utopia, he explained, "we have nowadays to acquire but two languages to talk to all peoples—our own, and the universal" (E, 257). This has not yet come to pass, but the widespread and growing use of English as an international tongue is a significant step in this direction, and a trend which will probably long continue, perhaps until Bellamy's forecast is belatedly realized.

6. On Technological Progress

The Nineteenth Century was a period of rapid technological progress in nearly all industries in all advanced countries. On the basis of this well-established trend, Bellamy predicted continued rapid technological progress in all countries (E, 44, 54, 187). While he deserves little credit for making this easy prediction, some of his specific technological predictions were more novel, or entirely original, as well as prescient.

For instance, he predicted the invention and common use of cable radio and television receivers which would provide each home with music, lectures, sermons, and entertainment 24 hours a day on many channels (LB, 87-91). He also foresaw the common use of the telephone, and the widespread use of electricity for domestic heating and lighting (LB, 94). In 1897 he predicted the invention and common use of the airplane, which he called an "air car," but noted that many others had made similar predictions.

He forecast the general replacement of the horse by automobiles and tractors, and the construction of "smooth, permanent, and clean roadways" throughout all advanced countries (E, 297-99). These roads would make travel by "electric motors" so convenient that most short and many long trips would be made by "private conveyance." Here we have a brilliant prevision of the coming age of the private motor car. But he failed to anticipate that gasoline motors would temporarily prove more efficient than electric motors.

Bellamy forecast a radical increase in the use of new, not yet invented, office machines, and a resulting decrease in the use of handwriting. In describing the new accounting system, he explained that "the accounts are kept automatically by a machine, the accountant merely playing the keyboard" (E, 32). Later, he added that, "practically speaking, handwriting has gone out of use. For correspondence, when we do not telephone, we use phonographs [records?], and use the latter, indeed, for all purposes for which you used handwriting...printed [typed?] matter is translated from phonographic copy..." (E, 123).

This was perceptive forecasting. However, he erred when he predicted that in 2000 A.D. most clothing would be made of paper, and, when soiled, would be recycled rather than cleaned (LB, 49).

He also erred when he forecast that, by the year 2000, "power, with all its applications of light, heat, and energy," would be "practically exhaustless and costless" due to use of "the tides, winds, and waterfalls..." and "natural inequalities of temperature" (E, 69).

7. On Agriculture

Bellamy was especially far-sighted concerning agriculture, which, he predicted, would become completely mechanized. In describing a farm of the year 2000 he wrote, "Over its surface was moving a row of great machines," which he called "electric plows" (E, 298-99). And he added that, "There was no tool, however small...used in agriculture or any other art, to which this [electric] motor was not applicable, leaving to the worker only the adjustment and guiding of the instrument."

He explained that, "With one of our [power] shovels...an intelligent boy can excavate a trench or dig a mile of potatoes quicker than a gang of men in your day, and with no more effort than he would use in wheeling a barrow." As a result, "it is estimated that about ten times the amount of power is nowadays given to the working of every acre of land that it was possible to apply in former times" (E, 299-300).

Bellamy even foresaw that the general use of tractors and autos would drastically reduce the farm acreage devoted to hayfields because there would be few horses to eat hay (E, 297).

In summarizing his agricultural forecasts, he claimed that "no industrial transformation since your day [1897] has been so complete...as that which has come over agriculture" (E, 302-03). I believe that most economists today would agree that this important prediction has largely come true.

On the other hand, Bellamy completely failed to anticipate the effects of this agricultural revolution on the size of the share of the U.S. work-force engaged in agriculture, which has fallen from over 50% to less than 5% since he wrote.

One of Bellamy's worst predictions was his forecast that all Americans would become vegetarians by the year 2000 because they would become much more sensitive to the feelings and rights of animals (E, 284-85).

8. On Retailing

Bellamy gave special attention to future trends in retailing. He predicted the continued growth in size and numbers of large department stores, and their establishment of branch stores. "The great city bazaar crushed its country rivals with branch stores, and in the city itself absorbed its smaller rivals till the business of whole quarter was concentrated under one roof" (LB, 39).

He anticipated that by 2000 A.D. all retailing would be done by a single state-owned chain of self-service sample stores offering the same goods at the same prices in each store throughout the nation. Advertising and aggressive selling would be almost entirely eliminated (LB, 79-84). These predictions have been partially verified. Advanced communist countries now have state retail monopolies which use little advertising and aggressive selling. And there has been a great growth of self-service retailing in the U.S.

Bellamy predicted the universal substitution of "credit cards" for money in the purchase of goods and services by consumers (LB, 67-69). There has been an enormous growth in the use of credit cards in advanced capitalist countries in recent decades, and many futurists now predict a continuance of this trend, facilitated by electronic transfer of bank deposits. However, the credit card industry has not yet become a state monopoly, as he expected. Moreover, he failed to predict the vast growth in the use of bank checks which has occurred in the U.S. and some other countries.

9. On Labor

Bellamy forecast a great improvement in the conditions of labor. For instance, factory workers would work in a "lofty, airy hall, walled with beautiful designs in tile and metal, furnished like palaces, with every convenience, the machinery running almost noiselessly, and every incident of the work that might be offensive to any sense reduced by ingenius devices to the minimum" (E, 54). We have not yet achieved such ideal conditions, but very great progress in this direction has been achieved in all advanced countries since 1897, and this trend is almost certain to continue indefinitely.

He predicted that by the year 2000 nearly all workers would retire at age 45. This has not come to pass. However, the average age of retirement has fallen in all advanced countries. And in the Soviet Union the legal age for retirement has fallen to or below 55, a very substantial verification of his forecast.

He forecast that by the year 2000 all "public services"—presumably including all retail and other services to consumers—would operate 24 hours a day, including holidays. "We have day and night shifts for all the public services—the latter, of course, much the smaller" (E, 67). This forecast has been partially verified by a marked lengthening of the hours of operation of many such services, but we still have a long way to go to fully realize this prediction.

Bellamy predicted the achievement of full employment (LB, 194), including all handicapped adults (LB, 104). I doubt that there has been any significant progress towards these goals in the U.S. since 1887, but they may be achieved before 2100 A.D. Moreover, they have already been almost fully achieved in the U.S.R.R. and some other communist countries. And in noncommunist Europe the level of unemployment from 1950 to 1980 was well below that from 1880 to 1900, when Bellamy was writing.

As previously noted, he expected that child labor would cease, and that all youth would remain in school to age 21. Then they would all serve for a time as "common or unskilled laborers...assignable to any work at the discretion of...superiors..." (LB, 53). This latter forecast was a bad one. In many advanced countries most or all young men are still required to serve a year or two in the armed forces, but no country has ever compelled all youth to serve a term as common laborers, and I doubt that any ever will. On the other hand, child labor has been radically reduced, and education radically prolonged, in all advanced countries since 1887.

10. On Social Insurance

Bellamy predicted the creation of a vast and comprehensive system of social insurance in all advanced countries. "No man anymore has any care for the morrow, either for himself or his children, for the nation guarantees the nurture, education, and comfortable maintenance of every citizen from the cradle to the grave" (LB, 70). This prediction was made in 1887, before any country, except perhaps Germany, had adopted even a small part of such a comprehensive system of social insurance, but it has been very largely verified by the subsequent great expansion of social insurance and welfare in all advanced countries.

11. On City Planning

Bellamy forecast that the cities of 2000 A.D. would be far more beautiful than those of his day. He anticipated "Miles of broad streets, shaded by trees and lined with fine buildings, for the most part not in continuous blocks but set in...inclosures.... Every quarter contained large open squares filled with trees" (LB, 27). While this prediction of urban improvement has been only very partially fulfilled, it will probably be more and more fully realized in the future.

He also forecast that every ward of the city would have its own large monopolistic general store, so that no residence would be "more than five or ten minutes walk from one of them" (LB, 80). The growth and spread of suburban shopping centers in the U.S. is a partial verification of this forecast.

In *Equality* (1897) he predicted that American cities would stop growing and become much smaller. "None of the great cities of your day have become extinct," the guide explained, "but their populations are but small fractions of what they were" (p. 293). After the peaceful revolution, "A large proportion of the old buildings and all the unsightly, lofty, and inartistic ones were cleared away and replaced with structures of the low, broad, roomy style..." (p. 294-95). Unfortunately, this prediction has not been realized. Indeed, the trend has been in the opposite direction. But I believe that his prediction will eventually be realized.

Bellamy expected that the people moved out of our large cities would be resettled "in the country." I expect them to be resettled in planned new or rebuilt garden cities, because urban life offers many advantages over rural life.

12. On Government

Bellamy predicted that by 2000 A.D. the U.S. government would be a novel combination of government by experts and retired persons. Government officials would rise from rank to rank, as military officers now do, so that all senior officials would be well-qualified experts. All but the three senior ranks would be appointed by their seniors, the President and his cabinet would be "chosen by suffrage," and the President must be an ex-cabinet member. For cabinet members, "chosen by suffrage" means elected by retired department staff (over age 45). The President would be chosen by all retired adults. He mentioned the Congress, which would merely propose laws, but did not explain how it would be elected (LB, 153-56). He expected that initiative and referendum elections would be conducted by telephone "a hundred times perhaps in a year" and that all elected officials would be subject to quick recall by their electors (E, 274-75).

In *Equality* (1897) Bellamy became more explicit in his prediction of government by experts. He remarked that, "it may seem like a paradox that the equalizing of economic and educational conditions, which has perfected democracy, should have resulted in the most perfect aristocracy, or government by the best, that could be conceived.... The people of today [2000 A.D.] ...are ready...to comprehend and to follow every better leading" (pp. 256-57).

Every growth of bureaucratic organization in business, government, and other fields increases the proportion of executives who are appointed by seniors rather than self-chosen or elected, and there has been a great growth of bureaucracy since 1887. Moreover, many large private firms have been nationalized. Thus his prediction of more government by expert bureaucrats has been partially realized. And the use of the initiative and the referendum by ballot, but not by telephone, has become more common in the U.S. But it will be a long time, if ever, before only former U.S. cabinet members can run for President, and before only persons over 45 can vote. These are among his least plausible predictions.

Bellamy predicted the creation of an international government including all nations. "The peaceful relations of these countries are assured by a loose form of federal union of world-wide extent.... Complete autonomy within its own limits is enjoyed by every nation" (LB, 112). The creation of the League of Nations and the United Nations demonstrated a trend in this direction, but the creation of a world federal union strong enough to preserve world peace is very unlikely before 2000 A.D. Here, as often elsewhere, the author correctly predicted a major social trend, but overestimated the rate of its movement.

He also anticipated that there would be virtually free immigration between all nations (LB, 115). International migration within Europe and within North America has increased sharply since his time, but free migration between all nations is most unlikely to occur in the foreseeable future because it would seriously depress real wages in all advanced states.

13. On Religion

Bellamy predicted a radical decline in American belief in sectarian Christian dogmas. The guide to his new society explained that, "It is a very long time since it has been customary for people to divide themselves into sects and classify themselves under different names on account of variations of opinion as to matters of religion" (E, 258). While this prediction has not been fully, or even largely realized, there has been a long decline in American belief in purely sectarian Christian dogmas.

He also forecast that the rise of religious broadcasting by radio and TV would produce a radical decline in church attendance and, therefore, in the relative number of church buildings. The guide asserted that, "we have little or no use for churches at all" (E, 255). Although the rate of church attendance has fallen substantially in most European states since 1897, it has fallen little if any in America. And it has certainly not come to be that Americans "have little or no use for churches at all."

Bellamy predicted that the invention and growth of religious broadcasting would enable the most intelligent and eloquent preachers to attract most religious listeners away from church sermons delivered by less competent preachers in churches (E, 256). There has been a trend in this direction in recent decades, but it has not moved nearly as fast as he expected it to move.

He also forecast that, "with a high degree of intelligence becoming universal the world was bound to outgrow the ceremonial side of religion..." (E, 258). This prediction too has not been verified by history.

Bellamy's greatest fault in religious forecasting was his complete failure to predict the growth of powerful anti-religious movements and governments. Today, one-third of mankind is ruled by such governments.

14. Final Comments

Although Bellamy successfully predicted many major 20th Century social trends, he failed to foresee some very important ones, including: (1) the rapid growth of U.S. and world population, (2) the continued decline in the U.S. birth rate, (3) the great movement of population from the country to the city in all advanced nations, (4) the growing provision of free medical care, and (5) the steady expansion of government control over private firms in all mixed economies.

He also failed to forecast the great wars and revolutions which devastated many countries, and the new military weapons used in these conflicts. In this respect he allowed his hopes to determine his predictions, a fault very common among futurists.

In spite of these and other faults, Bellamy was certainly one of the most successful scientific futurists of his century. Among his predecessors, only Condorcet and Marx may have excelled him.

H. G. WELLS AS A FUTURIST

Herbert George Wells (1866-1946) was one of the most famous and influential English authors of his time. He published over 100 books and many more articles. His Outline of History sold over 2,000,000 copies in several languages, and he often wrote about the future. It is impossible to note all his predictions and fictional suggestions about the future in a brief essay, so I shall concentrate upon his major explicit, nonfictional predictions.

Wells first established himself as a popular author by writing imaginative science fiction—The Time Machine (1895), The Island of Dr. Moreau (1896), The Invisible Man (1897), etc.—most of which has been made into popular films, but he soon became a serious, scientific futurist, and remained one for the rest of his life.

The close of the 19th Century prompted him to think more seriously about the future. So he wrote a series of magazine articles containing a realistic, comprehensive forecast of social trends during the coming century. The articles appeared first in the Fortnightly Review, and were then published in book form as Anticipations of the Reaction of Mechanical and Scientific Progress upon Human Life and Thought (1901), hereafter referred to as Anticipations. It was an immediate publishing success, being reprinted several times in its first year, and later translated into several foreign languages. It aroused widespread comment, and marked a major change in Well's career, from fiction to social thought and reform. My unattributed page references are to this book.

In his autobiography Wells claimed that Anticipations was "the first attempt to forecast the human future as a whole and to estimate the relative power of this and that great system of influence...sober forecasting, that is to say, without propaganda, satire, or extravaganza, was so much a novelty that my book... excited quite a number of people" (p. 551). Wells was either unfamiliar with Condorcet's Sketch, or had forgotten it, but Anticipations was probably the first such comprehensive nonfiction prediction of the future in English. As such, it was a most important contribution to the new science of futurism.

1. On the Need for Scientific Futurism

In an interview in Cassell's Saturday Journal (4-26-1899), Wells said, "I am strongly of the opinion that we ought to consider the possibilities of the future much more than we do. Why should four-fifths of the fiction of today be concerned with times that can never come up again, while the future is scarcely speculated upon? At present we are almost helpless in the grip of circumstances, and I think we ought to strive to shape our destinies."

In 1901 Wells gave a lecture at the Royal Institution with the significant title, "The Discovery of the Future," in which he asserted that, "It is our ignorance of the future and our persuasion that ignorance is incurable that alone has given the past its enormous predominance in our thoughts." He claimed that it is now possible "to attain to a knowledge of coming things as clear, as universally convincing, and infinitely more important to mankind than the clear vision of the past that geology has opened to us during the nineteenth century." He argued that a new kind of inductive history—which in his autobiography (p. 552) he later called Human Ecology, the working out of "biological, intellectual, economic consequences"—might be used both to chart the future and to help men use it (N. & J. Mackenzie, H.G. Wells, 163).

In his autobiography he proposed the creation of university "Professorships of Analytical History" to re-organize and teach history in such a way as to reveal major long-run social trends and permit their projection into the future. "Sooner or later Human Ecology, under some name or other, will win its way to academic recognition and to its proper place in general education—in America sooner than in Europe, I guess" (p. 553). Here we have a brilliant pioneer prediction of what has already begun to happen in American universities.

Let us turn now to some of his predictions.

2. On Transportation

The automobile was still relatively new and rare when Wells was writing Anticipations, but he foresaw a great future for it. He predicted "the organization of large carrier companies using...motor trucks to carry goods in bulk or parcels on the high roads," and described the future of private car use (p. 15). The latter "will add a fine sense of personal independance to all the small conveniences of first-class railway travel." He also expected the replacement of the horse omnibus by the motor omnibus, both in cities and on the highways (pp. 16-17).

He perceived that the growing use of automobiles would result in the construction of new through highways "very different from macadamized roads," highways which "will be used only by soft-tired conveyances." They will probably "be made of very good asphalt" or of "some quite new substance altogether," and "traffic in opposite directions will probably be strictly separated." Moreover, "streams of traffic will not cross at a level, but by bridges." When these new freeways have been built, "it will be possible to experiment with vehicles of a size and power quite beyond the dimensions prescribed by our ordinary roads..." (pp. 18-19).

He also predicted the widespread use of moving sidewalks in congested city shopping centers within 30 to 40 years (pp. 28-30). This was a bad prediction.

3. Urbanization and Suburbanization

Wells explained that "the general distribution of population in a country must always be directly dependant on transport facilities" and that, therefore, growing use of the automobile would result in a great expansion and thinning out or suburbanization of metropolitan areas. "Indeed, it is not too much to say that the London citizen of the year 2000 A.D. may have a choice of nearly all England and Wales south of Nottingham and east of Exeter as his suburb..." and "the vast stretch of country from Washington to Albany will all be 'available' to the active citizen of New York and Philadelphia before that date" (p. 46). Here we have a pioneer forecast of what modern futurists call the coming megalopoli.

This expansion of metropolitan areas will result in the creation of "suburban nuclei" or shopping centers. To them "will be drawn doctor and school-master, and various dealers in fresh provisions, baker, grocer, butcher; or if they are already...there they will flourish more...and about them the convenient home of the future with its numerous electrical and mechanical appliances...will gather a population of repairers...dealers" and mechanics. "The much more elaborate post office and telephone services" will improve communications (p. 56).

"In addition...many Londoners...may abandon the city office altogether, preferring to do their business in more agreeable surrounding. Such a business as book publishing for example..." (p. 57). This process of business decentralization within urban areas has continued ever since 1902, and is likely to continue indefinately.

4. More and Better Mechanics and Engineers

Wells predicted that the rise of the automobile and other new machines for factory, office, and home would continuously increase the demand for mechanics and engineers, who would increase in numbers much faster than the total population.

The bicycle was very popular when Wells wrote *Anticipations*. He foresaw that "the motors promise new difficulties, new rewards, and new competition. It is an ill look-out for the cycle mechanic who is not prepared to tackle the new problems that will arise. For all this next century this...body of mechanics will be picking up new recruits..." It, "and that larger multitude...concerned with motors," will make up "only a small...section of the general body of mechanics and engineers...who will tend to become an educated and adaptable class in a sense that the craftsmen of former times were not educated and adaptable" (pp. 85-87).

5. Rise of the Professionals

Wells anticipated a long-continuing rise in the proportion of professionally trained workers in the population (up to perhaps 20-25%). He expected them to become a "new, numerous, intelligent, educated, and capable...element" in society, new presumably only because of their increased importance. Unfortunately, he implied that this class would include few if any females.

This growing professional class "will probably dress with a view to decent convenience, they will not set the fashions...but will steady and sober them.... They will not be habitual promenaders, or greatly addicted to theatrical performances.... They will take a considerable interest in public affairs. Their menage ...will be servantless" (p. 106).

6. Fewer Servants

Wells predicted that, "within a reasonable term of years," the upper middle-class family "will probably not keep a servant for two...reasons...they will not want one, and...they will not get one if they do." They will not want one because technological progress —central heating, air conditioning, electric stoves, dish-washing machines, etc.—will make house-keeping far less laborious. And "there will be few servants available" because few women will want to work as domestic servants (pp. 106-111).

"It is the lack of proper warming appliances which necessitates a vast amount of coal carrying and dirt distribution.... The house of the future will probably be warmed in its walls from some power-generating station...air will enter...through...tubes in the walls, which will warm it and capture its dust...and by simple devices such sweeping as still remains necessary can be enormously lightened" (p. 107).

7. Feminist Progress

In _Anticipations_ Wells failed to predict the long process of feminine liberation which would occur in the next 80 years (pp. 118-23). He did not even forecast votes for women, which was only 16 years off in England. But in later years he became more perceptive.

In his novel _Ann Veronica_ (1909) he shocked Edwardian readers with his account of an emancipated modern woman, and thereafter he became a champion of equal rights for women. In a 1916 book, _What is Coming?_ he finally predicted the postwar granting of the vote to English women. He also predicted that the economic gains won by women during the war would not "be reversed after the war" (Wells, _Journalism and Prophecy_, p. 107-09). But even here he failed to even dimly foresee the long string of feminist victories that was coming.

On the other hand, he did foresee a "relaxation of the marriage law and of divorce...(p. 129). And he anticipated changes in "moral standards" which would permit acceptance of "physiologically sound _menages_ of very variable status" and also "vice and depravity, in every form that is not absolutely penal," in every social class (p. 133).

8. Eugenics and Population Control

Wells repeatedly predicted, implicitly or explicitly, that mankind will eventually adopt eugenic measures to improve the human race. Near the end of _Anticipations_ he forecast that, "man...will...select and breed for his embodiment a continually finer and stronger and wiser race" (p. 270).

This idea is elaborated in his novel, _A Modern Utopia_ (1905), where he proposed that the state should establish minimum requirements for legal parenthood. These should assure that a potential father has achieved a certain standard of personal competence by earning a living and by meeting certain physical requirements. Alcoholics, criminals, the insane, and other defectives should be segregated in order to prevent their having children (p. 136).

The need for national and world population control was often explained by Wells. In <u>Anticipations</u> he explicitly predicted that "man...will...control his own increase" (p. 270).

9. On Religion

Like the elder Huxley, his revered teacher, Wells early became a firm believer in biological evolution and agnosticism, but he did not reject the concepts of god and moral truth. He made few predictions about religion. Perhaps the most interesting was his prediction in the last pages of early editions of <u>The Outline of History</u> (1920) that "the coming world state ...will be based upon a common world religion, very much simplified and universalized and better understood. This will not be Christianity nor Islam nor Buddhism nor any such specialized form of religion, but religion itself pure and undefiled...brotherhood, creative service, and self-forgetfullness" (<u>J. & P.</u>, 399). This seems more like ethical humanism than any kind of religion, defined as belief in the supernatural. In his autobiography he called himself a "sturdy atheist" (p. 578).

10. On Languages

Wells predicted a continued, long decline in the importance and use of minor dialects and languages. "The 20th Century will see the effectual crowding out of most of the weaker languages" or "a supplementing of them by...one...of a limited number of world languages.... This will go on not only in Europe, but... over the whole world...except in China and Japan" (p. 230). He predicted that French would become the dominant European and world language because more good literary and scientific books were then being published in French (pp. 237-42). He failed to foresee that scientific publications in English would outnumber those in French by more than five to one before 2000 A.D., but he noted that the volume of such publications would determine which language became predominant (p. 232).

11. On Agriculture

Wells predicted that technological progress in agriculture "will render possible agricultural contrivances that are now only dreams" and could be well used only by better educated operatives. He anticipated that small family farms would survive for some decades, but asserted that, "I do not see how they can obstruct, more than locally, the reorganization of agriculture...upon the ampler and more economical lines mechanism permits, or prevent the development of a type of agriculturist as adaptable, alert, intelligent...as the coming engineer" (pp. 93-95).

12. Socialism

Wells became a member of the Fabian Society soon after the publication of Anticipations (1901), and remained a Fabian socialist for the rest of his long life. He often predicted or implied the eventual adoption of socialism, both in England and throughout the world. For instance, in the last pages of his Outline of History (1920), he explicity predicted that the "economic organization" of the coming world state "will be an exploitation of all natural wealth, and every fresh possibility science reveals, by the agents and servants of the common government for the common good. Private enterprise will be the servant...and no longer the robber master of the commonweal" (J.& P., 400).

13. Government by Experts

When Wells began to write, democratic government was still a new and rare thing, even in Europe, and nearly all political reformers advocated its extension and perfection. Wells was one of the first influential futurists to predict that such government would eventually be replaced by government by experts. In Anticipation he predicted that the function of government in "the New Republic" would be taken out of the hands of politicians elected by an ill-informed mass electorate and re-assigned to "capable men," mostly scientists and engineers with "a strong imperative to duty" (pp. 153-75). In a later book, A Modern Utopia (1905), Wells called such elite rulers samurai, an order of "voluntary nobility" open to any adult over 25 who has received a college or upper school degree. They would be the only voters.

In his Experiment in Autobiography (1934) he restated his belief in the need for a highly educated, nonhereditary ruling elite, and noted that Lenin's Communist party was the closest existing group to his proposed Samurai Order (p. 563).

If democratic government does in time give way to government by experts, as I believe it will, this prediction will prove to have been Well's most brilliant and significant long-run forecast. However, it has serious defects. The idea that engineers, pure scientists, and all other highly educated men are qualified to run a modern state is as unreasonable as the idea that lawyers are qualified to perform medical operations. Only educated persons who have majored in social science and have had years of experience in government are qualified to choose, or serve as, national legislators and executives. Moreover, Wells failed to predict the way in which democratic governments will gradually change into governments ruled by experts.

14. On Warfare

"The great change that is working itself out in warfare is the same change that is working itself out in the substance of the social fabric.... In warfare this takes the form of the progressive supersession of the horse and the private soldier...by machines...." For instance, "the rifle will probably also take on some of the characteristics of the machine gun. It will be used either for single shots or to quiver and send a spray of almost simultaneous bullets..." (p. 179). He forecast in detail the kind of stable trench warfare (pp. 180-87) and behind-the-lines mobilization of civilians which would occur in World War II (pp. 184-88). In 1901 he failed to anticipate the vital role of airplanes in future wars, but instead forecast heavy use of invulnerable balloons, including "steerable balloons" and "flying rams" (pp. 190-94).

On the other hand, in "The Land Ironclads," a short story published in 1903, he foresaw the future use of armored tanks. His tanks were to be "long, narrow, and very strong steel frameworks carrying the engines, and borne upon eight pairs of pedrail wheels, each about ten feet in diameter..." The armor was to be "twelve-inch iron-plating which protected the whole affair...." (J.& P., pp. 50-51).

In an imaginative novel, The War in the Air (1908), Wells not only suggested the possibility of destructive air warfare and airplane bombing of civilians, but implied that this possibility "must alter the ordinary man's attitude to warfare" (Autobiography, p. 569).

In The World Set Free, a scientific romance about world war published in 1914, thirteen years after Anticipations, Wells not only suggested the extensive use of airplanes to drop bombs on the enemy but even foresaw the use of "atomic bombs" which would spray long-active "radio-active substances" over wide areas (J.& P., pp. 54-56).

Leo Szilard read this romance in the early 1930s and was prompted to invent and patent an atom bomb. He assigned the patent to the British War Office, which kept it secret. Later (1939), he induced Einstein to write the letter to Roosevelt which initiated the American atom bomb program.

On the other hand, in <u>Anticipations</u> Wells could not "see any sort of submarine doing anything but suffocate its crew and founder at sea" (p. 200). "At the utmost the submarine will be used in narrow waters... it will simply be an added power in the hands of the nation that is predominant at sea" (p. 201). Few bad predictions have been so quickly disproven by history!

In his book <u>The Fate of Man</u> (1939), written in the summer of 1939, Wells foresaw the coming world war and predicted a terrible result. "No country...will emerge...at anything like the level of civilization at which it stands today.... The human process will go back...to a mechanically feeble barbarism.... It will be the Dark Ages over again, a planetary instead of a merely European Dark Ages" ($\underline{J}$.& $\underline{P}$., pp. 236-37).

He could hardly have been more wrong! The first three decades after World War II were by far the most progressive and prosperous mankind had known. Real wages and university enrollment rose by far more than 100% above the best prewar year in all advanced countries. However, Wells may have deliberately and grossly exaggerated the probable harm from this war in order to strengthen his case for peace.

15. World Government

In the last three chapters of <u>Anticipations</u> Wells confidently predicted the eventual creation of a world government able to maintain peace and order throughout the world, and explained the reasons for this firm prediction.

"We have seen that the essential process arising out of the growth of science and mechanism, and more particularly out of the still developing new facilities of locomotion and communication science...is" the decline of old social organizations and "the synthesis of ampler and still ampler...social unities...this process...will attain to the establishment of one world-state at peace within itself" (p. 267). He called this coming world government "the New Republic," and predicted that under it the world would have "a common language and a common rule." He added that, "all over the world its roads, its standards, its laws, and its apparatus of control will run."

In an article written in the winter of 1917-18 Wells asserted that, "Existing states have become impossible as absolutely independent sovereignties. The new conditions bring them so close together and give them such extravagant powers of mutual injury that they must either sink national pride and dynastic ambitions in subordination to the common welfare of mankind, or else utterly shatter one another. It becomes more and more plainly a choice between the League of

Free Nations and a famished race of men looking in search of nonexistent food amidst the smouldering ruins of civilization" (J.& P., p. 127). This argument is much more persuasive today than in 1918. Wells frequently restated and elaborated this argument in the years 1918-46. To persuade mankind to accept it became the chief purpose of the last decades of his life.

In A Modern Utopia (1905) he gave some details of the coming world state. It will be a vast world bureaucracy, "the sole landowner of the earth," which directly maintains order, highways, communication and courts of law. It will be ruled by a meritocratic elite, inaptly called the samurai. It will assure cradle-to-grave education, social security, and welfare for all the people in the world (pp. 88-92). It will create and maintain a central world identification file listing every person on earth, with their identifying traits and personal history (p. 162).

In his Autobiography (1934) Wells wrote that "I remain persuaded that there will have to be a last conflict to inaugurate the peace of mankind. Rather than a war between sovereign governments, however, it is far more likely to be a war to suppress these whenever they are found" (p. 570). The first prediction still seems plausible.

16. Comments

H. G. Wells was the first English-language writer to state the case for a new science of futurism, and the first to write a nonfictional book devoted to predicting the future. Unfortunately, he failed to note and comment on the many perceptive forecasts made by earlier futurists.

He may have been the first futurist to predict the major effects of the growing use of motorcars upon social evolution in advanced countries.

He explained more fully than any earlier writer the reasons why creation of a strong world government is almost certain. One of his reasons was his brilliant forecast of the invention of nuclear weapons.

KEYNES AS A FUTURIST

John Maynard Keynes (1883-1946), the greatest modern English economist, wrote many articles for popular magazines and newspapers, as well as learned treatises on economics. Thirty-seven of his articles were reprinted, in whole or in part, in Essays in Persuasion (Norton Library, 1963). In his preface Keynes wrote that "the volume might have been entitled "Essays in Prophecy and Persuasion, for the Prophecy... has been more successful than the Persuasion" (p. v). All page citations given here are to this edition, unless otherwise attributed.

As this quotation suggests, the book contains a number of verified prophecies, which I prefer to call scientific predictions. A brilliant social scientist like Keynes does not waste his time on unsupportable guesses and prophecies. His forecasts are bound to be more or less scientific.

Keynes first came to public attention as the author of the widely read Economic Consequences of the Peace (1919), in which he predicted both that the Germans would never pay the reparations provided for in the Treaty of Versailles, and that the Allies would never repay their war loans from the U.S. I do not discuss these soon verified predictions because I am interested here mainly in long-run predictions, especially those which deal with trends which will continue well beyond 2000 A.D.

1. The Liberal Party and New Political Questions

Although Keynes was a liberal in English politics, he wrote in 1926 that, "I do not believe that Liberalism will ever again be a great party machine in the way in which Conservatism and Labour are great party machines" (p. 344). He also explained that, "I do not believe that the Liberal Party will win one-third of the seats in the House of Commons in any probable or foreseeable circumstance" (p. 339).

In 1925 Keynes gave an address to the Liberal Summer School at Cambridge, entitled "Am I a Liberal?" in which he offered a variety of implicit and explicit predictions about future political, economic, and social trends. He began by asserting that "the historic party questions of the nineteenth century are as dead as last weeks' mutton," which implies the prediction that they will receive far less attention in England in the future than they had received in the past. As examples he cited "Civil and religious liberty, the Franchise, the Irish Question, Dominion Self-Government, the Power of the House of Lords, steeply graduated taxation of Incomes and Fortunes, the lavish use of the Public Revenues for...Social Insurance...Education, Housing and Public Health..." (p. 325). This forecast was largely mistaken. Most of these issues have remained live political issues to the present day in England, and even more so in the U.S.

Keynes urged the Liberal Party to replace these old issues with five new classes of issues, which he was confident would attract increasing public attention in the future, namely:

"1. Peace Questions
2. Questions of Government
3. Sex Questions
4. Drug Questions
5. Economic Questions"

He devoted only eight pages to a discussion of these coming political issues, but each class deserves separate consideration here.

2. Peace Questions

"On Peace Questions," he urged, "let us be Pacifist to the utmost. As regards the Empire, I do not think that there is any important problem except in India. Elsewhere...the process of friendly disintegration is now almost complete.... But as regards Pacifism and Armaments we are only just at the beginning" (p. 330).

This statement implied that "the progress of friendly disintegration" of the Empire would continue until it was complete, as in fact it has. And his implicit forecast that the issue of armament limitation would become or remain a major political issue has also been verified.

3. Questions of Government

"I believe that in the future government will have to take on many duties which it has avoided in the past" (p. 331). In a separate essay, "The End of Laissez Faire" (1926), he specified five of these new duties: (1) "deliberate control of the currency and of credit" in order to stabilize price levels and the rate of economic growth"; (2) "the collection and dissemination on a great scale of data relating to the business situation"; (3) determination of "the scale on which...the community as a whole should save"; (4) control of "the scale on which these savings should go abroad"; (5) control of the size of the nation's population and (6) perhaps "a little later" eugenic progress (pp. 318-19).

Since this was written, the U.K. and other advanced countries have taken on many new duties, including most of the six specified above. Thus this very important prediction has been largely verified by the course of history, and I believe is almost certain to be even more fully verified in the future.

4. Sex Questions

Keynes wrote that "The questions which I group together as Sex Questions have not been party questions in the past," but "I cannot doubt that...[they] are about to enter the political arena." They include "Birth Control and the use of Contraceptives, Marriage Laws, the treatment of sexual offenses and abnormalities, the economic position of women, [and] the economic position of the family." He claimed that "in all these matters the existing state of the Law...is still medieval...[and] out of touch with civilized opinion and...practice." He implied that many reforms in sex laws were inevitable because public opinion had long been growing more favorable to such reforms. This is a good method of predicting the future, but has been little used by futurists.

Keynes was remarkably prescient when he forecast that sex questions would arouse more and more interest among voters and politicians. And he was one of the first to make this sound and significant prediction. Almost every issue of a modern newspaper or news magazine contains evidence of the great contemporary political importance of his sex questions. And there have been many important liberal reforms in laws on marriage, divorce, abortion, birth control, homosexual behavior, etc., in all advanced countries since 1925, the year he made his perceptive forecast on sex questions.

5. Drug Questions

Keynes had less to say about his prediction on drug questions than about any of his five other classes of questions. He explained that the "Drink Question" was by far the most important drug question in the U.K., and did not mention heroin, cocaine or other hard drugs (p. 333). However, if we include these drug questions in his "Drug Questions," his prediction that they would receive greatly increased attention from voters, politicians, and government officials has certainly been verified by history.

6. Economic Questions

As an economist, Keynes naturally elaborated his predictions on economic questions more fully than any of the other four listed above. He quoted with approval Professor Commons," who has been one of the first to recognize the nature of the economic transition amidst the early stages of which we are now living." Commons had listed "three epochs, three economic orders, upon the third of which we are now entering. The first is the Era of Scarcity.... Next comes the Era of Abundance...[including] the victories of laissez faire and historic liberalism.... But we are now entering on a third era, which Professor Commons calls the period of Stabilization.... In this period, he says, 'there is a diminution of individual liberty, enforced in part by government sanctions, but mainly by economic sanctions through concerted action...of associations, corporations, unions..." (p. 335).

According to Keynes, the period of stabilization will include "the transition from economic anarchy to a regime which deliberately aims at justice and social stability..." (pp. 334-35). He did not advocate or predict socialism, but he clearly expected a great increase in government efforts to achieve continuous full employment and to reduce income differentials.

He specifically forecast that government control over monetary policy would expand. "It is not an accident that the opening stage of this political struggle, which will last long and take many different forms, should center about monetary policy. For the most violent interferences with stability and with justice...were...brought about by changes in the price level" (p. 337). Both the general stabilization forecast and the monetary policy forecast have proven true in all advanced countries since 1926.

7. Economic Growth

In an article, "Economic Possibilities for our Children" (The Nation and Atheneum, 1930), Keynes asked and answered the question: "What can we reasonably expect the level of our economic life to be 100 years hence?" He asserted that "the average standard of life in Europe and the U.S. had been raised...about fourfold" since 1500 (p. 363), and predicted that "the standard of life in progressive countries 100 years hence will be between four and eight times as high as it is to-day" (p. 364). Since he made this daring prediction, real income per person has already risen well over 100% in "progressive countries," and seems likely to at least double again in the next 50 years. To date his long-run prediction has been fully verified.

Unfortunately, in 1930, the year the Great Depression began, Keynes rejected as "wildly mistaken" the then widely voiced short-run forecast "that a decline in prosperity is more likely than an improvement in the decade which lies ahead of us" (p. 358). This bad prediction of his was the kind that supports a basic principle of futurism, namely, the principle that it is usually much more difficult to predict the continuance of any trend for a short period than for a long period. Most futurists have ignored this very important principle.

Keynes foresaw the coming extraordinary technological and economic progress in European and American agriculture. "There is evidence that the revolutionary technical changes, which have so far chiefly affected industry, may soon be attacking agriculture. We may be on the eve of improvements in the efficiency of food production as great as those which have already taken place in mining, manufacture and transport" (p. 364). He should have written will instead of may in this uncertain forecast. The context clearly suggests that he was very confident of such economic progress.

8. Solution of the Economic Problem

Keynes repeatedly asserted or implied that continued economic growth would in time solve, or virtually solve, the economic problem, and that this in turn would have radical effects on human behavior. "This means that the economic problem is not—if we look into the future—the permanent problem of the human race," and, "If the economic problem is solved, mankind will be deprived of its traditional purpose," which will require "readjustment of the habits and instincts of the ordinary man, bred into him for countless generations..." (p. 366).

I predict that the economic problem will be a "permanent problem of the human race" because human wants are insatiable, population will grow, and natural resources will become scarcer. Moreover, men have always had, and always will have, traditional purposes other than solution of the economic problem—for instance, procreation, self improvement, artistic creation, power over other men, public approval, etc.

Continued economic progress will of course reduce the time and effort men devote to purely economic activities, especially to boring or unpleasant work, but this readjustment will be pleasant and gradual, not harmful or shocking, as Keynes implied, and will certainly not change human instincts.

9. Unemployment

Keynes claimed that "technical efficiency is increasing by more than 1% per annum compound," and that, as a result, "We are afflicted with a new disease... technological unemployment (p. 364). He implied that both technical progress and the growth of technological unemployment would long continue.

I believe that such unemployment was still insignificant in 1920, and that it has not grown since 1930. European unemployment rates were much lower in the years 1950-80 than in the years 1919-39, in spite of rapid technological progress. Keynes' forecast on technological unemployment was one of his worst predictions.

Although Keynes predicted that technological unemployment would continue to grow, presumably for many decades, he also predicted in The General Theory of Employment, Interest, and Money (1936) that "the world will not much longer tolerate the unemployment which... is associated with present-day capitalistic individualism" (p. 381). There is some conflict between these predictions, neither of which has proven true. The world continued to tolerate the excessive unemployment associated with capitalistic individualism for another 48 years. However, I believe his prediction on such unemployment will eventually be verified, probably before 2100 A.D.

10. The Growth of Leisure

Keynes' greatest fear, however, was not the fear of technological unemployment but the fear that economic progress would create too much leisure, which he thought might be misspent.

"To use the language of today—must we not expect a general 'nervous breakdown'? We already have a little experience of what I mean—a nervous breakdown of the sort which is already common enough in England and the United States amongst the wives of the well-to-do classes, unfortunate women, many of them, who have been deprived by their wealth of their traditional tasks and occupations..." (pp. 366-67).

It was stupid prejudice, not wealth, which deprived these women of useful work, and this prejudice has steadily weakened since 1930. As a result, more and more wives of well-to-do men have gone to work outside the home, and this trend will continue until nearly all harmful idleness among well-to-do women has ended. Moreover, every increase in real wages and economic equality reduces the supply of domestic servants.

Keynes feared that economic progress would greatly increase harmful leisure among men, as well as among women. He feared that economic wants would be too few and too weak to assure even three hours of work a day. "Now it is true that the needs of human beings may seem to be insatiable. But they fall into two classes—those needs which are absolute in the sense that we feel them whatever the situation of our fellow human beings may be, and those which are relative in the sense that we feel them only if their satisfaction lifts us above, makes us feel superior to, our fellow. Needs of the second class...may indeed be insatiable;... But this is not so true of the absolute needs—a point may soon be reached...when these needs are satisfied in the sense that we prefer to devote our further energies to non-economic purposes" (p. 365).

Subsequent history has not borne out this prediction. Real wages have risen by 100 to 200% in all advanced countries since 1930, but the hours of labor have fallen only to 40 hours a week. Moreover, every government agency and every social class in Europe and America is still eager to greatly increase its real income. Reformers eager to abolish slums and build beautiful cities tell us that enormous, almost incredible, sums will be required merely to replace housing which is now considered greatly inadequate.

What Keynes called our "absolute needs" or wants expand with every new invention—automobiles, television, stereophonic phonographs, small moving-picture cameras, etc.—and with every increase in real income. In America the well-to-do, as well as the poor, are eager to earn more in order to buy more consumers' goods, travel abroad more often, buy more expensive meals in fine restaurants, etc. There is no evidence that the well-to-do American is satiated with consumers' goods, and new and more expensive consumers' goods are invented every year.

Furthermore, most Americans are aware of the benefits and pleasures of the work they perform. For many workers, the greatest tragedy of their lives is their compulsory retirement at age 65.

Of course, the well-to-do have always had the most interesting work. But economic progress steadily increases the numbers of interesting jobs. In advanced countries it demands more and more professional employees and fewer and fewer unskilled workers and machine tenders. And wise government and business policies will promote this trend. As real wages rise, men will become ever less willing to do dull work, and employers will find it ever more profitable to eliminate dull jobs. Jobs can be redesigned to meet workers' needs as easily as hats and automobiles can be redesigned to meet consumers' needs. Unfortunately, under Capitalism it has to date been far more profitable to please the consumer than to please the worker. Once full employment at high wages has been achieved, it will become as profitable to please workers as to please consumers. Thereafter, if not before, constant job improvement will increase the pleasure of work as fast as product improvement increases the pleasure of consumption.

For all of these reasons, it is quite unlikely that mankind will ever suffer long from an undue amount of leisure. Keynes ignored these reasons, but he finally reached a similar conclusion. "I feel sure that with a little more experience we shall use the new-found bounty of nature quite differently from the way in which the rich use it today..." It seems odd that he here referred to the benefits of man-made technological progress as "the new-found bounty of nature."

11. Reduced Hours of Labor

Keynes predicted that in advanced countries the hours of labor will be radically reduced in order to provide a little work for all who need work. "But... we shall endeavor...to make what work there is still to be done to be as widely shared as possible. Three-hour shifts or a fifteen-hour week may put off the problem for a great while" (p. 369).

As I have previously explained, there is no basis for the prediction that there will be a shortage of work or jobs when our economy is rationally organized. But the hours of labor will long continue to decline slowly in advanced countries because, with rising affluence, men will voluntarily choose to enjoy more leisure at the expense of potential increases in real output and income. However, it will be a very long time, probably centuries, before most workers voluntarily choose to work only 15 hours a week, if they ever do so. In the 52 years since Keynes made this forecast, the average hours of labor of full-time workers in affluent America have declined only from about 48 to about 40 hours per week. And many workers are still eager to work overtime or hold two jobs in order to increase their real income.

12. Interest Rates

In his classic work, <u>The General Theory of Employment, Interest, and Money</u> (1936), Keynes asserted that "there are no intrinsic reasons for the scarcity of capital" and that "it would not be difficult to increase the stock of capital up to the point where its marginal efficiency had fallen to a very low figure," so low that it would yield no interest. He implicitly forecast that this would be done, and concluded, "I see, therefore the rentier aspect of capitalism as a transitional phase which will disappear when it has done its work," perhaps "within one or two generations" (pp. 375-77).

Six years earlier, in his "Economic Possibilities for our Grandchildren," he had foreshadowed these predictions. "When the accumulation of wealth is no longer of high social importance, there will be great changes in...social customs and economic practices, affecting the distribution of wealth and of economic rewards..." (pp. 369-70).

Since Keynes made these forecasts, the real rate of interest has risen in all advanced countries; it has not declined radically or become zero, as he predicted. It may soon begin a long-run decline, but I doubt that it will ever fall much below the average rate in Keynes era. The chief reason why interest rates have not, and will not, decline as rapidly as he predicted is that the progress of technology continuously opens up new profitable investment opportunities in all industries, and such progress is certain to continue indefinitely. Moreover, world population will long continue to grow, and human wants as a whole are insatiable.

13. Length of Life

In a 1927 review of H. G. Wells' book, <u>The World of William Clissold</u>, Keynes noted and approved Wells' forecast that the average length of life will continue to increase. Keynes correctly predicted that "we shall somewhat rapidly approach to a position in which, in proportion to population, elderly people...will be nearly 100%...more numerous than in the recent past." As a result, "We are threatened...with the appalling problem of the able-bodied 'retired'..." Moreover, by 2000 A.D. "effective power" will be in the hands of men on average fifteen years older than those who had such power in the nineteenth century (pp. 352-53).

Keynes feared that the idle able-bodied aged would waste or misuse their leisure, like "the regular denizens of the Riviera." Here again he mistakenly assumed that it would become increasingly difficult to provide jobs for all persons who need and want work. I have already explained why this implicit prediction was unsound in 1927, and is still unsound today.

14. On Communism as a Religion

In 1925, after a visit to the Soviet Union, Keynes published a book, <u>A Short View of Russia</u>, reprinted in part in Essays in Persuasion. In it he claimed that "Leninism is a combination of two things...religion and business," and stressed the importance of the religious element (pp. 297-98). On the basis of this premise, he made some novel forecasts. "I feel confident of one conclusion—that if Communism achieves a certain success, it will achieve it, not as an improved economic technique, but as a religion...as a religion what are its forces? Perhaps they are considerable.... For modern capitalism is absolutely irreligious" (pp. 305-06). "The decaying religions around us...have lost their moral significance just because...they do not touch in the least degree on these essential matters ...[namely] the love of money...the universal striving after individual economic security," etc. (p. 308). "Perhaps, therefore Russian Communism does represent the first confused stirrings of a great religion" (p. 309). "Russia will never matter seriously to the rest of us, unless it be as a moral force" (p. 311).

Since Keynes wrote this, the U.S.S.R. has achieved full employment, free health care and education for all, comprehensive social security and other social reforms which Keynes might have considered to be moral advances. I prefer to call them economic welfare advances.

Unfortunately, he made other dubious predictions in the field of morals.

15. Moral Theory and Behavior

According to Keynes, further economic progress, especially the elimination of interest, will radically change ethical theory and behavior. "When the accumulation of wealth is no longer of high social importance, there will be great changes in the code of morals.... All kinds of social customs and economic practices, affecting the distribution of wealth and of economic rewards and practices...we shall then be free to discard" (pp. 369-70).

To illustrate this forecast, he predicted that "avarice...usury...and the love of money," which are now considered moral, will eventually be considered immoral. I believe these abnormal attitudes and/or practices are now considered immoral or harmful, and that they will always be so considered, but this will not affect the accumulation or distribution of wealth.

Future economic progress may make thrift, industry, and economic efficiency less essential or beneficial, but it will never make them personally or socially harmful, and it will make saving much easier. In any case, it is meaningless to call any behavior moral or immoral because these terms have no accepted meaning, and it is impossible to conceive of a way of verifying any moral claim.

16. Comments

It is both remarkable and paradoxical that Keynes, a brilliant economist, made his worst predictions in the field of economics. He mistakenly forecast that interest rates would fall drastically, that technological unemployment would rise significantly, and that the hours of labor would fall to 15 hours a week.

On the other hand he correctly predicted rapid economic growth, a great increase in the functions of government, and increased political discussion of drugs, sex, and peace issues.

J. B. S. HALDANE AS A FUTURIST

John Burton Anderson Haldane (1892-1964) came from an artistocratic intellectual Scotch family. His father and a great uncle were Oxford dons, and an uncle was Secretary of State for War. He himself was an eminent biologist and geneticist who taught first at Cambridge and later at the University of London. He was a widely-read popularizer of science.

In 1924 he published a 15,000-word essay in book form, Daedalus, or Science and the Future, which was twice reprinted within five months, and was quoted by Gerard O'Neill in 1981. All page references in this essay are to this book.

1. Methods of Prediction

Haldane rarely if ever used data on past social trends to project future social trends. Instead, he relied largely on information concerning recent past trends in science and technology to predict future advances in these fields and their probable effects on social events and trends. He was by no means the first to stress the technological basis of social evolution but he was probably the first important futurist to stress the advance of science as a more fundamental cause of social evolution. However, this new emphasis is implicit rather than explicit in his essay. He did not discuss the methodology of futurism.

2. Comments on Earlier Futurists

Unlike most futurists, Haldane offered some brief comments on earlier futurists. He noted one especially bad forecast by G. K. Chesterton. "Mr. Chesterton in The Napoleon of Notting Hill [1909]...prophesied that hansom cabs would still be in existence 100 years hence owing to a cessation of invention" but, "Within six years there was a hansom-cab in a museum..." (p. 8).

On the other hand, he praised H. G. Wells "as a serious prophet, as opposed to a fantastic romancer" and called him "singularly modest" and "conservative" in his predictions. He cited Wells' daring forecast in Anticipations (1902), "that by 1920 there would be heavier than air flying machines capable of practical use in war" as an example of a conservative prediction.

He commented, "I propose in this paper to make no prophecies rasher than the above" (pp. 9-10). In fact he offered some much more daring predictions or suggestions.

He also noted, and implicitly rejected, Samuel Butler's "horrible vision...in which man becomes a mere parasite of machinery...which will successively usurp his activities, and end by ousting him from the mastery of this planet" (p. 4).

He did not refer to the forecasts of any other writers. He mentioned Condorcet, Bentham and Marx, but only as critics of metaphysics, not as futurists (p. 17).

3. On the Growth of Research

In sharp contrast to Chesterton, Haldane was confident that scientific research and progress will continue. "I think...that so long as our present economic and national systems continue, scientific research has little to fear. Capitalism...will always protect him [the scientist] as being one of the geese which will produce golden eggs.... And competitive nationalism... will hardly forego the national advantages accruing from scientific research" (p. 6). He also predicted that the socialist British labour party, which had not yet come to power, would foster scientific research in the hope that it would lead to "shortened hours rather than to unemployment."

4. Einstein's Future Influence on Philosophy

In a brief initial comment "on the future of physics" Haldane praised Einstein as "the greatest Jew since Jesus" and predicted that his "name will still be remembered and revered when Lloyd George, Foch, and William Hohenzollern share with Charlie Chaplin the ineluctable oblivion which awaits the uncreative mind" (p. 11). This was an early (1924) and prescient forecast of the coming world fame of Einstein.

Haldane went on to predict that growing acceptance of Einstein's theories would compel the majority of scientific men to reject "the materialism...of the last few generations" and "adopt a very extreme form of Kantian idealism." Indeed, "we are in for a few centuries during which many practical activities will probably be conducted on a basis, not of materialism, but of Kantian idealism" (pp. 11-15). Later, "physiology will invade and destroy mathematical physics" and "The basic metaphysical working hypothesis of science and practical life will then...be something like Bergsonian activism" (p. 16).

In the sixty years since these predictions were made, the main trend in philosophy has been the continued rise of positivism (as predicted by Condorcet and Comte), not the rise of Kantian idealism, and I believe this trend will long continue. Moreover, as positivists have long argued, science has no need for any metaphysical foundations. All basic scientific premises must be verifiable in order to be meaningful and useful, and are verified by the useful and verifiable scientific discoveries they facilitate. Metaphysical premises are unverifiable by definition, and therefore senseless and useless to scientists. It follows that Haldane's predictions on future trends in philosophy and the basic premises of science are not likely to be verified by history.

5. The Cost of Light

Haldane explained that electric light bulbs were very inefficient in 1924 because 95% of their radiation was invisible. "To light a lamp as a source of light is about as wasteful of energy as to burn down one's house to roast one's pork. It is a fairly safe prophecy that in 50 years light will cost about a fiftieth of its present price, and there will be no more night in our cities" (pp. 18-19).

The real cost of light did decline almost continuously from 1924 to 1984, but probably by less than 80%, not by the 98% he forecast. And night has remained far darker than day in our cities. Like most futurists, Haldane grossly overestimated the rate and extent of future change.

6. The Speed of Transport

According to Haldane, the speed of transport is "only limited by the velocity of light. We are working towards a condition when any two persons on earth will be able to be completely present to one another in not more than 1/24 of a second. We shall never reach it, but that is the limit which we shall approach indefinitely." This trend will "bring mankind more and more together,...render life more and more complex, artificial, and rich in possibilities..." (pp. 19-20).

There has been a strong trend in this direction ever since 1924, and it is very likely to continue forever, as he forecast, but the end or limit he suggested still seems incredible.

7. Industrial Integration and Stability

Haldane predicted that, "As industries become more and more closely interwoven, so that a dislocation of any one will paralyze a dozen others (and that is the position towards which we are rapidly moving), the ideal of the leaders of industry, under no matter what economic system, will be directed less and less to the indefinite increase of production in the intervals between such dislocations, and more and more to stable and regular production, even at the cost of reduction of profits and output..." (pp. 20-21).

He explained that it had taken "some thousands of years to produce the stable agricultural society" and predicted that, "It should take a shorter time to evolve a stable industrial society" (p. 22). Here he surely did not overestimate the speed of future social change. And his prediction that the problem will be solved still seems very plausible.

He went on to forecast that the people who first learn to stabilize their economy "will inherit the earth" (p. 22). But Soviet Russia was the first nation to stabilize its economy, and it has not yet inherited the earth. Moreover, "inherit the earth" is the kind of vague prediction futurists should not make.

8. Energy

Haldane wrote, "it is axiomatic that the exhaustion of our coal and oil fields is a matter of centuries only" (p.22). But such resources are never "exhausted." What can and will happen is that the real costs of coal and petroleum will rise as less productive sources are exploited.

He predicted that, "Ultimately, we shall have to tap those intermittent but inexhaustible sources of power, the wind and the sunlight" (p. 23). This was a prescient as well as a sound prediction in 1924. He was the first of the futurists discussed here to make this forecast.

He elaborated this forecast by explaining that "400 years hence...England...will be covered with rows of metallic windmills working electric motors which... supply current...to great electric mains." The surplus power generated in windy weather "will be used for the decomposition of water into oxygen and hydrogen" which "will be liquified and stored" for use as fuel in calm weather and in vehicles (pp. 24-25). These predictions may still come true, but, like most other predictions of technological change, they are relatively dubious.

He noted and explicitly rejected the prediction that energy would in time be commercially produced by means of "induced radio-activity" (p. 27). This forecast has already been clearly disproven.

9. Synthetic Food and Agriculture

Haldane predicted that chemists would be able to produce cheaply nearly all essential foods, including protein. "I...allow 120 years...before a completely satisfactory diet can be produced...on a commercial scale" from coal, plant cellulose, atmospheric nitrogen, and other abundant materials. Within a "century sugar and starch will be about as cheap as sawdust" (p. 38). It is still possible that these predictions will be largely verified, but I think he should have allowed at least twice as long for their fullfillment.

On the basis of these forecasts, he went on to predict that "agriculture will become a luxury and that mankind will be completely urbanized." This will be socially beneficial because "Human progress in historical time has been the progress of cities dragging a reluctant countryside in their wake. Synthetic food will substitute the flower garden and the factory for the dunghill and the slaughterhouse..." (p.39).

In the meantime agriculture will become far more efficient due to "the application of various chemical manures...[and] most of all by the results of systematic creation of hybrid plants, including new plants such as algae which fix nitrogen in the soil (p. 60). This will result in an "enormous fall in [real] food prices and the ruin of purely agricultural states" before 1944 (p. 61). Agriculture did become far more efficient.

Moreover, the escape of new nitrogen-fixing algae to the sea will result in "an increase of the fish population...so great as to make fish the universal food...and to render even England self-supporting in respect of food by 1960" (pp. 61-62). These predictions were not fulfilled.

10. Aluminum

In 1924 aluminum was little used. Haldane predicted that the process of extracting aluminum from clay would be greatly improved, and that, as a result, aluminum "and its alloys will certainly take the second, and possibly the first place as industrial metals" (pp. 31-32). This prediction has already been verified. Aluminum has become the second most important industrial metal in advanced countries.

11. Ectogenesis and Eugenics

Haldane predicted that ectogenesis—the creation and care of fetuses outside the womb—would be developed and would become more common than natural conception, pregnancy, and birth in advanced countries before the year 2074. He specified that France would be the first to adopt ectogenesis and by 1968 would be producing 60,000 ectogenic chidren a year, in spite of a future Papal Bull condemning ectogenesis (pp. 63-65). He should have specified much later dates, perhaps 2500.

He also forecast that the general adoption of ectogenesis would greatly facilitate the adoption of eugenic policies which would yield "enormous" advantages, because only the ovaries removed from genetically very superior women would be used in ectogenesis. He explained that "The small proportion of men and women who are selected as ancestors for the next generation...[will be] so undoubtedly superior to the average that the advance in each generation...[will be] very startling." Moreover, without such eugenic policies, "there can be little doubt that civilization would...collapse within a measurable time owing to the greater fertility of the less desirable members of the population..." (pp. 66-67).

12. Mood-Changing Drugs

As a physiologist, Haldane claimed that products like coffee, tea, tobacco, and alcohol are physiologically beneficial and "civilizing influences of incalcuable value," and predicted that other such products will be discovered and generally used (pp. 33-37). In fact, the consumption of coffee, tea, and tobacco is probably nearly always physiologically harmful, and that of alcohol is very harmful, to millions of people. If other such drugs are discovered and widely used, the results are very likely to be equally harmful. Every nervous stimulation is followed by an equal and opposite reaction, usually depression. Moreover, most such drugs are habit-forming. Therefore, men ought to discontinue their use, and probably will in the long run. However, since 1924 several harmful new drugs have been discovered or popularized and become widely used, as he predicted.

13. Health Care

Haldane forecast that the continued progress of medical care would "practically abolish infectious diseases...all over the world" before 2000 A.D. (p. 58).

He suggested that, as our knowledge of the functions of human glands increases, "we may be able...to control our passions by some more direct method than fasting and flagellation" i.e., by the use of new drugs (pp. 70-71). He specifically predicted that doctors would learn how to ease or end the pains of menopause and thus prolong a woman's youth and allow her to age as gracefully as the average man" (p. 74).

He implied that nearly all causes of premature death will be eliminated, and predicted that, "The abolition of disease will make death a physiological event like sleep. A generation that has lived together will die together." As a result, old people will become much less reluctant to die, and mourning for the dead will diminish (pp. 73-74). These predictions are being verified.

14. World Government

Haldane was confident that mankind will eventually create a world government strong enough to preserve world peace, but feared that, "It may take another world war or two to convert the majority" of men to the need for such a government. He warned that "there is a fair chance that the possibility of human organization on a planetary scale may be rendered impossible by such a war" or wars. In which case, "mankind will probably have to wait for a couple of thousand years for another opportunity" (pp. 84-85). The subsequent invention of nuclear weapons has made these predictions seem prescient.

15. The Social Effects of Scientific Progress

According to Haldane, "the tendency of applied science is to magnify injustices until they become too intolerable to be borne, and the average man...turns at last and extinguishes the evil at its source" (p. 85). War is but one such evil. Thus, "the late war is only an example of the disruptive results that we may constantly expect from the progress of science. The future will be no primrose path. It will have its own problems" (p. 57).

Moreover, "virtues are means between two extremes ... It follows that an alteration in the scale of human power [due to scientific progress] will render actions bad which were formerly good." For instance, it may transform resignation and inaction in the face of disease from a virtue to a crime (p. 89).

16. The Effects of Science on Morals and Religion

Haldane predicted that the continuing progress of science would alter morals and religion. "The time has gone by when a Huxley could believe that while science might indeed remould traditional mythology, traditional morals were impregnable... We must learn not to take traditional morals too seriously. And it is just because even the least dogmatic of religions tends to associate itself with some kind of unalterable moral tradition, that there can be no truce between science and religion" (p. 90).

In the last paragraph of Daedalus the author forecast that, "The scientific worker of the future will more and more resemble the lonely figure of Daedalus as he becomes conscious of his ghastly mission [deicide] and proud of it. He quoted eight lines of an ode to Daedalus, the last of which describes him as "Singing my song of deicide" (pp. 92).

17. Comments

Haldane was perhaps the first well-known natural scientist to write a book on the future. Since then several others have followed his example. All have been seriously handicapped by their lack of professional training and experience in history and the social sciences. Realizing this handicap, Haldane largely restricted his predictions to the effects of scientific advances, especially in biology, but this left large areas of future social change undiscussed. Moreover, his book was much too small to permit proper discussion of most of the future events and trends he did discuss. Finally, the formulation and organization of his predictions appears to have been very carelessly done. It seems more a preliminary draft than a finished version of his ideas.

Haldane's serious prediction of the invention and general use of ectogenesis was taken up and elaborated by Aldous Huxley and made a leading feature of his brilliant dystopia Brave New World (1931). Haldane had foreseen that his prediction would arouse fierce criticism (p. 67).

C. C. FURNAS AS FUTURIST

When he wrote his first book on the future, Clifford Cook Furnas (b1900) was an associate professor of chemical engineering at Yale. Later he became Chancellor of the University of Buffalo.

In 1932 he published America's Tomorrow, An Informal Excursion into the Era of the Two-Hour Working Day. In 1936 he published The Next 100 Years, The Unfinished Business of Science. Both books featured future technological change rather than probable social progress. They were among the first, perhaps the first, American nonfiction books explicitly devoted to a realistic prediction of the future.

In his two books on the future, and especially in the second, Furnas discussed many technological and social problems without making any predictions. He often explained what should or might be done, but failed to predict what would be done. On the whole, he was a reluctant futurist.

This essay is largely based on America's Tomorrow because it was his most comprehensive treatment of the future. All page references not otherwise credited are to this book.

1. Methods of Prediction

Furnas explained that America's Tomorrow "is not ...a scientific discourse, tho it is written from the fortification of a scientific background..." (p. xiii). In fact it was largely based on scientific evidence—statistical trends, knowledge of technological progress, etc. I think he meant that his scientific forecasts were not as certain as his forecasts concerning the results of chemical processes. But a prediction is not less scientific merely because it is less certain. It is unscientific only when it is not based on scientific evidence and reasoning.

Like most futurists, Furnas was apparently unfamiliar with the literature of futurism. The six-page bibliography to The Next Hundred Years does not list a single book reviewed here, or any other futurist book or article. He could have greatly improved his picture of the future by making use of ideas developed by earlier futurists.

Furnas stressed the role of technological progress as a major cause of social change. He also noted that the full effects of many past technological advances had not yet occurred. In his opinion, "we have long since passed the peak in discovery and invention of fundamentals: but "the social upheaval caused by technological change...is actually only beginning" because it takes many decades to fully exploit fundamental advances (NHY, p. 339).

Some futurists have asserted or implied that certain social changes will occur because rational men are likely to consider them rational or beneficial. Furnas explicitly rejected this method of prediction. "Unfortunately," he asserted in The Next Hundred Years, "No one has ever moved the social mass by powers of reason...No movement of history was ever driven by anything but emotion—mob emotion" (p. 356).

It is of course true, or likely, that all conscious human acts have emotional causes, but emotions do not tell us how to act or solve social problems. I believe that reformers who use rational arguments have had a great influence on human history, and will have even more influence in the future, as people become better educated. Therefore, one good way to help predict the future is to determine what future social policies will be rational.

1. Education and Research

Although he was an educator by profession, Furnas had very little to say about the future of education. For instance, he failed to forecast the prolonged and radical growth of secondary and higher education which occurred in all advanced countries from 1931 to 1981.

However, he did forecast a great expansion of vocational secondary education in the U.S. "I anticipate that there will be an increasing number of public trade schools, so that nearly everyone can enter life's productive age with some sort of definite equipment for earning a living" (pp. 237-37). I doubt that there has been much progress in this direction since 1931. Certainly the vast majority of U.S. high school students still leave school with little if any "definite equipment for earning a living."

Since 1931 there has been more than a tenfold increase in relative private and public spending on research and development, i.e., in the share of national income invested each year in R and D. Although Furnas was a professor of chemical engineering, and must have hoped for such an increase, he largely failed to predict it, and certainly failed to properly emphasize it.

3. Technology

Furnas confidently predicted continued and indefinite technological progress in the form of new and improved machines. "I am all for the machine, and I am certain that eventually it will reach its fullest possible development...and that the world will be an infinitely more satisfactory place in which to live because of it. We are a long way from that now" (NHY, p. 357). He claimed that the "replacement of men by machines has only begun" (NHY, p. 343). In fact, machines have caused no net replacement of men to date. They have merely helped workers to increase their output.

In 1931 Furnas predicted that men would soon land on the moon. "I do not doubt that some day a great crowd will gather...to watch a man be locked into a peculiar bullet-like machine on the first...trip to the moon. I hardly expect it in my day... I do not think he will get back..." (p. 23). He also forecast that the machine would be a rocket (p. 24). In fact, Furnas lived to see the first man on the moon by TV, and the first moon visitors returned alive. Nevertheless, this prediction was largely verified.

Furnas also correctly anticipated the common home use of television in his lifetime (p. 38). On the other hand, he mistakenly forecast that man would never "unlock the atom" and obtain nuclear power (pp. 52-53), and he failed to foresee the development of computers.

4. Agriculture and Synthetic Food

Furnas correctly expected that U.S. farms would become larger and larger. "The farmer will gradually pass through the process of consolidation" (p. 270). "The fences will come down and each field will embrace thousands of acres" farmed by machinery. Moreover, farming will become even more scientific (p. 272).

As a result of these trends there will be a continued decline in the role of the family farm in food production. "As the farmers become fewer in number—and they will—they will move to the cities. The independent farmer as we know him probably is doomed; machinery means capital, and capital means big business" (p. 47).

He went on to suggest a much more radical trend affecting the role of agriculture, its replacement by synthetic food factories. "There may not be very much to be done on the land anyway. Plants and animals are laboratories.... Man is learning chemistry very rapidly...it may become less and less profitable to raise foods as such...they can be made in vats and kettles cheaper" (pp. 48-49). There has been a weak trend in this direction ever since he wrote, but it is still unlikely that synthetic foods will largely replace natural foods in the next century or two.

5. Transport

Furnas wrote that "We may reasonably expect that most of our transportation will always be the agencies we now have..." (p. 27). A futurist should rarely if ever say "always," but his prediction would have been plausible if it had been made for the short run.

He correctly anticipated that "the airplane will, in a relatively few years, be our most common means of long-distance hired travel" (p. 28), and added that "mail and fast express, too, are the natural heritages of the plane" (p. 29).

He successfully forecast a great increase in the use of pipe-lines and power lines. "All the dirty work of the fuel business will be done at the coal mines; the solid coal will be completely gasified or liquified, and the product pumped to the cities..." (p. 31). This prediction has not yet been verified, but it may still come true.

He also wrote that, "The motor trucks are destined to take over local freight" (NHY, p. 243), a forecast that has already been largely verified in the U.S.

6. Resources

Although he did not foresee the invention of nuclear power, Furnas was not worried about future energy and material supplies. "There will always be a great sufficiency of energy available for us," he asserted, but eventually, after another thousand years or more, we will have to rely entirely on solar power (p. 56).

He correctly predicted that "as our supply of each metal becomes leaner, there will be...substitution of a more abundant material" (p. 61). For instance, aluminum will be increasingly substituted for iron (p. 62). And we may dig much deeper for ore (p. 63).

7. Feminism

Furnas was well aware of the rise of feminism and foresaw its long continuance. "We have some very notable examples of women who have a career, children and a husband—all three. We shall have more and more of them" (p. 217). "There will be a gradual change in attitude towards work on the part of those women who are married" (p. 216). He also forecast increased public welfare support for poor mothers with children but without a husband (pp. 217-18). However, he failed to predict how far or how fast these trends would go,

which minimizes the importance of these forecasts. He
also failed to explain that his predicted decline in
the hours of labor would make it much easier for mothers to work outside the home. And he failed to foretell the coming great growth of kindergartens and other
child-care agencies, which had the same effect.

8. Population and Eugenics

Furnas asserted that "we are willfully limiting
our population, and we will continue to do so more and
more, until we get it down to a decent figure" (p. 96).
He did not explain what such a "decent figure" will be.
Nor did he anticipate heavy and prolonged illegal immigration.

9. Urban Growth

Although he expected that many more farmers would
move to towns and cities, Furnas mistakenly predicted
that the largest U.S. cities would soon begin to shrink.
"As the cities become smaller—and they will—there
will be more of them" (p. 47). In his only reference
to the work of other futurists, he noted and rejected
Stuart Chase's dubious prediction that our largest cities are headed for mechanical breakdowns which will
teach us the proper size limits. Furnas forecast "human and not mechanical" breakdowns in large cities
(pp. 43-44). I doubt that either will ever occur in
the U.S., but I expect that American voters will eventually limit city size for a variety of sound reasons.

10. Welfare Capitalism

Furnas discussed in some detail the contemporary
competition between capitalism and socialism, and
correctly predicted the rise of a comprehensive welfare economy under capitalism in the U.S. He forecast that ever larger U.S. corporations would increasingly provide free health care, old-age pensions, and
stable jobs at good wages for their employees. Business firms will give new young employees lifetime contracts (pp. 183-85).

For "the average worker the wages will never all
be paid at once but part will be held in trust by those
who know how to hold it," the employers (p. 187). Furnas did not anticipate the subsequent rapid growth of
social insurance, apparently because he feared the
growth of government. In fact, since he wrote, the
growth of government social insurance has been much
more rapid than the growth of business worker-welfare
programs. But he was correct in predicting a great
further expansion of the latter.

Furnas noted that the predicted growth of corporate welfare programs would require a further growth in the size of business firms: "It will mean operation in large units; that is inevitable. The small capitalist cannot afford the losses entailed in stabilizing commerce by calling on reserves" (p. 185). He here ignored the fact that small firms can shift such risks to private insurance companies.

Furnas explained that the rise of free, employer-financed health care "will mean socialized medical practise of a sort...private corporations will develop a satisfactory system just to keep professional practise out of the hands of the state" (p. 188). But, since 1931, public support of health care has grown much faster than private business support in all advanced countries.

Furnas clearly implied that labor unions would not play a major role in the predicted rise of welfare capitalism. He forecast a decline in union membership, and asserted that, "It is very doubtful if the labor and trades unions will ever rise to great power... [because] they have shown themselves incapable of shouldering social responsibility" (p. 196). In fact, since 1931, U.S. union membership has grown substantially, and unions have been largely responsible for the great growth of fringe benefits which make up much of welfare capitalism.

Furnas predicted that government ownership of U.S. public utilities would never expand significantly (p. 205). To date, such ownership has not expanded much in the U.S., but has expanded greatly in most other advanced countries, which suggests that it is very likely to do so in the U.S. in the next 50 years. Few in any major long-run European social trends fail to occur in the U.S.

Furnas expected that the rise of welfare capitalism and increased taxation of the highest incomes would make personal income less unequal in the U.S. "There probably will be a considerable redistribution of the nation's wealth, with a decrease in the number of... our lesser millionaires" and "considerable government curbing of the upper reaches of material wealth" (p. 184). Since 1931 there has been a slight, but not a "considerable" redistribution of wealth in the U.S., but this redistribution may continue indefinitely.

11. Communism

According to Furnas, the U.S. economy already had a large communist sector in 1931—free public schools, free highways, free libraries, etc. He explained that, "It is hard to say how great a communistic control of our life we shall witness in the future, but we must be approaching the limit now..." (pp. 197-78). However, he also predicted the rise of comprehensive, employer-financed free health care, which alone would notably expand communist or free distribution. And in fact there has been a notable and almost continuous growth of free distribution since he wrote—more free higher education, health care, child care, legal care, etc.

Furnas predicted that Russia would abandon communism after achieving "a reasonably prosperous state" because communism limits individualism (p. 201). But Russia is now more prosperous than was the U.S. in 1931, and has not abandoned communism. However, it may still do so. It is impossible to disprove a prediction that has no time limit. That is why such predictions are far less important than those with a time limit.

12. Health Care

As previously noted, Furnas foresaw the rise of health insurance and health care financed by employers. He also expected great technical progress in health care. As a result, he asserted that "Our future generations may grow up in an apparently aseptic world so far as the infectious diseases are concerned. The childhood diseases will have disappeared, the common cold will have gone the way of the dodo, smallpox will only be a matter of record..." (pp. 55-56). Later he forecast that "disease will be practically eliminated" (p. 78). He has already been proven largely right on infectious diseases and on smallpox, but his forecast on the common cold has not yet been verified.

13. Length of Life

One of the most important and most emphasized forecasts in America's Tomorrow is that concerning the length of human life. "Most important of all, there will be a prolongation of life," partly because "disease will be practically eliminated." These were plausible predictions, but the author went on the predict an incredible average life span: "I believe that my grandchildren many generations removed will come to look upon death as a horrible curiosity, rather than an inevitable penalty for living" (p. 94). This is a very implausible prediction, and such predictions weaken the reader's confidence in the author's forecast on other subjects.

Four years later, in The Next Hundred Years Furnas became ultra-cautious in predicting prolongation of the average human life span in the U.S. He predicted a rise only from 60 to 70 years by the year 2036 (p. 95). I predict it will be closer to 80 than 70. He did not explain the reasons for the radical change in his forecast.

14. The Hours of Labor

As the subtitle of <u>America's Tomorrow</u> suggests, Furnas heavily emphasized the effect of future progress on the length of the working day. He asserted that, "The most important thing that our industrialism will give us will be leisure" (p. 5). He predicted that the average length of the U.S. working day would continue to decline until it reached two hours. "Even two hours may be too many. I use that as a first approximation..." (p. 13). He did not explain when this end would be achieved, nor why two hours is the probable ultimate standard.

Since 1931 the length of the average U.S. working day for non-agricultural firms has declined from about 45 hours to about 39 hours, but the rate of decline has been falling. It now seems very unlikely that average hours will fall below 25 hours in the next century or two. The forecast of a two-hour work day therefore seems grossly unrealistic. It may eventually be technologically feasible, but it will never be adopted, both because men need several hours of work each workday for psychological and health reasons, and because after the hours of labor have fallen to 4 or 5 hours, workers will always want additional goods and services more than they desire additional leisure.

He noted and flatly rejected a Brookings Institute claim that Americans can, and eventually will, consume an output per person "many times that achieved in...1929" (<u>NHY</u>, p. 359). Actually, output per person has much more than doubled since 1929, and will probably double again and again without causing workers to prefer leisure after 2, 3, or 4 hours of work a day.

To support his prediction of a two-hour working day, Furnas claimed in 1932 that, "It is becoming increasingly difficult to invent something that the public will desire to buy..." (p. 12). I believe that history has completely disproven this claim.

15. Leisure Use

As a result of his forecast of a radical decline in the average hours of labor, Furnas devoted considerable space in both books to future changes in the use of leisure. He predicted that nearly all the customary uses of leisure—travel, sport, reading, writing, study, art, hobbies, etc.—would grow indefinitely (pp. 234-43). As a professor, he naturally expected special increases in intellectual and cultural activities. "The future will be filled with writers..." and "many more readers" (p. 241). Here, as often elsewhere, he probably allowed his desires to overinfluence his predictions.

16. Standardization and Westernization

Furnas predicted increased standardization of economic goods and methods of production throughout the world. "The kind of food we eat, our mode of travel, the type of dwelling and kind of clothes may be expected to become more standardized..." (p. 258). Moreover, standardization will result in westernization. "We are not going to have the great variety of peoples and groups of customs which we now have.... Clothing all over the world is now merging into the standards set by Europe and America, and means of transportation and ways of doing things are rapidly following suit" (p. 264). Those predictions have been increasingly verified by history since 1931, and will, almost certainly, be further verified for centuries.

17. Comments

Although Furnas made some very bad major predictions—most notably those on the two-hour day and length of life—most of his forecasts have been partially verified in the years since 1931, and/or are still plausible. However, most of his good predictions were vague and incomplete. He rarely specified how far or how fast any predicted trend would go, or whether he was predicting a nominal or a relative growth. And he did not make any sound and significant new predictions about the future, except perhaps that concerning welfare capitalism. Nor did he repeat and stress any such predictions made by his contemporaries.

In spite of such faults, Furnas deserves great credit both as a pioneer American futurist and as one of the first to foresee the rise of welfare capitalism. On the whole, he made outstanding contributions to the science of futurism.

JAMES BURNHAM AS A FUTURIST

James Burnham (b1905) was probably the most influential American futurist of the first half of this century. His masterpiece, The Managerial Revolution (1940) was widely reviewed, and was translated into most major foreign languages. It is remarkably lucid, persuasive, and daring in its predictions.

When he wrote it, the author was a young professor of philosophy at New York University, who had been an active literary critic, editor, and Trotskyite for several years.

The Managerial Revolution resembles The Communist Manifesto more than any other previous futurist work, but it is anti-Marxist in several basic ways, and Marxist in others. Like Condorcet, Marx, Bellamy, and Wells, Burnham predicted a social revolution, but the revolution he described and predicted, the managerial revolution, differed in many ways from that forecast by any of these predecessors. However, he based most of his predictions upon a Marxist economic theory of social evolution. He too claimed that economic trends are the basic causes of social, political, and ideological trends.

1. The Decline of Capitalism

Burnham asserted that world capitalism had been in decline since 1914. "The curve of the extension of capitalist control, which had risen without interruption from the fourteenth century, abruptly broke downward [in 1914] and has sunk continuously ever since, heading swiftly toward zero" (p. 99). He predicted that this decline would continue. "The theory of the managerial revolution predicts that capitalist society will be replaced by 'managerial society.'" Indeed, "the transition is already well under way" (p. 29).

Burnham asserted that capitalism cannot survive because it will continue to result in: (1) "mass unemployment," (2) "recurring economic crises," (3) an unmanageable "volume of public and private debt," (4) growing restriction of "free monetary exchange transactions," (5) "a permanent agricultural depression," (6) large unused "investment funds," (7) the failure of colonialism and imperialism, (8) failure to use "technological possibilities," and (9) a decline in popular acceptance of "the ideologies of capitalism" (pp. 31-35). These nine predictions haved been largely confirmed to date.

Burnham treated the growth of government ownership and control of industry as evidence of the decline of capitalism and the rise of a managerial society. "Government is moving always more widely into the economy...every incursion of government into the economy means that one more section of the economy is wholly or partially removed from the reign of capitalist economic relationships" (p. 106). He repeatedly implied or predicted that such incursions would continue until capitalism had been replaced by a managerial society (p. 112).

Burnham claimed that capitalism reached its peak in the U.S. in 1914, and had been declining since then. In fact, it continued to expand its share in the U.S. mixed economy for many decades after 1914, and may not yet have reached its peak. He erred because he failed to distinguish between capitalism and individualism, the economic system which was dominant in nearly all advanced countries from 1600 to 1900. The individualistic (family firm) share of the U.S. economy has been declining for over 200 years, but the capitalist sector (private firms with four or more employees) has been growing for 200 years, and may not yet have ceased growing.

However, this criticism does not refute his subsequent claim that the managerial sector (including all government, all non-profit, and some large corporate enterprises) has been growing steadily since 1914. The decline in the individualistic sector has been rapid enough and large enough to permit both the other sectors to expand simultaneously.

2. The Bleak Future of Socialism

After predicting that capitalism would decline rapidly in advanced countries, Burnham predicted that it would not be followed by socialism. He based this prediction on an arbitrary definition of a "socialist society" as one that "is classless, fully democratic, and international," and on arbitrary definitions of "classless" and "fully democratic." For him a "classless" or "fully democratic" society was one in which all members have equal income and political influence (p. 39). No such society has ever existed, or can exist, because every feasible system of government distributes income and political power unequally. Thus his argument was purely verbal or philosophic, i.e., armchair reasoning from arbitrary definitions or premises.

3. The Managerial Revolution

The main thesis of The Managerial Revolution is that "we are now in a period of social transition... from the type of society which we have called capitalist or bourgeois to a type of society which we shall call managerial.... What is occurring...is a drive for social dominance, for power and privilege, for the position of ruling class, by the social group or class of the managers.... This drive will be successful." It began about 1913, and will probably end before 1964 (p. 71). This transition will amount to a social revolution because it will drastically change the most important social institutions, will cause parallel changes in cultural institutions and ideologies, and will bring a new social group to supreme political power (p. 5).

"The economic framework in which this social dominance of the managers will be assured is based upon the state ownership of the major instruments of production...there will be no direct property rights in the major instruments of production vested in individuals.... The managers will exercise their control over the instruments of production and gain preference in the distribution of the products...indirectly, through their control of the state. The state...will...be the 'property' of the managers... The control of the state by the managers will be suitably guaranteed by appropriate political institutions..." (p. 72). In other words, the managers will not be elected in democratic elections, but will be self-appointed or chosen by their group or their supervisors. Burnham did not predict the precise method of choosing national chief executives, but he suggested a method like those used by the Roman Catholic Church and the Russian Communist Party.

Burnham claimed that in predicting a managerial revolution he was projecting into the future a social trend which had already existed for some time. "The theory is...an interpretation of what *already* has happened and is now happening. Its prediction is simply that the process which has started and which has already gone a great distance will continue and reach completion" (p. 75).

He referred to the famous study, The Modern Corporation and Private Property by Berle and Means, to support his claim that professional business managers had long been gaining business power at the expense of stockholders in large corporations (pp. 88-89). He also cited the rise of communism and fascism as evidence that capitalists were losing out to managers.

It is noteworthy that, in trying to explain the past and predicted growth of the managerial sector, Burnham failed to use the plausible Marxist argument that the invention of large and expensive machines has tended to cause a great increase in the scale of production, which in turn has brought about a great increase in the number and power of professional managers, and will long continue to do so.

He also failed to note that the growing demand for goods and services which cannot or should not be sold for a price—education, health care, child care, highway use, etc.—has caused, and will continue to cause, an increase in the size of government, and therefore of the managerial sector.

4. The Nature of the Managerial Economy

In Chapter IX Burnham forecast the nature of the economy of a managerial society. He began by explaining that, "When, finally, the major part of the instruments of production come under governmental ownership and control, the transition is, in its fundamentals, completed" (p. 118). He then asked, "What kind of economy will this be?.... What group will be the ruling class?" (p. 119).

In answering these questions, he first claimed that, "there is not the slightest reason for believing that the particular form of state-owned economy now in the process of development will be economically classless." Rather, he predicted that managers would use their power to make themselves a new social class, i.e., that the managers of a managerial society would "exploit" it. "By 'exploitation' is meant the processes...whereby...an unequal distribution of income comes about" (p. 123). In other words, he merely anticipated that the managers would fix their own salaries above the average level in the managerial society, a very plausible prediction. But such use of the term _exploitation_ is misleading. The term always connotes excessive earnings.

He went on to explain that this coming managerial exploitation would create a partly hereditary new ruling class, "...the managers will exploit the rest of society...through the possession of privilege, power, and command of educational facilities [they] will be able to control, within limits, the personnel of the managerial recruits, and the ruling class of managers will thus achieve a certain continuity from generation to generation" (p. 126).

Burnham noted that, "many, perhaps most, of the present managers do not consciously want or favor state ownership," and he explained that "We have here an irony that is often repeated in history" (pp. 127-28).

He meant that those who will benefit from proposed social reforms often oppose them. He forecast that state ownership and control of the economy would continue to grow primarily because capitalism will fail to solve many serious economic problems—unemployment, inflation, growth, etc.—not because the managers will demand it.

He explained that, in a state-owned managerial economy, "it is no longer necessary for each branch of industry, as a whole, to operate at a profit...branches of the economy or the whole economy can be directed towards aims other than profits. The managerial economy will no longer be 'the profit system'" (pp. 129-30). Rather, "the regulation of production...will be carried out deliberately and consciously by groups of men.... Under the centralized economic structure of managerial society, regulation (planning) is a matter of course" (p. 132).

Burnham predicted that, "In a managerial economy, the role of money will be considerably restricted... money will no longer function as individual capital... even in exchange transactions the use of money...will be limited" (p. 130). He suggested that barter would partly replace monetary payment in internatinal trade, and that "An increasing number of consumer goods and services will be supplied without...direct...money payment," i.e., as free goods (p. 131). The last prediction deserves special attention because it is important, is probably sound, and is novel. So far as I am aware, no previous futurist had forecast a "vastly enlarged" distribution of free goods.

He also forecast in 1940 that "money will become increasingly and perhaps altogether divorced from any metallic base" (p. 131), a perceptive forecast which has already been verified in nearly all advanced countries.

Burnham predicted that the freedom of workers will be "greatly altered" in the coming managerial economy. "There being only one major employer (the state) there will be no bargaining among competing employers; and the assignment and transfer of jobs, as well as the fixing of rates of pay, will not be left to the accidents of market bargaining" (pp. 131-32).

He failed to realize that the rulers of a managerial economy could use their great powers to achieve wage rates which are ideal because they balance supply and demand, and which orthodox economists claim would exist under pure and perfect competition. The elimination of market bargaining over wage rates does not require state assignment of workers to jobs. Proper allocation of labor could, and eventually will, be achieved by proper variation of wage rates, not by coercion of workers, even in a managerial or socialist economy.

Burnham forecast that the coming managerial economy will not be subject to "the capitalist type of economic crisis, since the factors involved are related to the profit requirements of a capitalist economy" and "will be done away with." However, it will be subject to its own form of crisis" which will be technical and political," caused by "breakdowns in bureaucratized administration" (p. 132).

He claimed that "mass unemployment is the most intolerable" of all economic difficulties, and predicted that a managerial economy will "do away with" it "or reduce it to a negligible minimum," as Germany and Russia had already done (p. 133).

Moreover, he forecast that a managerial economy would make better use of new inventions and technological devices, and would assure the investment of idle capital funds. As a result of all these reforms, the long-term production curve will resume its advance, interrupted by the Great Depression (pp. 133-34), and "there will be a greater total output...in relation to the total population than under capitalism" (p. 136).

On the other hand, he asserted that economic planning could not and would not be scientific, and that therefore "there will continue to be, as there always has been, fighting over the spoils" (p. 138), which the managers would win.

5. The Locus of Political Power

Chapter VII, "Who Are the Managers," describes the managers who will rule the coming managerial society. They will not be the lawyers, who are now so numerous in legislatures and government bureaus, or the engineers who technocrats have proposed as the new ruling group (p. 80). Instead, "the managers are simply those who are, in fact, managing the instruments of production nowadays" (p. 77). They are engaged in "the tasks of the technical direction and coordination of the process of production." They may now be called "production managers, operating executives, superintendents, administrative engineers, supervisor technicians; or, in government...administrators, commissioners, bureau heads..." (pp. 79-80). He explicitly excluded "finance-executives" because they do not manage operations (p. 84).

Burnham predicted that the coming managerial society would "do away with the representative political institutions of the old society" (p. 149). Parliaments will be abolished. Political power will be "localized in administrative bureaus." They will "proclaim the rules, make the laws, issue the decrees.

The shift from parliament to the bureaus occurs on a world scale" (p. 148). Unfortunately, he did not explain how national leaders or bureau chiefs would be chosen after representative government had been abolished, so his picture of the coming managerial government was not very clear.

Burnham predicted that, "In spite of the fusion between the state and the economy, there will remain a certain differentiation between the 'politicians' and the 'managers.' ...a...differentiation in function..." Politicians will control the military and police forces. Nevertheless, "the managers, not the bureaucrats," will be "the leading section of the new ruling class." To carry out their policies, the political bureaucrats will "require enormous resources...these can be assured only through their...subordinating themselves to...the managers" (pp. 157-58). This prediction seems very dubious. Neither Stalin nor Hitler found it necessary to subordinate himself to the managers in their semi-managerial societies.

The chief objection to Burnham's prediction that governments will eventually consist of, or be controlled by, professional managers is that management or administration is only one of the three major functions of government, the others being policy determination or legislation, and adjudication. Managers may be well qualified to determine administrative structures and policies, but they are quite unqualified to determine other social policies, such as those concerning: (1) income distribution or redistribution, (2) taxation, (3) foreign trade, (4) price determination, (5) free distribution, (6) immigration, (7) abortion, (8) inflation, (9) unemployment, (10) national saving, (11) investment fund allocation, (12) defense expenditures, (13) crime, (14) social security, (15) pollution, and many other social problems. In advanced countries, democratically elected politicians and their social scientist assistants and advisors are far better qualified by education and experience to determine nearly all government policies. It is very likely that the power or influence of professional managers in industry and government will long continue to increase, as Burnham predicted, but it is very unlikely that they will ever replace politicians and generals as supreme national policy makers. In this function politicians will be increasingly replaced by social scientists, not by professional managers.

6. On Democratic Government

Burnham predicted that the period of transition from capitalism to a managerial society will usually

be a period of dictatorship (pp. 166-67). On the
other hand, "Historical analogy [the transition from
feudalism to capitalism] suggests that with the consolidation of the structure of managerial society,
its dictatorial phase (totalitarianism) will change
into a democratic phase." Two additional reasons for
this prediction are: (1) "the state of mind of the
people" must be known and considered by rulers, and
(2) some democracy allows political opponents "to let
off steam" harmlessly (p. 167).

In any case, "In spite of wider democracy...con-
trol by the ruling [managerial] class can be assured
(as under capitalism) when major social institutions
upholding the position of the ruling class are firmly
consolidated, when ideologies contributing to the
maintenance of these institutions are generally accepted, when the instruments of education and propaganda are primarily available to the ruling class, and
so on" (p. 168).

Nevertheless, "It is not yet clear whether the
social relations of the new [managerial] society could
be guaranteed in any other way than through a one-party
democracy" (p. 169). And the coming managerial democracy "would have to be a nonparliamentary democracy"
(p. 170).

Burnham concluded this discussion by asserting
that, "The democracy of capitalist society is on the
way out, is, in fact, just about gone, and will not
come back. The democracy of managerial society will
be some while being born; and its birth pangs will include drastic convulsions" (p. 171).

7. International Relations

According to Burnham, "Experience has shown that
the existence of a large number of sovereign nations,
especially in Europe...is incompatible with contemporary economic and social needs." There is not "the
slightest chance for the restoration of the pre-1939
system in Europe" (p. 173).

"Nevertheless, it is extremely doubtful that the
world political systems of managerial society will be
organized as a single world state" because: (1) centralized world rule is technically impossible, and (2)
no state could "organize a military group sufficiently
large and cohesive to be able to patrol the whole
world" (p. 174). Both of these reasons are unpersuasive. A world federal state could easily delegate most
government functions to member governments, and, with
modern planes and nuclear weapons, could patrol the
world and enforce world peace. However, as he predicted, no single world state has yet been created.

Writing in 1940, Burnham predicted that, "The comparatively large number of sovereign states under capitalism is being replaced by a comparatively small number of great nations, or 'super-states' which will divide the world among them." Later, he became more specific, forecasting that, "the world political system will coalesce into three primary super-states," based upon: (1) Japan and eastern China, (2) the U.S., and (3) Europe, especially its northeastern and north-central regions, excluding eastern Europe (pp. 175-76). He did not expect the Soviet Union to become a postwar superpower.

He predicted that the creation of this new world order would require more than one war after World War II. "It should go without saying that the mechanism whereby this new political system will be built is and will be war...the war of 1939 is the first great war of managerial society" (p. 176). But it "is only the first, not the last..." (p. 178).

"What will be actually accomplished by these wars will not be a decision as to who is to rule the bases —for Americans are going to rule here, Europeans in Europe, and Asiatics in Japan and east China—but decisions as to what parts and how much of the rest of the world are going to be ruled by each of the three strategic centers" (p. 179). Each of these great superpowers will enjoy a nearby zone for natural preeminence, but will periodically fight over more marginal areas, apparently indefinitely, for he anticipated no world government. These coming wars will help in "completing the destruction of capitalism."

He also forecast that World War II would produce "at least two more of the major political leaps towards managerial society: first, the political consolidation of the European Continent; and, second, the breakup of the British Empire,..." (p. 177, see also p. 183).

8. "The Russian Way"

According to Burnham, "the pattern" of the Russian revolution and subsequent evolution "may well be reproduced elsewhere" (p. 210). Moreover, "In its economic and political institutions, Russia comes closest to the institutional types of the future.... It is along such lines that the institutions of established and consolidated managerial society will evolve" (p. 221). He added that, "there is not going to be a capitalist restoration in Russia" (p. 223).

Nevertheless, he clearly implied that Russia would be badly defeated in World War II because it was technologically and culturally inferior to Germany. "The advantages which the managerial structure gave

Russia against capitalist nations disappears when Russia is confronted with other managerial or near-managerial states which are not burdened by Russia's weaknesses." Therefore, "during the course of the next years Russia will split apart into an eastern and western section, each section gravitating toward one of the key areas...of the super-states of the future" (p. 225). In other words, he implied that European Russia would become part, or a satellite, of the coming European super-state, probably dominated by Germany, and that Siberia would be similarly ruled by an East Asian super-state. These predictions turned out to be very bad short-run predictions, but it is still possible that they will be largely verified in the next century or two.

9. "The German Way"

Burnham believed that the Nazis had started a major social revolution, the change from capitalism to managerialism, in Germany. As a result, "Germany is today a managerial state at an early stage," even though it retains more capitalist elements than Russia (p. 239). That is why "Nazi Germany had a better, a more effective, war economy than her rivals..." (p. 240), and was able to easily overrun Poland and France.

He asserted that, "The general outcome of the... war is...assured...because it does not depend upon a military victory by Germany, which is...likely.... England, no matter with what...allies, cannot conceivably hope to conquer the European Continent;... Nor could they repartition Europe into independent, fully sovereign states" (p. 247). Here we have three bad major predictions in a single paragraph.

If the Hitler regime is defeated or replaced, "it will give way to...a regime differing from Hitler's not by being capitalist but by being a more matured representative of the managerial future...the social revolution in Germany cannot be reversed" (p. 250).

Whether or not Nazism survives, "What will emerge...will be a super-state based upon the European area of advanced industry. The Germany...of now is the nuclear first stage in the development of that super-state" (p. 251).

10. The Future of the U.S.

Burnham predicted that government control over, and government ownership of, U.S. industry would continue to grow. He regarded the New Deal as a major step towards a managerial society. He forecast that corporate managers would continue to take over the business and political power previously held by capitalists: "...in the U.S., the tendency away from capitalism and toward managerial society has received a specific native ideological and institutional expression...the 'New Deal'..." (pp. 252-54).

He correctly predicted that the U.S. would soon take part in World War II (p. 269), and that this participation would speed up the movement towards a managerial society (p. 262). He asserted that the 1940 presidential election had been the last, or "at most, the next to last" U.S. democratic election (p. 261).

He anticipated that after World War II the U.S. would begin to consolidate its political and military domination over its own strategic base (North and South America) and to struggle for domination of marginal areas like Viet Nam. "From her continental base the U.S. is called on to make a bid for maximum world power..." (p. 262). It will strive for control of "the rest of South America, the Far East (including conspicuously the Far Eastern colonies of formerly sovereign European states) and in fact the whole world.... This struggle is bound to be inconclusive" since "no one state can...rule the world" (p. 264).

The capitalist social structure cannot hold its own in these scheduled conflicts because: (1) a managerial system is more efficient, (2) "Adequate arming ...is no longer profitable," and (3) capitalist ideologies will not attract enough popular support (pp. 265-66).

Burnham wrote that, "it is...possible that the U.S. could accomplish the transition to managerial society in a comparatively democratic fashion," but stated that, "It is more likely than not" that this transition would include "revolutionary mass movements, terror, purges..." (p. 272). Fortunately, this prediction has not yet been verified."

11. Comments

On the whole, Burnham was less original, comprehensive, and successful as a futurist than any of the major pioneer scientific futurists previously discussed. Several able writers had called attention to the growing power of managers before he recklessly predicted a very rapid further growth in the economic and political power of managers. Moreover, he ignored many vital social trends recognized and projected into the future by earlier futurists. And he failed in his effort to draw a sharp distinction between the trend towards a managerial society and that towards socialism.

Writing in 1939-40, Burnham gave undue weight to the recent short-run trend towards fascism and totalitarianism, and much too little weight to the far longer and more general trends towards capitalism and democratic government.

He was correct in projecting into the future the long-run trends towards government ownership and control of business and towards managerial dominance in large corporate and government organizations but, like most futurists, he grossly overestimated the rate of future social change. And he frequently implied that managers and administrators are, or will be, competent to solve major social problems which they have not been trained to solve, and which should be left to politicians and/or social scientists.

JOSEPH A. SCHUMPETER AS A FUTURIST

Joseph Alois Schumpeter (1883-1950) was an Austrian economist and ex-minister of finance (1919) who joined the Harvard faculty in 1932. In 1942 he published a lucid and brilliant book, Capitalism, Socialism, and Democracy, which contains not only many predictions about the future but also a theory of social evolution which explains why major social changes occur and why they are predictable. This essay is based on this book, to which all page references refer.
In his predictions Schumpeter was almost as daring as James Burnham, and some of their predictions are similar, but Schumpeter's analysis was far more sophisticated and persuasive, partly because Schumpeter was a social scientist.

1. His Metholodogy

Although he was not a socialist, Schumpeter was an admirer of Karl Marx, especially of his economic interpretation of history. Like Marx he stressed the thesis that economic progress in a capitalist society inevitably creates new social conditions and attitudes which will lead to the eventual destruction of capitalism. But he stressed changes in attitudes among the upper classes, not the creation of a working class hostile to capitalism, as causes of the continuing rise of socialism.
Schumpeter asserted that mere unexplained prediction "is not science but prophecy," because "What counts in any attempt at social prognosis is not the Yes and No that sums up the facts and arguments which lead up to it, but those facts and arguments themselves. They contain all that is scientific in the final result" (p. 61). This implies that a scientifically justified conclusion is not scientific, an unsound idea, but the distinction between prophecy and scientific prediction is plausible and useful. Some writers have treated forecasters like Nostradamus as futurists.
He also claimed that futuristic analysis "never yields more than a statement about the tendencies present in an observable pattern" (p. 61), which implies that one cannot scientifically predict future changes in these tendencies, a dubious theory. It also implies that all predictions must be based on trend projection,

another dubious idea. I believe that mere comparison of contemporary conditions in advanced and backward countries can help us to predict the future of backward countries. Also, comparison of the current opinions of more and less educated people is often useful.

In spite of this emphasis on trend projection as a method of prediction, Schumpeter later claimed that "a historical record...over any...period does not itself justify any extrapolation at all" (p. 72) because "the very concept of historical sequence implies the occurrence of irreversible changes..." (p. 72n). This reasoning seems both unclear and unsound. Predictions based on extrapolation of long social trends are never certain, but they are far more likely to be true than false, which explains why such extrapolation is a very common and very useful method of predicting the future.

He asserted that "Prognosis does not imply anything about the desirability of the course of events that one predicts" (p. 61). But most social trends continue because more men want them to continue. Moreover, it is usually safe and scientific to predict that a desired social trend will begin or continue. And the belief in future social progress, well grounded on past social progress, implies that most future social trends will be beneficial. Therefore, scientific prognosis does usually imply that the trend or event predicted is regarded as desirable by most people in the region concerned.

2. Economic Growth under Capitalism

Schumpeter reported that the Day-Persons index of total U.S. production showed an average annual growth rate of 3.7% from 1870 to 1930, and predicted that this rate of growth would continue for another 50 years, indeed indefinitely, if the capitalist system was not changed and weakened by new government regulation (pp. 64-65). He claimed that if this future growth were permitted, nearly all reforms desired by social reformers "would be fulfilled automatically or could be fulfilled without significant interference with the capitalist process" (p. 69). But he implicitly forecast that the U.S. government would adopt "anti-capitalist policies which would greatly reduce the rate of economic growth" (p. 71). This last forecast proved to be a bad one because U.S. economic growth from 1930 to 1980 was as rapid as from 1870 to 1930.

On the other hand, his conditional forecast that numerous social reforms would be achieved if economic growth continued at past rates has been verified. He specifically forecast the adoption of unemployment insurance (p. 70) and increased provision of free goods

(p. 71), and his general forecast covers many other reforms—social security, safety laws, pollution control, drug regulation, etc.

3. The Decomposition of Capitalism

The most significant general prediction in Capitalism, Socialism, and Democracy is the prediction that "a socialist form of society will inevitably emerge from an equally inevitable decomposition of capitalist society" (p. ix). He repeated this forecast in several versions. "The thesis I shall endeavor to establish is that the...performance of capitalism is such as to negative the idea of its breaking down under the weight of economic failure, but that its very success undermines the social institutions which protect it, and 'inevitably' creates conditions in which it will not be able to live and which strongly point to socialism as the heir apparent" (p. 61).

Schumpeter stated and elaborated several major reasons for the past and prospective future decomposition of capitalism, including: (1) the rise of rationalism, (2) the multiplication of intellectuals, (3) the obsolescence of entrepreneurship, (4) the decline of the landed aristocracy, (5) the destruction of the capitalist framework, (6) the evaporation of the substance of property, and (7) the decline of the bourgeois family. He made predictions on all of these points, as explained below.

4. The Role of Rational Calculation

One major general reason for "the inevitable decomposition of capitalist society" is that capitalist economic activities teach men to be more rational because they require the constant calculation of costs and of profits and losses. Capitalist calculation "turns the unit of money into a tool of rational cost-profit calculation, of which the towering monument is double-entry bookkeeping" (p. 123). And, once such rational economic calculation is perfected and applied to any competitive capitalist society, it reveals more and more serious economic wastes or inefficiencies— unnecessary advertising, duplication of facilities, unemployment, etc.

"The capitalist process rationalizes behavior and ideas, and by so doing chases from our minds, along with metaphysical belief, mystic and romantic ideas of all sorts." It weakens religion and "our inherited sense of duty...becomes focused in utilitarian ideas about the betterment of mankind" on earth, a socialist ideal (p. 127). Later, he explained that, "the bourgeois finds to his amazement that the rationalist attitude does not stop at the credentials of kings and popes but goes on to attack private property and the whole scheme of bourgeois values" (p. 143). He clearly implied that this attack would continue and grow as long as capitalism survives.

5. The Role of Intellectuals

Moreover, the very success of capitalism creates a larger and better educated class of independent intellectuals capable of applying rational economic welfare calculation to capitalist economies. Thus, "rising capitalism produced not only the mental attitude of modern science...but also the men and the means" (p. 124). And a growing number of such men have become informed critics of capitalism and advocates of socialism. Schumpeter implied that this process would continue and grow.

In a later chapter, he repeated this important implicit prediction. He claimed that, "unlike any other type of society, capitalism inevitably, and by virtue of the very logic of its civilization, creates, educates, and subsidizes a vested interest in social unrest" (p. 146). This interest includes critical intellectuals, who enjoy growing influence but feel neglected, underpaid, and powerless in a capitalist society (pp. 147-52).

According to Schumpeter, "One of the most important features of the later stages of capitalist civilization is the vigorous expansion of facilities for higher education" (p. 152). He implied that this expansion would continue as long as capitalism lasts. This expansion will continue to increase the number of critical intellectuals, eventually "beyond the point determined by cost-return considerations" which will cause "sectional unemployment...unsatisfactory conditions of employment" and even "unemployability of a particularly disconcerting type." The resulting disappointment makes intellectuals ever more critical of capitalism. Thus the commendable success of capitalism in expanding higher education favors the rise of socialism.

Moreover, intellectuals have radicalized the labor movement. "Capitalist evolution produces a labor movement" (p. 153), Schumpeter wrote, implying that this movement will continue to grow. He did not repeat or revise the Marxian explanation for this growth, which he apparently accepted. Instead, he asserted that "intellectuals invaded labor politics...they verbalized the movement, supplied theories and slogans for it—class war is an excellent example—made it conscious of itself, and in doing so, changed its meaning...they naturally radicalized it..." (pp. 153-54).

He apparently expected that this process would continue indefinitely.

6. The Obsolescence of Entrepreneurship

According to Schumpeter, the progress of technology and business administration under capitalism tends to make the entrepreneurial function obsolete. "This social function is already losing importance, and is bound to lose it at an accelerating rate in the future, even if the economic process itself, of which entrepreneurship was the prime mover, went on unabated...innovation itself is being reduced to routine...becoming the business of teams of trained specialists..." (p. 132). As a result, "economic progress tends to become depersonalized and automatized. Bureau and committee work tends to replace individual action" (p. 133). He implied that such routinized innovation and management can be performed as well under socialism as under capitalism.

"The perfectly bureaucratized giant industrial unit not only ousts the small or medium-sized firm and 'expropriates' its owners, but in the end it also ousts the entrepreneur and expropriates the bourgeoisie as a class, which...stands to lose not only its income but also...its function. The true pacemakers of socialism were not the intellectuals and agitators who preached it but the Vanderbilts, Carnegies, and Rockefellers" (p. 134). He implied that the number and size of such giant industrial units would continue to grow and make capitalist entrepreneurs more and more obsolete. He explained that, "so far as prognosis goes," his new analysis yielded the same result as the Marxian analysis.

7. The Decline of the Landed Aristocracy

According to Schumpeter, an aristocrat, the European bourgeoisie never acquired the lordly attitude and habit of command characteristic of feudal rulers. They therefore allowed the surviving landed aristocracy to continue to rule, or share in national rule, throughout most of the era of high capitalism. However, eventually, "the capitalist process, both by its economic mechanics and by its psycho-sociological effects, did away with this protecting master or, as in this country, never gave him, or a substitute for him, a chance to develop" (pp. 138-39). It also weakened the political influence of village artisans and the tenants of great landlords. "In breaking down the pre-capitalist framework of society, capitalism thus broke not only barriers that impeded its progress but also flying buttresses that prevented its collapse"

(p. 139). "But, without protection by some non-bourgeois group, the bourgeoisie is politically helpless" (p. 138), and will be unable to prevent the continued growth of socialism.

8. Destruction of the Capitalist Framework

Schumpeter claimed that "the capitalist process, in much the same way in which it destroyed the institutional framework of feudal society, also destroys its own" (p. 139). He implied that this destruction would continue.

Capitalism destroys its framework because it "attacks the economic standing ground of the small producer and trader" by concentrating economic activities in ever larger industrial concentrations, as Marx had predicted. "The political structure of a nation is profoundly affected by the elimination of a host of small and medium-sized firms" whose owners have great political influence (p. 140).

Moreover, large firms will be increasingly managed by salaried executives who "tend to acquire the employee attitude, and rarely if ever identifies itself with the stockholding interest." Most stockholders "do not care much about what for them is but a minor source of income" and "almost regularly drift into an attitude hostile to 'their' corporations" and to "big business in general" (p. 141).

Finally, the growth of big business and big unions will continue to restrict or eliminate freedom of contracting, both between firms and between firms and employees. For instance, collective bargaining restricts the freedom of individual workers to bargain and contract (p. 141).

9. "Evaporation of the Substance of Property"

Schumpeter explained that the multiplication and growth of corporations will increasingly replace the direct ownership of real estate and inventories with the ownership of paper claims to a share in corporate assets. As a stockholder, the capitalist's "will to fight and to hold on is not what it was with the man who knew ownership and its responsibilities in the full-blooded sense of these words.... Thus the modern corporation...socialized the bourgeois mind: it relentlessly narrows the scope of capitalist motivation; not only that, it will eventually kill its roots" (p. 156). I believe he meant that a great corporation is more like a socialist trust than an owner-managed firm, and that corporate securities resemble government bonds more than tangible private property.

10. The Decline of the Bourgeois Family

According to Schumpeter, one of the chief motives for capitalist accumulation and enterprise is the desire to found or preserve an "industrial dynasty" (p. 156). But "the rationalization of everything in life" is steadily weakening this motive, and will long continue to do so. As soon as the bourgeois "introduce into their private life a sort of inarticulate system of cost accounting" (p. 157), they become increasingly aware of the costs and inconveniences of bourgeois family life. Moreover, "capitalist inventiveness produces contraceptive devices of ever increasing efficiency" (p. 158). Therefore, the bourgeois desire to accumulate and invest in order to create or preserve an industrial dynasty will continue to weaken.

"In order to realize what all this means for the efficiency of the capitalist engine of production, we need only recall that the family and the family home used to be the mainspring of the typically bourgeois kind of profit motive." This mainspring is weakening, and will continue to weaken. "With the decline of the driving power supplied by the family motive, the businessman's time-horizon shrinks, roughly to his life expectations...He drifts into an anti-saving frame of mind..." (pp. 160-61).

11. The Economic Trend to Socialism

Schumpeter summarized his main conclusion on the future of capitalism and socialism as follows: "Faced by the increasing hostility of the environment and by the legislative, administrative, and judicial practice born of that hostility, entrepreneurs and capitalists --in fact the whole stratum that accepts the bourgeois scheme of life--will eventually cease to function" (p. 156).

Furthermore, "the capitalist process not only destroys its own institutional framework but it also creates the conditions for another.... The outcome of the process is not simply a void...things and souls are transformed in such a way as to become increasingly amenable to the socialist forms of life.... In both these respects Marx's _vision_ was right" (p. 162).

These processes are inevitable but incomplete. Thus, "the various components of the tendency we have been trying to describe, while everywhere discernible, have as yet nowhere fully revealed themselves. Things have gone to different lengths in different countries .... Industrial integration is far from being complete. Competition...is still a major factor.... Enterprise is still active.... The middle class is still a political power.... From the standpoint of immediate practice...[and] short-run forecasting—and in these things, a century is a 'short run'—all this surface may be more important than the tendency towards another civilization that slowly works deep down below" (p. 163). Here Schumpeter displayed a realization—rare among futurists—that major social trends move slowly.

12. The Political Transition to Socialism

Schumpeter predicted that "in the case of mature socialization," i.e., in very advanced capitalist societies like England and Germany, the problems of moving from nominal capitalism to real socialism will not be "insurmountable," indeed "not even very serious. Maturity implies that resistance will be weak, and that cooperation will be forthcoming from the greater part of all classes...there might be revolution. But there is not much danger of this" (p. 221).

On the other hand, when socialism comes to power prematurely by revolution, in capitalist states which have not yet largely socialized themselves, the transition will require violent and ruthless suppression of capitalists and other dissidents. "It should be obvious that socialization in any situation immature enough to require revolution...[and] a subsequent reign of terror cannot benefit, either in the short or in the long run, anyone except those who engineer it" (p. 225).

Karl Marx had predicted that the proletariat would provide the basic or sole political support for the coming drive towards socialism. By contrast, Schumpeter predicted that intellectuals and bureaucrats would become at least equally strong supporters of the move towards socialism. He asserted that "the state, its bureaucracy and the groups that man the political engine are quite promising prospects for the socialist looking for his source of political power... they are likely to move in the desired direction with no less 'dialectical' necessity than are the masses." He cited the rise of English Fabian Socialism to illustrate this trend (pp. 310-11).

He also forecast that "whatever the political method a nation may adopt," the expansion of bureaucracy "is the one certain thing about our future" (p. 294). This corresponds to Marx' prediction concerning the future growth of the proletariat.

Writing the last pages of this book in July 1942, Schumpeter asserted that, "there cannot be any doubt that the present conflagration will—inevitably everywhere, and independently of the outcome of the war —mean another great stride toward the socialist order. An appeal to our experience of the effects of the First World War on the social fabric of Europe suffices to establish this prognosis. This time however the stride will be taken also in the U.S." (p. 374). This prediction proved to be accurate for Europe, but not for the U.S.

He elaborated these general predictions by forecasting that, "In no country will war taxation of business and of the business class be reduced in the proportion in which it was reduced after 1914.... Moreover, nowhere will war controls be liquidated to the extent" they were "after 1918. They will be put to other uses.... Finally, there is no reason to believe that governments will ever relax the hold they have gained on the capital markets and the investment process" (pp. 374-75). In fact, this hold was greatly relaxed in both the U.S. and the U.K.

13. The Future Socialist Society

After explaining why "the economic process tends to socialize *itself*," Schumpeter described the eventual result as follows. "Business, excepting the agrarian sector, is controlled by a small number of bureaucratized corporations. Progress has slackened and become mechanized and planned. The rate of interest converges toward zero, not temporarily only...but permanently, owing to the dwindling of investment opportunities. Industrial property and management have become depersonalized—ownership having degenrated to stock and bond holding, the executives having acquired habits of mind similar to those of civil servants" (p. 219).

As previously explained, the prediction that investment opportunities will dwindle and economic progress will slacken is very dubious because future technological progress may continue indefinitely to open up new profitable investment opportunities.

He described the coming socialist society as "an institutional pattern in which the control over means of production and over production itself is vested with a central authority" (p. 167). He "avoided the terms state ownership of, or property in, natural resources, plant and equipment" because, like Marx, he predicted that the state, as an entity separate from the economy, will cease to exist in a fully socialist economy. Private property and taxation will cease to exist for the same reasons (p. 169).

He devoted Chapter XVI, "The Socialist Blueprint," and the next two chapters, to a persuasive and sophisticated explanation of the way in which wages, rents, interest, saving, outputs, profits, etc., could and should be determined in a socialist society. Since the analysis is technical, and since he did not predict the adoption of his proposals, they are not discussed here.

He did note that, "I...cannot visualize...a socialist organization in any form other than that of a huge and all-embracing bureaucratic apparatus." He added that, "surely this should not horrify anyone who realizes how far the bureaucratization of economic life—of life in general even—has gone already..." (p. 206).

He also forecast that "the socialist order presumably will command that moral allegiance which is being increasingly refused to capitalism" because of anti-capitalist propaganda and "the class-war complex" (p. 211). Moreover, he predicted that although "the socialist management may bungle, it certainly will not pay any premium to anybody for the express purpose of inducing him not to produce." And "every comrade will realize the true significance of restiveness at work and especially of strikes.... If he struck...he would do so with a bad conscience and meet public disapproval" (p. 212).

14. The Future of Democracy

Schumpeter discussed five necessary conditions for the success of democratic government: (1) a supply of able potential leaders, (2) proper limitation of "the range of political decision," (3) "a well-trained bureaucracy," (4) "democratic self-control, i.e., public respect for democratic methods, and (5) "tolerance for differences of opinion" (pp. 290-95). He concluded that his analysis "suggests a pessimistic prognosis for...democracy" in capitalist countries," primarily because "the democratic method never works at its best when nations are much divided on fundamental questions of social structure" (like socialism versus capitalism) and because the bourgeoisie "did not produce a successful political stratum of its own ..." (p. 298). This pessimistic prognosis seems unjustified to me because I believe that most of his five prerequisite conditions have been increasingly achieved in all advanced capitalist nations since 1900.

After repeatedly predicting that "democracy is bound to work with increasing friction" under capitalism (pp. 298, 301), Schumpeter suggested that democratic government might function better under socialism because there will be more agreement on "the tectonic principles of the social fabric" and because the number and importance of "clashing capitalist interests," for instance "between agriculture and industry," will diminish. "Thus far socialism scores." But "socialist democracy may eventually turn out to be more of a sham than capitalist democracy ever was" (pp. 301-02).

He was much more certain about the future of "economic democracy," worker control over and within individual plants. "It is safe to say that much of this economic democracy will vanish into thin air in a socialist regime" (p. 300n). This was a shrewd forecast. The history of economic democracy in both communist and democratic countries has largely verified this prediction to date.

15. Anglo-American Imperialism

Schumpeter forecast that in the case of a "complete victory of the Anglo-American-Russian alliance—that is to say, a victory that enforces unconditional surrender but with all the honors held by England and the U.S.—...the consequence...will be Anglo-American management of the affairs of the world—a kind of... Ethical Imperialism. A world order of this kind... can be established only by military force...this would mean for these two countries a social organization that is best described as Militarist Socialism" (pp. 373-74). As history has shown, he overestimated the future role of the U.K., and underestimated that of the U.S.S.R., on the international scene. And "Military Socialism" has not yet developed beyond a very early stage in either England or America.

16. Final Comments

The economic, sociological, and historical analysis contained in Capitalism, Socialism, and Democracy is much more sophisticated and persuasive than that contained in any other 20th Century book reviewed here. Its chief defect as a futurist classic is that the author deliberately concentrated his analysis on a few major long-run social trends, and ignored a very large number of other significant trends. For instance, he had little or nothing to say about sexual, criminal, medical, population, agricultural, financial, monetary, city planning, social insurance, and free-distribution trends.

His worst mistake was his prediction that postwar economic growth in capitalist countries would slow down because of increasing government interference with and taxation of private business. In fact, economic growth rates in nearly all advanced capitalist countries were much higher in the first three decades after after 1945 than ever before, in spite of, or because of, increased government interference and taxation.

MORRIS L. ERNST AS A FUTURIST

Morris Leopold Ernst (1888-1976), an eminent New York City lawyer, served for many years as the national director of the American Civil Liberties Union. He published over a dozen popular books on a variety of social problems. One of them, Utopia, 1976 (1955), was about future social events and trends. It is significant because it was one of the first American nonfiction books entirely devoted to predicting future social events and trends.

1. Methods of Prediction

Ernst claimed that his book was "based for the most part on nothing more than an extension of present trends" (pp. 3-4), and he quoted a great many statistics, which suggests that he was trying to be far more realistic and scientific than utopian authors. However, he often used utopian terms. His first sentences were: "This book is my utopia. It is a dream for our republic in 1976." He should have explained that this book is a realistic prediction of the future, as scientific as I can make it, and that the predicted society would be so much improved as to justify calling it a utopia.

In addition to projecting past trends into the future, Ernst often argued or implied that certain things would happen because, in his opinion, they would benefit mankind. But he did not explicitly state and justify this method of scientific prediction.

Ernst paid little attention to the previous efforts of scentific futurists like Condorcet and Wells, but he claimed to "have read Utopias from Plato...to Bellamy..." Unfortunately, he did not explain how his methods of prediction differed from theirs. He claimed that the "writings of these entrancing speculators endured through the centuries because the authors were men of hope" (p. 3), which suggests that he too may have deliberately allowed mere hope to influence his predictions.

2. Economic Progress

Ernst asserted that "our annual per capita income in present dollars was about $320" a century ago, and had risen to $1500 in 1955. He predicted that it would rise to $2000 in 1964 and $4000 in 1976, presumably in 1955 dollars (pp. 34-35). As usual, he greatly overestimated the speed of social change. The growth of real per capita income from 1955 to 1976, about 70%, was abnormally high, but far less than the 167% he forecast.

He explained this forecast by stressing the coming use of nuclear power, which has so far been disappointing. He even predicted that, "Travel by air, by boat and by car will rely on atomic fission" in 1976 (p. 39), a prediction that has been largely disproven. He also claimed that, "Atomic batteries are not far off" (p. 38), still a very dubious claim.

Ernst forecast that U.S. coal production would rise by 50% between 1955 and 1976 (p. 42). It actually rose by less than 20%. He even expected that, "Coal if used at all will be gassified underground, with pipe-line transmission as a gas or liquid" which seems inconsistent with his forecast on coal production. Such coal gassification may become common in a century or two, but there has been very little of it to date.

On the other hand, he noted that, "The demand for electricity has doubled in our land every ten or twelve years..." and predicted that, "By 1976 our generating capacity will be eight or ten times as great as in 1950" (p. 47). It actually rose to about seven times the 1950 figure.

He also predicted that, "Telephone...lines are to give way to microwave radio" (p. 38); "Foods will be sterilized by split-second exposures" to fission rays, which will also "immunize seeds, oats, and other grains against disease.... Clothing will be produced impervious to stain, unmussable and durable for the lives of consumers. Plastics subjected to atomic radiation" will be developed and widely used (p. 39). "Our paint bill will be eliminated by smokeless power and nontarnishing and nonfading materials" (p. 40). I could cite more such overoptimistic predictions, most of which may be largely verified in the very long run.

3. The Growth of Leisure and Recreation

Ernst noted that the normal hours of labor in the U.S. had gradually declined from 80 hours in 1776 to 40 hours in 1953, and predicted that they would fall "to 30 hours or less" in 1976 (pp. 14, 15).

He predicted that the growth of leisure time would greatly increase the time and money devoted to leisure-time activities. He claimed that "our people are already shifting with great speed from an audience society to a participating society," and implied that this trend would continue (p. 19). The great increase in TV viewing and in attendance at sporting events since 1950 suggest that his claims were mistaken. Unfortunately, he forecast that, "attendance at sports will decline" (p. 29).

He forecast that spending on pets, which is a "substitute outlet for affection, domination, or company, is likely to diminish as loneliness declines" (p. 21). I believe that such spending has probably grown much faster than GNP since 1955, and that loneliness may have increased due to the continued growth of large cities.

He predicted that "photography will decline as painting, etching and water-color work increases..." (p. 23). Photography has certainly not declined, either absolutely or relatively, since 1955.

He expected that the growth "of leisure will reinvigorate our 10,000 weekly newspapers..." (p. 33). In fact the number fell to 8824 in 1975.

On the other hand, his predictions that Americans would spend more time and/or money on travel, sports, museums, libraries, gardening, amateur science, etc. (pp. 27-30) have probably all been verified by history.

4. Population

Ernst correctly forecast the creation of a new "contraceptive pill or equivalent" and, largely on this basis, predicted that in 1976 the U.S. population would be only 190 million (p. 58). In fact it rose to 214 million. He correctly forecast that both birth and death rates would continue to decline, but did not offer figures (pp. 62-63).

He anticipated that the growth of birth control would eliminate orphan asylums (p. 64)—this prediction was largely verified—and increase "the joys of sexual marital contacts" (pp. 61-62).

He predicted that U.S. population movement "from big cities to suburbs will be less significant than the flow to newly created centers of population" (p. 66). In fact, it was far more significant.

He foresaw the growth in the relative share of the aged in the U.S. population, but foolishly asserted that, "Retirement in present terms will not exist in 1976. The old folks will not be condemned to wasted, useless existences" as in 1955 (p. 63). In fact, the growth of pensions encouraged increased idleness.

He hopefully forecast that, "The color of skin

will no longer be, by 1976, a strong bar to social, sexual, or marital bonds" (p. 65). While discrimination did decline from 1955 to 1976, the decline was far less than he had predicted.

He predicted that, "From now on immigration will play a smallish role" in the U.S. (p. 56). In fact, legal immigration grew steadily from 1955 to 1976, and illegal immigration soared.

He optimistically expected that, "our present fearsome insistence on visas and other documents permitting entrance or exit will have disappeared" by 1976 (p. 57). Actually, the change was slight. The "joint passport" he forecast has not been adopted.

5. Food Production

According to Ernst, "We are approaching in agriculture a change as dramatic as the shift from water power to atomic fission" in industry (p. 68). The major feature of this revolution will be the achievement by 1976 of effective general weather control. "Man will master weather. Weather will be his servant.... We will place rain where we want it and move it from areas...where it is unwelcome" (p. 73). "The contribution to our food production by...rain- and weather-making will...be on a magnificent scale. But...also...we will say 'Halt' to the torrid zone in its northward march...and arable land will become available in the now Frozen North" (pp. 74-75). Unfortunately, there has been no significant creation or use of weather control since 1955.

He also forecast that ocean water is about to be desalinated for use in agriculture (p. 75), that many fish farms will be developed, that algae will become an important new food, that synthetic foods will be created and widely used, and all this by 1976 (pp. 77-79). He should have specified a much later date, perhaps 2076. Little progress in these directions occurred betwen 1955 and 1976.

He correctly foresaw notable increases in the use of improved chemical fertilizers, herbicides, and insecticides, but overestimated their effects. "Undesirable growth...if it is allowed...will be cheaply exterminated.... Soon we will say 'finish' to the boll weavil by using a poison to be absorbed, not sprayed" (p. 76). I could cite several other equally unrealistic predictions on farm technology, but will not do so.

Ernst forecast a great increase in the production of home-grown home-eaten vegetables. "The home (in the decent-sized community) will be a miniature chemical vegetable farm" by 1976 (p. 80). Actually, the output of such vegetables probably declined steadily from 1955 to 1976, in nearly all American cities and towns.

6. Economic Organization

Ernst began his chapter on economic organization (#6) by remarking that, "I would be less than frank if I did not state the high values I place on competition, the fears I have of excessive power and the certainty that a too-big state spells loss of human individuality" (p. 83). Largely for these reasons, he predicted that the long decline of business competition would reverse itself. "The vertical trust will be broken up and competition will once more become significant" (p. 105). "Our banks will be curtailed as to branches and deposits" (p. 103). "Our largest companies of multiple products will 'spin off' parts of products and assets into separate companies..." (p. 97). "The leader in the battle for economic freedom will be the Secretary of Commerce. He will desert his present role of protecting the giants.... He will be the proponent of antitrust laws with teeth..." (pp. 103-04).

It is always risky to predict the reversal of a well-established social trend. The trend towards oligopoly did not reverse itself, and Ernst's predictions on competition were proven false.

In addition, he forecast a radical change in the patent system, one intended to promote competition. "Since patents are...monopoly grants...before 1976 there will be a split-up of the present patents into two kinds of protection," one "for fundamental leaps of the brain" and the other for less important inventions (p. 100). No such split-up occurred or now seems likely in the near future.

He expected that "bankruptcy court proceedings for large corporations will be a thing of the past" and that "There will be no issue of bonds" to finance corporations (p. 108). These changes may occur within another century or two, but they did not occur before 1976, as he predicted.

He also forecast that unions would become more democratic and would assume more managerial functions. "Democracy within trade unions is fast growing.... With the shift...to widespread worker-owner participation, labor leadership with preferential balloting will soon be associated with the management of business" (pp. 93-94). Unfortunately, there has been little if any increase in union democracy or in union participation in management in the U.S. since 1955.

Ernst asserted that protective tariffs are uneconomic and, apparently for this reason, predicted that they will be largely or completely abolished. "By 1976 we will be free trade nation..." (p. 101). Tariffs were significantly reduced between 1955 and 1976, but the U.S. is still far from being a "free trade nation."

7. Home and Family

According to Ernst, "with respect to appliances and gadgets, our homes will be unrecognizable in 1976 by the people of today. We are on the march toward mechanized homes; by 1976...all housing will be fully supplied with basic plumbing" (p. 111). He then cited relevant statistical data on these trends. These are among his most successful predictions.

He correctly forecast that such mechanization "will greatly reduce" the labor of housekeeping (p. 113) and that "the American home will enjoy more space and convenience" (p. 117). Unfortunately, he also predicted that, "All cabinet, ice box and stove doors will slide open by a mere touch or by a photo-electric eye.... Homes will be heated by atomic or solar power, or by...heat pumps.... All our power and heat will come into the home by way of the ether, with the entire removal of all wire and telephone poles.... The light and power...will be so cheap that it won't pay to meter it" (p. 119). Here we have several forecasts that grossly overestimated the speed of technological progress.

However, he successfully predicted "Increasing development of group nurseries" and more "participation of the husband-father in...homemaking..." (p.120). He also foresaw that, "Males will employ more color" in their clothing and wear hats and ties less often (p. 122), presumably because these trends were already apparent. He noted the growing trend for women to work outside the home, and implied that it would continue (p. 127), as in fact it did.

Ernst correctly forecast that both the sexual and the feminist revolution would continue. He foresaw "more value in more premarital sexual experience in 1976" (p. 294); "a reduction of censorship" in sexual matters (p. 295); "the closer identification of men and women in jobs, in the home, and...in the education of children" (p. 296); and more understanding of and toleration for homosexuals (p. 293).

8. Education

Ernst forecast a revolution in American education. "The new home, the doubled income, the [increased] time for parents to watch over education...will create more change between 1954 and 1976 than [occurred] between 1854 and 1954" (p. 158). A great increase in the proportion of youth who attended high school, and, even more, of those who attended college, did occur during these years, as he had predicted (p. 133), but the increases in elementary, secondary, and college enrollments between 1854 and 1954 were much larger and more significant. Moreover, Ernst apparently expected a revolution in teaching methods and curriculum from grade one through college (pp. 140-48), and no such revolution took place.

He predicted that the U.S. federal government would vastly expand its scholarship program for college students so that nearly all qualified students would be able to enter college and secure a degree (pp. 150-51). He expected that this reform would free every college president from fund-raising before 1976. "With money supplied by the students" the president's "major time-consuming duty of cajoling money out of rich alumni, big corporations, and government agencies will be ended. He will concentrate on changes in educational techniques" (p. 152). There was a great expansion of government scholarship and loan programs for college students between 1955 and 1976, but it was not nearly as large as Ernst forecast. And the fund-raising activities of college presidents probably increased.

Ernst expected that, "Education will be extended through life.... Moreover, compulsory education will go through high schools, junior colleges and ultimately colleges" (pp. 154-55). He did not specify a date for these reforms, but 1976 was his usual limit. Compulsion was applied to more high-school-age youth, but not to more college-age youth, during the period 1955 to 1976.

He forecast that, "By 1976 close to one half of our people will, all through their adult lives, take courses by correspondence or otherwise..." (p. 155). I doubt that this percentage rose above 5% by 1976.

He anticipated that by 1976, "there will be no segregation because of race, creed, color, or national origin.... Even the voluntary religious Jim Crow schools will be finished, because the majority is hurt equally with the minority by segregation" (p. 156). Unfortunately, this prediction was not verified.

He also predicted that the "teaching profession will attract more of the best types in...1976" (p. 142), and that professors of education will acquire a professional status above that of any college faculty" (p. 143). Neither of these predictions has been verified by history.

On the other hand, he successfully forecast an increase in teachers' relative earnings (p. 142), and in the proportion of males (p. 145) and of married females (p. 149) in the U.S. teaching force.

He predicted a radical decentralization in the U.S. public school systems because, "No group...is competent to run education for a population of 25,000 or more." Therefore, in cities like New York there will be a school board...by 1976, for each school" (p. 149). Actually, the average size of U.S. school districts continued to grow from 1955-76, as it had long been growing.

9. Health Care

Ernst noted the recent rapid growth of U.S. health insurance, and asserted that, "By 1976 we will all be covered for all health disabilities" (p. 165). While such insurance did grow substantially between 1955 and 1976, the growth was far less than he predicted. He added that, "With universal insurance we will have more medical schools, more doctors, and more facilities." We did. Also, he foresaw that, "Our chemists will learn many more short cuts" to health by creating new drugs.

He claimed that, "few...would deny that all of the present important diseases will be detectible, preventable, and curable by 1976" (p. 165). I believe most experts would have denied this forecast in 1955, and it proved to be very mistaken.

He specifically predicted that a cure for the "common cold" would be found. "The surrender of the common cold to our new magic will enhance our national productivity ten times more than the licking of arthritis" (p. 169). Unfortunately, neither disease was "licked".

He expected a vast increase in mental health care and research. "Long before 1976 the number of draftsmen in this field—researchers, psychiatrists, psychologists, and psychoanalysts—will reach unbelievable numbers, and the research expenditures will run into billions of dollars a year" (p. 176). These predictions were only very partially verified.

10. Transport and Travel

Ernst anticipated that by 1976, "Relocation of plants" nearer the sources of materials and/or customers "will make for shorter hauls" and "cut down the cost of living" (pp. 181-82). I doubt that much such relocation occurred.

He forecast that passenger planes would fly from New York to London in two hours, and that "rockets will carry mail from Cleveland to Chicago," that "airfields will be converted for vertical-rising travel," that nuclear-powered planes would be developed, that "The North and South poles will be used for landing bases," and that "all new post office buildings will be constructed with roof platforms as landing fields"

(pp. 182-84). None of these forecasts came true.
He also predicted that by 1976, "We will regain local control" over spending on highways (p. 185). This did not happen.

On the other hand, he predicted that, "The private car will...shrink in size, will be designed for functional uses...will have engines in the rear, tubeless tires, visibility of the road, with less power, and greatly decreased cost of upkeep and propulsion energy" (p. 185). Cars did not begin to shrink in size until after 1976, and did so for a reason he failed to forecast, but the other forecasts in this paragraph were partially verified by 1976.

11. Religion

According to Ernst, "There is little doubt that the churches are in for trouble" (p. 192). Governments, psychiatrists, and others will take over church functions. As a result, "The membership in the sense of dues-paying, or regular church attendance—of all sects will greatly decline" (p. 197). This did not occur.

He also noted that church statistics on membership and contributions had long been unreliable (pp. 191-92), and predicted that they would be improved before 1976 (pp. 191-92). He expected that "the present secrecy in regard to income and disbursement will be abandoned" and that "soon some national Protestant church will make clear to the public the details of its own bookkeeping," which will prompt other churches to do the same. (p. 193).

Ernst predicted that religious people would become much more interested in "mental telepathy, precognition, the growth of intuition, the processes of introspection, reflection, and awareness..." Moreover, "scores of trained scientists will enter religious fields by delving into the character of extrasensory powers" (p. 195). These predictions were verified.

He also forecast correctly that "interdenominational marriages will increase" and that "parochial schools ...will decline" (p. 198).

He expected that religious opposition to "birth control, smoking, ...dancing, ...playing on the Sabbath" and other such allegedly immoral behavior will diminish. Such activities "will be appraised as personal virtues or vices unbecoming as subjects of religious morality" (p. 194).

I believe that nearly all these predictions on religious trends have proven at least partially accurate. He was more cautious and prescient in this field than in any other.

12. Trends in the Media

Ernst predicted that both chain ownership of U.S. daily newspapers and newspaper ownership of forests and paper mills would become illegal by 1976 (p. 209). He asserted that "Boilerplating will be reduced" (p. 208), and that the number of weekly newspapers will increase greatly (p. 207). None of these changes occurred.

He mistakenly forecast that "Radio will be divorced in ownership and management—from television," and that "pocket or wrist receivers" will be "in common use" by 1976 (p. 213).

He anticipated the rise of pay-TV and pay-radio. "In the days to come, radio and television will in part be unsponsored, and the consumer will pay—on his telephone bill or by gadgets attached to the...set—for what he wants to buy over the air" (p. 266). In fact, pay-TV was still insignificant in 1976, but it is now growing. Pay-radio is still some decades in the future, if it is ever adopted.

Ernst predicted that "By 1976...we will abolish tariffs on paper and devise machines to print and bind an entire volume in a single operation....The accent on best sellers will be reduced....Rental libraries...will grow [from 100,000] to at least half a million," authors and publishers will share in rental fees (p. 205), and many more books will be produced photostatically (p. 206). Only the last prediction was verified.

He expected that "the present [U.S. postal] subsidies to newspapers and magazines on advertisements will be abolished" (p. 206), but that such subsidies on the export of U.S. scientific and scholarly journals will be increased (p. 213). He mistakenly predicted a world-wide elimination of tariffs on newspapers, magazines, newsprint, radio sets, films, and recording instruments (p. 220).

13. Government

Ernst forecast a radical decentralization of our government. "As standards of living show less disparity between states, the function of the national government as collector-distributor will diminish..." (p. 238). And states will "relinquish power over cities..." (p. 237). Within cities, separate independent boards of control will be established for each public school, library, park, playground, etc. Such decentralization "will result in 80% voting at national elections (pp. 231-32). In fact, the old trend towards centralization accelerated, and voting participation declined from 1955 to 1976.

He mistakenly asserted that, "The last of our

skyscrapers has already been built" because "No one who lives above the fourth...floor has roots in a democracy and skyscrapers for business will be recognized as economically unsound." Moreover, "The slums of big cities are so costly that...we will decide it is cheaper to raze them." Also, "The streets will be for traffic, and not employed as free garages" (p. 235).

On the other hand, he correctly predicted a great increase in female participation in government. "By 1976 women will hold far more important posts in the judicial system, elective and executive branches" (p. 236). And he also successfully predicted great increases in federal spending on education and research (p. 245).

He mistakenly forecast that "we will adopt the plan...to have the state, and only the state, pay campaign costs for all candidates," that "bicameral annual legislatures will give way to unicameral biannual (p. 239), and that "the Cabinet will sit on the Senate floor..." (p. 243).

14. Legal Reforms

As a lawyer, Ernst was especially qualified to predict legal changes, but here, as elsewhere, his excessive optimism weakened his judgment. For instance, he forecst that, "Judges and jurors will be held strictly to...weighing evidence and finding guilt," leaving determination of penalties to others (p. 262), and that the handling of divorces will be transferred from courts to marriage counsellors (p. 266). He also mistakenly expected that, "<u>Stare</u> <u>decisis</u>—the rule that some old case decided the point forever and a day—will be discarded" (p. 269).

On the other hand, he successfully predicted that radio and TV reporting of U.S. trials would not be adopted (p. 261), that capital punishment would cease by 1976 (p. 263), and that the use of arbitration would increase greatly (p. 267).

He mistakenly forecast that the use of public defenders would decline (p. 259), that "prompt congressional review of all opinions of the Supreme Court" on the constitutionality of congressional laws will be adopted (p. 264), and that nearly all accident cases will be transferred from the courts to special new administrative agencies (p. 265).

Ernst expected that by 1976 the training of judges would be different from that of lawyers, and that, "Judges in the upper courts will be selected only from those who have had judicial experience in the lower" (p. 265). Unfortunately, these desirable reforms have not yet been adopted.

15. World Government

Ernst predicted that the U.N. would be strengthened by giving it increased power over "the three major points of deepest concern...the free flow throughout the planet of people, goods and ideas." He wrote: "I suggest that, within less than ten years...a formula for selected partial surrender of sovereignty on immigration will be...approved in the U.N." (p. 283). In fact no such surrender concerning people, goods, or ideas has yet been approved in the U.N.

He also asserted that, "What man is now working toward, is the biggest possible government in area and peoples" and claimed that "the U.N. is on its way," presumably towards this goal, which, he explained, would almost certainly not be achieved by 1976 (pp. 286-87).

He expected that, "Universal military training... will be adopted" in the U.S. by 1976, and that this training would prepare men for civilian as well as military life (pp. 279-80). This did not occur.

16. Comments

Ernst probably made many more predictions than any previous would-be scientific futurist, so many, indeed, that I have felt compelled to ignore many of them, and to discuss many others very briefly. Unfortunately, he apparently gave little thought to most of his forecasts, and often made obviously dubious or unreasonable predictions. For instance, he predicted the sudden reversal of well-established trends. He grossly overestimated the speed of normal social change, and frequently allowed his hopes and desires to determine his forecasts. His mistakes are especially apparent because he chose to make predictions for a very short period of time which has already come to an end.

Ernst did not develop any new, or elaborate any old, methods of scientific prediction. Nor did he make any surprising but plausible original predictions.

GUNNAR MYRDAL AS A FUTURIST

Gunnar Myrdal (b1898) is a distinguished Swedish economist and politician. He has been a professor of political economy at the University of Stockholm and a minister of the Swedish government. He is well known in America for his influential study of the U.S. race problem, An American Dilemma. He also wrote Beyond the Welfare State (1960), a major contribution to futurism. My essay is entirely based on this book, to which all page references refer.

Although the title, Beyond the Welfare State, clearly implies that the author can and will predict the future, and the book contains many important implicit and explicit predictions, late in his book he largely repudiated futurism: "...prognostications on the really large and fateful issues are valueless—" he asserted, "they have always proved grossly inaccurate in the past,..." His chief justification for these extreme and erroneous claims was that, "The future is continually our own choice. There is no blind destiny ruling history" (p. 226).

I believe, on the contrary, that many sound predictions on "really large and fateful issues" can be made. For instance, I predict that the birth rate in all poor countries will decline almost continuously for at least 100 years, and that the urban population in these countries will grow faster than the rural population throughout this period.

Moreover, it is false to claim that such predictions by earlier writers "have always proved grossly inaccurate." Many thoughtful men predicted the rise of political democracy, the progress of science, the growth of public education, the abolition of slavery and other "large and fateful" social changes long before these changes took place.

Karl Marx was one of the greatest pioneer futurists. According to Myrdal, "Marx shared the common destiny of all prophets: to be belied by events" (p. 4). The term prophet is properly used only to denote persons who rely on revelation or intuition to predict the course of events. To apply it to a man like Marx, who rejected all divine revelation and unsupported intuition, is both inaccurate and belittling.

Moreover, Myrdal went on to say about Marx that "it is a sign of his genius that he foresaw so many relatively important things as accurately as he did"

(p. 5). This admission is far more significant and accurate than the charge that Marxian predictions were "belied by events." Some were, and some were not. Marx's overall score was high compared with his predecessors, Condorcet apart.

Myrdal claimed that the idea of introducing far-reaching socialist reforms in a democratic capitalist state "peacefully and without revolution" is "entirely foreign to Marx's way of thinking" (p. 6). This is a very questionable claim. Most democratic European socialists have long called themselves Marxists and practiced gradualism. Marx lived and wrote before European workers had won the vote, and naturally concentrated his attention upon the problem of how to achieve political power in undemocratic states.

1. Methodology

Myrdal did not discuss the methods which he used to predict the future, but they are fairly obvious. Like previous futurists, he relied heavily on the projection of well-established recent social trends. Most of his book is devoted to a discussion of such trends. He often implied, rather than asserted, that such trends would continue.

He also repeatedly claimed that most men have common basic wants or needs for economic progress, social security, liberty, equality, fraternity, etc., which will largely determine future social trends (p. 96). He explained that the continued growth of education and knowledge will make men more and more rational in their methods of satisfying these needs (p. 104). Therefore, he implied, but did not explicitly claim, that a well-trained social scientist who knows what methods would be rational can use such knowledge to predict what men are likely to do. However, he rarely quoted the predictions of other recent or contemporary social scientists. Marx and Engels were the only futurists he referred to.

The most distinctive features of his method of prediction were his repeated claim that most major long-run social trends have mutually supported each other, and will continue to do so. For instance, economic progress favors the rise of democracy, and vice versa.

He also occasionally explained that less advanced countries are likely to adopt successful reforms already adopted by more advanced countries.

2. The Rise of State Intervention

A welfare economic policy is one which requires government intervention to prevent or minimize the anti-welfare effects of unregulated market or business determination of outputs, prices, wage rates, interest rates, pollution levels, accident risks, etc. According to Myrdal, "the total volume of state intervention has been steadily increasing, and at an increasing rate" (p. 21), for many decades, due to ever-growing recognition of the anti-welfare effects of unregulated business policies. These trends are almost certain to continue indefinitely, until all advanced countries have achieved a fully developed welfare economy. "The Welfare State is nowhere, as yet, an accomplishment; it is continually in the process of coming into being" (p. 62).

One of the major reasons for the increasing need for state intervention to increase economic welfare has been, and will continue to be, the decline of price competition due to the spread of oligopoly and monopoly. "This development compels the state to large-scale measures of intervention" (p. 32).

Another reason is that, due to industrialization, the spread of knowledge, secularization, and other factors, men have become, and will continue to become, "more enterprising, more experimental...more 'economically rational'" (p. 33). As a result, they will become more aware of the need for such state intervention.

Later Myrdal elaborated his theory on the probable effects of increased education. He asserted that "everywhere the Welfare State has preserved its faith in education and is now devoting more and more efforts —and public funds—to raising educational levels..." (p. 112). As a result, "the individual...will...become more 'propaganda safe'.... He will reform taxation and everything else" (p. 111).

Thirdly, "this growth of...state intervention... has been tremendously accelerated by the unending upheavals in international relations" since 1914 (p. 23). He was referring to hot wars, cold wars, decolonialization, radical fluctuations in export demand and foreign exchange rates, etc. As a result, "all states have felt themselves compelled to undertake new, radical intervention..." And, "Looking toward the future, we have to reckon with a continuation of this influence from international relations..." (p. 24).

Fourth, "the democratization of the political process" has resulted in growing political pressure "for redistributional state intervention on a large scale" (p. 37), and, presumably, will continue to do so in all incompletely democratic countries. "Generally speaking, the less privileged groups in democratic society, as they become aware of their interests and their political power, will...press for ever more state intervention in practically all fields" (p. 38).

Moreover, "Whenever new measures of state intervention...are introduced, even if their purpose is quite a different one, they will tend to be utilized as a means of equalization as well" (p. 39). And "the appetite" of the poor "for intervention is bound to grow as they get more of it. With the greater rationality of attitudes and increasing knowledge, they will also press forward with more effectiveness" (p. 40).

Finally, public demand for continuous full employment will continue to grow until all advanced countries adopt interventionist welfare-economic policies which insure such full employment. After describing past efforts to reduce unemployment and aid the unemployed, Myrdal asserted that, "These developments represented only steps toward demanding that the state should...create demand for labor sufficient to liquidate mass unemployment..." (p. 65). Thus, "It is safe to predict that in none of the Western countries will a period of severe unemployment ever again be tolerated by the people" (p. 69). Since he did not precisely define "a period of severe unemployment" we cannot conclude that the high unemployment rates of 1983 disprove this prediction, but I doubt that he expected the reoccurrence of 9% unemployment rates.

3. The Decline of the Gold Standard

To illustrate his general prediction that state intervention to increase welfare will long continue to grow, Myrdal discussed the reasons for the recent and prospective abandonment of the gold standard and free international movement of gold. He explained why free gold flows could disturb national economies, and concluded that, "No country today—and certainly not the U.S.—is willing any longer to accept a level of economic activity and employment determined by the automatic repercussions, through the banking system, of changes in its international payment situation." A new international monetary system may be created, but "it could not be the old automatic system under the gold standard" (p. 28). A few years after this prediction was made, President Nixon broke the last ties between the U.S. dollar and gold, and no country has since returned to the old gold standard. As a result, nearly all governments frequently intervene in once-free foreign exchange markets.

Since 1960, when Myrdal predicted a long further growth in government intervention in private business, all advanced countries have expanded old kinds of intervention and adopted new ones to limit pollution, protect consumers, prevent accidents, restrict imports, control foreign exchange rates, influence private investment, etc., etc. Thus, this prediction has been fully verified to date, and seems likely to be increasingly verified for many years to come.

4. The Growth of Nonstate Intervention

According to Myrdal, the need for intervention in and control over private business and market determination of prices, wages, outputs, etc., has become so great and so increasingly recognized that private-group intervention (including, but not limited to, collective bargaining) by unions, professional associations, trade associations, etc., has grown and will long continue to grow, in all advanced welfare economies, as a supplement to increased state intervention.

"Many of the most important policy decisions, then, are taken outside parliament, and put into effect by other organs than those of state administration...general price and income agreements, covering many different markets...are made after multilateral collective bargaining...as the years pass by, such forms of general income settlements...will gradually become the rule" (pp. 46-47).

This prediction has been partially verified in Western Europe, but not in the U.S., where union influence on wage rates has probably declined slightly since 1960.

5. The Growth of Economic Planning

According to Myrdal, the continued spread of state and private-group intervention in business and social affairs will lead inevitably to the adoption of more and more economic planning, i.e., to rational coordination of different interventionist policies. "Coordination leads to planning or, rather, it *is* planning.... Coordination of measures of intervention implies a reconsideration of them all from the point of view of how they combine to serve the development goals of the entire national community..." (p. 63). Moreover, such coordination "constitutes a steadily developing approach to planning which tends to become firmer and more embracing as present tendencies work themselves out" (p. 64).

Myrdal forecast that the governments of welfare states would find it necessary to coordinate the policies of unions and trade associations, as well as those of state agencies. "The government...will then gradually find it is important to lead the negotiations and to control the compromises between the nationwide organized power groups, as it is to lead parliament itself" (p. 47).

He considered in some detail the claim that the growth of planning will weaken or destroy political democracy, and concluded that this is very unlikely because men will become more rational and more stable. He explained that, "we have, so far as I know, never seen a democracy fail because of too much planning" (p. 105).

The chief fault in Myrdal's prediction that economic planning or coordination would spread and mature in advanced noncommunist countries was that he did not explain how it could be verified. A few national planning agencies have been created in Western Europe since he made this prediction, but they have engaged only in indicative planning, and there is little if any evidence of increased coordination of government policies. And what would such evidence be? Nevertheless, the need for such coordination is so great, as Myrdal made clear, that his hard-to-verify prediction still seems very plausible.

6. Decentralization of Power

In spite of his forecast that both welfare programs and economic planning will increase, Myrdal also predicted eventual growing decentralization of state intervention. This would be achieved by delegating more and more government functions to regional and local state agencies, to national and regional labor unions, and to private nonprofit organizations. Indeed, this development is well under way.

"As a result of this development, the whole character of our national communities is changing," and presumably will continue to change. "What in reality ...constitutes public policy is now decided upon and executed in many different sectors and on different levels: not only directly by the central state authorities and by provincial and municipal authorities ...but also increasingly by a whole array of 'private' power groups.... Even individual business firms, if they become so big...have to be included in this institutional infrastructure...in charge of what in effect is public policy" (p. 47). This process "represents a decentralization of the making and implementation of public policies" (p. 49).

Later he suggested that, "As the trade unions become entrenched...they might in time be prepared both to see the end of a lot of detailed legislation on hours of work, vacations and the like, and to take over, in cooperation with the employers' unions, much inspection of sanitary and other conditions, which is now still carried out by state...organs" (p. 89).

He also explained that, "I am confident, too, to take another example, that there will come a time in America, perhaps not as very far off as many believe, when there will be no practical need to retain legislation, courts, and administration to defend Negroes against discrimination..."

He concluded that, "in the immediate future I am convinced there are many fields where we should prepare ourselves for a radical diminution of state regulations" (p. 91).

These predictions on decentralization of control functions seem very dubious, because there has been a long, world-wide trend towards centralization and the creation of uniform national standards.

7. The Growth of Democracy

Myrdal forecast that the decentralization of public policy formation will call for and result in a growth of democracy in trade unions, trade associations, cooperatives, etc. Moreover, mere decentralization itself will bring policy determination closer to the people and thereby make it more democratic.

"In the advanced Welfare State, the increasing strength, number, and activity of these organizations, as well as of the authorities for provincial and municipal self-government, has meant a spreading out of participation, initiative, and influence over what is, in reality, legislation and administration to ever larger sections of the people themselves in their various localities and occupations" (p. 49). He restated this theory later (p. 87).

He also explained that "economic progress...has made possible a lessening of internal inequalities. The generally wider elbow room that follows economic progress, and the lessening of inequalities...have also laid a firmer basis for political democracy, which has become ever more effectively the form of government in the rich countries" (p. 153). Since he predicted separately both continued economic progress and continued lessening of inequalities, he clearly implied continued growth or intensification of political democracy in rich countries.

He went on to discuss the low level of active participation in local elections, union elections, etc., in the U.S. He explained this by the large volume of immigration into the U.S. and concluded that, "This line of explanation should make us optimistic in regard to the future development of the democratic organizational state in the U.S. As...integration proceeds, it should be fairly safe to assume that the intensity of active participation by the Americans in their organizations and...communities...will rise" (pp. 54-55).

8. Economic Progress

Myrdal devoted little space to the prospects for continued economic progress, but he frequently assumed or implied that such progress would continue indefinitely. For instance, he asserted that, "everybody also is aware...that production, incomes, and particularly the levels of living of the broader strata of our national communities have been rising more rapidly than ever, and that the prospects of the young are brighter than were those of their parents.... Economically, as well as socially, the Welfare State has been a conspicuous success" (p. 86).

Later he asserted that "the few rich countries... have experienced spectacular progress..." and "this fortunate development is continuing with unabated force." Moreover, "further economic progress has become almost automatic" (p. 152), which clearly implies a prediction that it would continue. Apparently he failed to make this prediction explicit and emphasize and elaborate it because he considered it obvious and almost universally accepted, as indeed it was. But, since this forecast can provide an essential part of the basis for other important, less obvious predictions, he should have made it explicit and explained the reasons for it.

9. Inflation

Myrdal clearly implied that the inflationary trend will continue. "In the present transitional period, this tendency can almost be said to characterize the democratic welfare state" (p. 112). The trend will continue as long as "people are mostly organized for bargaining in their capacity as earners, not as consumers" (p. 114). He should have added that the growth of monopolistic competition is a major inflationary factor which will long continue to operate. As noted earlier, he had previously explained that this factor is a major cause of the growth in state intervention (p. 32).

He asserted, mistakenly I believe, that inflation cannot be controlled by "financial and monetary measures" (p. 116), and implied that it can and will be controlled "when the citizens become equally effectively organized in their role as consumers" (p. 118). This prediction is not very plausible. I predict that state intervention will be required.

10. Public Ownership

Myrdal forecast that the adoption of more and more interventionist economic welfare policies and proper coordination of them would continue to weaken the socialist demand for nationalization of industry. "It is apparent that as the Social Democrats gradually won popular support...they generally tended to play down the nationalization issue.... It now plays an ever decreasing role...and may be on the way to disappearing" because the socialist goals "were...largely attained by other means..." (p. 74). He went on to specify some of the means already successfully used to redistribute incomes more equally, and concluded that, "In all these aspects public control can be tightened, without resort to nationalization.... Therefore, I would expect that...nationalization will disappear from the [socialist] program..." (p. 75). One unstated possible reason for this prediction is that he was thinking of West European states where nearly all public utilities, railroads, airlines, coal mines, oil companies, etc., were already publicly owned and operated (p. 94).

However, on the next page he conceded that, "It is possible that, in the Welfare State of the future, public ownership and public managership will come to play a somewhat larger role, perhaps in the very long run a much larger one. But the change will...not come suddenly...and will not usually be of great importance. Actually, public ownership of industry has continued to grow significantly in most advanced countries since 1960.

Myrdal noted that "in almost all undeveloped countries there is a strong dislike of foreign control of large-scale enterprises," and predicted that, "in all probability, we shall soon see a good deal more nationalization of foreign holdings in these countries" (p. 259). This prediction has been increasingly verified by events since 1960, and I expect that future events will continue to confirm it. This is the kind of important predictions which futurists find it easiest to make because it can be supported by both social analysis and by obvious statistical trends.

11. Income Equalization

According to Myrdal, "The urge for economic equalization is everywhere present, and it is commonly proclaimed as a principle. Its sphere of operation is not limited to taxation and to redistributional expenditure schemes. It enters into, and determines, the scope of all other state intervention" (p. 38). As a result, "state intervention is seen to be in the interest of the lower income groups and, in general, actually is so..." (p. 39). Moreover, the "appetite" of the poor "for intervention is bound to grow as they get more of it. With the greater rationality...and increasing knowledge, they will also press forward with more effectiveness" (p. 40).

In a later chapter he claimed that there is already a general consensus in advanced noncommunist countries on the need for more redistribution of income, and that therefore, "more redistributional reforms are becoming an almost automatic consequence of economic progress" (p. 73). He explained that, "In the cumulative social process, economic progress, equalization of opportunities, and political democracy are interrelated by circular causation, each being both cause and effect of the others" (p. 153).

The spread and strengthening of social security is a major part of the income-equalization trend whose continuance Myrdal forecast. "Sweden is now inaugurating...a compulsory provident and pension scheme.... It is probably taking the lead in a reform movement which other Western countries will soon join. All old people will, by legislation, be guaranteed an income corresponding to two-thirds of their earnings during the best 15 years of their working life" (p. 66). Since this prediction was made, social security programs have been enlarged and made more generous in most Western countries, as he predicted, but it will be a long time before this liberal Swedish pension level is achieved in all advanced countries.

12. The Creation of Social Harmony

Myrdal asserted that the growth of state intervention and coordination had gradually reduced social tension and strife and was well on the way to creating a general social harmony in advanced welfare economies. "The examples I have given—in regard to the now largely undisputed, and consequently almost automatic, progress of further redistributional reforms...educational and health reforms, etc., and the virtual disappearance of the nationalization issue—point to the increasing political harmony that has come to exist much more generally...in the advanced welfare state" (p. 79). Later he wrote of "the created harmony of interests and opinions, which we can now see coming into being" (p. 81). Clearly he implied that this trend would continue, and it will take a very long time to fully achieve social harmony.

Much later he explained that, "The ordinary citizen, living in these happy [rich] countries has experienced the steady improvement of his own economic fortunes, and sees in the future ever brighter openings for himself and his children in a national community that is continuously getting richer, and is at the same time approaching by gradual reform, those ideals of social democracy he has been brought up to cherish"

(p. 154). Obviously, such experiences help to create feelings of social harmony, and Myrdal implied that they would continue to do so. He added that the kind of social harmony he predicted was quite different from that anticipated by old-fashioned liberals because it would be due to state intervention, not to unregulated competition.

The chief defect in his prediction on social harmony is that he suggested no method of verifying it. Perhaps he meant that a decline in the number of serious riots and social revolutions could verify it. However, a good scientific prediction should be more easily and clearly verifiable.

13. U.S.-Soviet Convergence

Although he stressed the radical differences between Communist and Western economies, Myrdal predicted that these differences would diminish. He explained that, "In the Western countries the trade unions are certainly more and more coming to function in a role which in reality is that of public authorities" when they help to fix wage rates and the conditions of labor, like Soviet unions (p. 128). He also noted the growing Soviet efforts to decentralize economic decision making. He concluded that, "It is not altogether improbable...that with the higher levels of living and education...the system will be loosened up. We might in 10 or 20 years see a very different Russia. In important respects it will come closer to the Western world..." (p. 129). He should have added that the Western world will become much more like the U.S.S.R. if his numerous predictions on future social reforms in the West are verified. But, of course, great changes are rarely if ever achieved in 20 years or less.

14. The Decline of Colonialism

In discussing "The Liquidation of Colonialism" Myrdal claimed that, "The ascendency of this world revolution is irresistable.... Its repercussions will fill the history of the rest of the century" (p. 149). This was an easy prediction to make in 1960. Condorcet was far more perceptive when he made a similar forecast in 1794.

Political colonialism resulted in economic colonialism, extensive foreign influence over the economic life of colonies and former colonies. Myrdal predicted the economic colonialism would decline. "This process of the liquidation of economic colonialism has not yet, by a long way, run its full course" (p. 150).

15. International Disintegration

According to Myrdal, the growth of state and private-group intervention in the private economy, and the resulting growth of government economic planning, has helped to integrate and stabilize the economies of all advanced welfare economies, but has also caused growing international disintegration. For instance, the growth of state control over domestic monetary expansion has reduced domestic economic fluctuations but has increased fluctuations in foreign exchange rates. In his words, "It is...undeniable that the larger part of the complex system of public policies in the interest of national progress, and of the growth of equality and security for the individual, which today make up the welfare state, have on balance tended to disturb the international equilibrium" (pp. 160-61). Since he had predicted much more progress towards a complete welfare state in advanced noncommunist countries, he clearly expected, and implicitly predicted, a long further continuation of the trend towards international disintegration.

It is true that some domestic stabilization programs cause international friction and disintegration. The current U.S. high interest policies are an example. But there is no good reason to claim that domestic welfare measures like old age pensions and unemployment insurance cause international disintegration. Thus Myrdal should not have attributed such effects to "the larger part of the complex system of public policies" in welfare states.

He did emphasize that the growth of economic nationalism—tariffs, quotas, export subsidies, etc.—is the major cause of international economic disintegration. It has played a positive role in promoting industrialization in advanced countries, he claimed, and, "There are thus good reasons why underdeveloped countries should give their foreign economic policies a pronounced nationalistic direction" (p. 106). But such nationalism "is a dangerous drug.... It is, indeed, only natural that nationalism tends to mount and then turn sour: into displaced aggression" (p. 209). He clearly implied that this is likely to happen often. In any case, all economic nationalism will continue to cause international disintegration.

Myrdal went on to predict or imply also that the failure of rich welfare states to adopt policies which would hasten the development of poor countries and reduce international real income differences would result in growing international friction and disintegration. Such a failure may result in more and more confiscation of foreign property in poor countries and in the blackmailing of rich countries. Long before the creation of OPEC, he claimed that poor countries "have available blackmailing powers of considerable efficiency" (p. 216). Moreover, "the feeling of being powerless is a temptation to reckless nationalism, and to the indiscriminate use of all the means a poor country has...to assert its interests" (p. 217). As previously noted, he explicitly predicted "more nationalization of foreign holdings" in poor countries. He added that the compensation paid will probably be arbitrary and inadequate (p. 214).

16. A Democratic Welfare World

Myrdal claimed that the only solution, and implicitly the eventual solution, to the problem of international disintegration and conflict is the creation of a democratic welfare world. "Only insofar as real advances could be made towards a democratic Welfare World—implying a growth of international solidarity on the part of both the rich and the poor nations and, on this basis, a rising trend towards international cooperation to equalize opportunities on a world scale —can it reasonably be expected that, in the long run, the political leaders of the poor countries will feel that they can afford to abstain from breaking rules and using their powers to blackmail the rich" (p. 220). He explicitly refused to predict adoption of this ideal solution (p. 226). However, he went on to suggest many details of this preferred solution.

It is remarkable that he did not even mention any other possible solution of the cold war or the race to a nuclear war. He never discussed the creation of a Russo-American Condominion or of an undemocratic world government able to maintain world peace. These are probably the most serious omissions in his analysis.

17. Comments

Myrdal's analysis of recent and current politico-economic trends was sophisticated and plausible, but he sometimes failed to explicitly predict the continuance of thse trends, in part because he believed men are able, by acts of free will, to reverse such trends. In fact, his analysis usually made clear the reasons why men are very unlikely to reverse these trends, and he often explicitly predicted their continuance. After all, trends created for good reasons are likely to continue for the same reasons. And the chief merit of his analysis is that he explained, far more fully and plausibly than most recent futurists, the good reasons for many recent major social trends.

It is also noteworthy that, unlike most futurists, Myrdal did not grossly overestimate the rate of social change. However, his emphasis on gradualism did not prevent him from predicting that gradual social change will in time produce radical results. "I have intentionally meant to depict a utopia," he wrote, after describing the results of the predicted continuation of current social trends (p. 96).

FERDINAND LUNDBERG AS A FUTURIST

Ferdinand Lundberg (b1905) is a sociologist, a liberal, and a best-selling author (<u>Imperial Hearst</u>, <u>America's 60 Families</u>). His book, <u>The Coming World Transformation</u> (Doubleday, 1963), is a serious effort at predicting major social trends in a wide variety of fields and countries, primarily during the years 1960-2110. About two-thirds of the book is devoted to trends in population, economics, government, and education.

Although he predicted continued rapid technological progress, Lundberg devoted only four pages of his book to specific "expected technological developments" (pp. 4-7), which include such often-predicted achievements as thermonuclear fusion, solar power, purification of sea water, superior batteries, new plastics, weather control and better birth-control pills.

Unlike most futurists, Lundberg devoted 20 pages of his book to a review of predictions made by earlier futurists—Condorcet, Malthus, Godwin, Ricardo, Marx, Wells, Keynes, etc. He rated Condorcet as the greatest of these, and listed 19 of his predictions.

1. Is the Future Predictable?

Lundberg discussed "the widely prevalent view that one cannot predict the future" (p. 69), and quoted two advocates of this unsound thesis—Drucker and Toynbee. He noted that, after denying the possibility of prediction, Toynbee went on to make several predictions, a common paradox.

Lundberg claimed that physical scientists do not hesitate to make predictions, and cited several cases in which they predicted the social consequences of technological changes (pp. 70-71). He also asserted that "the logicians of science hold that one can" make predictions, and quoted Nagel to this effect. He added that "our personal relations with other men, our political arrangements and social institutions, our transportation schedules...could not be what they are unless fairly safe inferences were possible about the human past and future" (p. 72). I believe this reasoning is sound.

Although Lundberg argued that "piecemeal social developments can be predicted by appropriate methods," he agreed with Karl Popper that the future is not fully determined. In other words, he rejected the theory of universal causation, the basic principle of all science. Apparently he believed that both individual and social behavior are largely, but not completely, determined.

Like Popper, Lundberg claimed that the theory of historicism, which holds that "future history can be prophesied on the basis of past history," directly contradicts the theory of "empirical-minded social scientists" who "believe that the impending future can be altered by appropriate action in the present..." (pp. 103-04). I see no contradiction. The past determines the future precisely because it determines "appropriate action" intended to affect the future.

2. Methods of Prediction

Lundberg's chief method of predicting the future was the projection of past social trends. But, he also anticipated effects of past events. "Many changes to come...will be no more than the further effects and extensions of changes and innovations in...earlier ...periods" (p. 1).

In many cases Lundberg referred to the opinions of experts concerning probable future social trends and reforms. And he obviously considered himself an expert whose opinion helps to justify certain predictions. Finally, he repeatedly assumed that desirable social reforms will be adopted because men will become better educated and therefore more responsive to sound arguments for needed social reforms.

Like Marx and Engels, Lundberg stressed the claim that changes in the technology of production are the most basic and powerful causes of major economic, political, and social trends (pp. 9-10). For him, the full effects of the industrial revolution have not yet been felt, even in the most advanced countries, and are just beginning to be felt in the least advanced countries. He implied that one can predict the future of all undeveloped countries by assuming that they will experience nearly all of the industrial revolution and its effects which have already occurred in advanced countries. However, lack of industrial fuels and raw materials, he added, will prevent some countries from achieving "full industrialization" (pp. 10-11). I believe that the success of Japan refutes this last point.

3. The Rate of Social Change

According to Lundberg, we are "on the threshold of some of the most spectacular changes ever seen" and "the beginnings of many of these changes will be clearly visible within from 25 to 50 years" (p. 1). Over 20 years have passed since he wrote this, but no such spectacular changes are yet visible, and I doubt that any will be clearly visible in advanced countries in the next hundred years. These countries have just completed several such changes—the agricultural revolution, the industrial revolution, the spread of literacy, the rise of radio and TV broadcasting, the scientific revolution, etc.—but they are far less likely to experience such radical changes in the next century. Moreover, Lundberg did not predict and describe any equally "spectacular changes."

Lundberg even expected that "the changes to come ...will make those witnessed in the momentous historical periods 1500-1650, 1650-1800, 1800-1950 appear by contrast to be far less remarkable." This prediction may well be valid for very backward countries like China, India, and Nigeria, because they have yet to experience the great social changes which advanced countries have already experienced, but it is very unlikely to come true in the most advanced countries, for whose readers Lundberg wrote.

4. The Future of Education

Lundberg devoted more space (70 pp.) to education than to any other subject, but most of it is a history and criticism of education.

His major prediction on education was that adult education will grow faster than other forms of education. "The most novel line of development in education...will be seen in adult education, now in its infancy" (p. 282). "Well within...150 years...the educated people, perhaps 25% of adults, will be those still going to school. Government officials, for example, will be given leaves of absence to attend university courses..." (p. 284).

He failed to anticipate the vast expansion in higher education which occurred in all advanced countries from 1960 to 1980, but he did predict a relative increase in the public funds available for student aid. "Very probably before A.D. 2000 total subsidization of select students will occur: the better students, no matter what their economic status, will have all their expenses paid..." (p. 281). He was right on the direction of this trend, but overestimated its tempo. I doubt that his prediction will become true in the U.S. before 2000 A.D.

Lundberg forecast that, "By the years 2000-25 there will be a virtually total decline in graduates specializing in business and commerce" (p. 257). This was a very bad prediction. There has been a rise, not a decline, in such U.S. graduates since 1960, and this rise may continue through 2025 A.D.

He predicted "a massive increase in the number of psychologists turned out by the schools" (p. 259). Here he was right on the trend from 1960 to 1980, and perhaps on that from 1980 to 2110 A.D.

He anticipated "substantial increases in the number of scientific personnel," especially of "behavioral scientists," a "relative decline in the number of graduates in journalism and religion" (pp. 260-61), and a relative increase in the numbers of engineers and health-care professionals (pp. 258-59).

It is noteworthy that Lundberg failed to predict the expansion of preschool education which occurred in most advanced countries between 1960 and 1980, and is likely to continue for many decades.

5. On Religion

Lundberg offered a brief, but lucid and plausible, statement of several reasons for the almost continuous decline of religious faith in advanced countries since 1500, and predicted that this trend "may ...be expected to continue...for the next 150 years" and that, "as a very long-term trend, religion as we know it appears to be on the way out." However, "it is possible that natural piety will organize around itself some new form of religion" which will incorporate into itself the outlook of science," because scientists are the "most faithful votaries" of the works of any sort of creator (pp. 321-22).

6. The Future of the Family

In Lundberg's opinion, "The family as an institution is in fact near the point of complete extinction" due to industrialization, urbanization, divorce, etc. (p. 295). Therefore, governments will increasingly perform functions once performed by the patriarchal rural family. "To deal with the problem of neglected and disoriented children, government will greatly extend present measures" (p. 297), and adopt new ones. It will establish new requirements for marriage (including raising the minimal age to 18), will employ more social workers to interview and educate pregnant women and new mothers, will assign psychologists to all schools, will increase the number of children's recreation centers and summer camps, will assure vocational training and/or jobs for all school leavers, will provide free health care for poor children and will single out and favor all gifted children (pp. 300-01). Moreover, "school children of the future will not be sent to their homes in midafternoon, as at present..." (p. 310).

Writing during the post-war baby boom, Lundberg presciently forecast that the U.S. birth rate "will fall and will...resume its pre-1940 trend." Furthermore, "Public policy will...everywhere favor the practice of birth control and probably abortion as well," and "immature and irresponsible" parents will be "surgically sterilized" (p. 299). His daring forecast on abortion was very quickly verified.

He also predicted that the proportion of women attending college and holding professional jobs outside the home would continue to rise because the average female I.Q. is as high as the average male I.Q., and because the need for able professionals will grow (p. 282).

7. Mechanization and Automation

Lundberg predicted that mechanization and automation would long continue in all countries. In advanced countries (a qualification he omitted), "Both the factory worker and the office worker are on the way out as dominant categories of the labor force;..." As they become relatively less numerous, "There will be many more persons engaged in highly skilled occupations requiring elaborate education" (p. 155), in repair and maintenance work (p. 31), and in "domestic employment" (p. 156).

He forecast that the number of U.S. factory workers would fall from 12 to 3 million by 2110 A.D., a very dubious prediction. I also doubt that domestic employment "may be counted on to absorb a large slice of those refused employment in offices and factories" (p. 156) because this implies that personal incomes will become more unequal. If incomes become less unequal, as I expect, the relative demand for domestic workers will decline.

Lundberg was very pessimistic about economic progress. He did not expect continued mechanization and automation to result in continuously rising real wages. "There will be little if any relative increase in profits and no lowering of product prices through automation except, perhaps, very temporarily...because "nearly all of the gain from...automation is going to be absorbed in taxes" (p. 341). I believe that this was his most serious error. In fact, real wages after taxes have risen very substantially in all advanced countries since he wrote, especially in Japan, where automation has probably been most rapid.

8. More-Unequal Incomes

Lundberg expected that automation would compel "unskilled, low-skilled and so-called semiskilled" workers to accept "relatively lower wages than at present" because it would increase the supply of them and reduce the demand for them (p. 159). He ignored the possibilities that control of immigration and births could reduce the supply of such workers, and that more vocational education could transform many of them into skilled workers.

Furthermore, governments may deliberately increase the number of highly skilled and professional workers enough to reduce their relative earnings, which would help to make earnings less unequal. For these and other reasons, I think his prediction that earnings will become more unequal by 2110 will be disproven.

9. The Decline of Labor Unions

According to Lundberg, "Labor unions...[face] a significant reduction in size and influence.... Automation, auto-computation, and telemation are all bound to reduce memberships as they eliminate jobs," especially factory jobs (p. 157). "What all this foreshadows is the gradual slow decline of the labor-union boss" (p. 159). Labor unions will be replaced in part by associations of "workers of higher skill...more like the American Medical Association" (p. 159). These trends did continue from 1963 to 1983 in the U.S. However, I doubt that automation, autocomputation, telemation, and the growth of professionalism will tend to decrease the relative number and power of union members world-wide. They are much more likely to merely shift workers from one union to another.

10. The Future of the City

The future of the city received more attention from Lundberg than from most previous futurists. He forecast that, "Eventually all cities...will be under the manager form [of government], with the manager either chosen by or approved by the national government" (p. 303). He explained that "political scientists, almost to a man, testify to the lower cost and greater efficiency of the city-manager scheme" (p. 304).

He anticipated the continuance of the trend "toward a few super-cities or megalopolises," some over 200 miles long (pp. 305-06).

He predicted a gradual reconstruction of large American cities, with the building of many more centers like Rockefeller Center, New York, and with the creation of neighborhoods which consist of "clusters of apartment buildings into which schools, hospitals and churches may in time be incorporated without external distinguishing marks." He expected that, "Individual dwellings in suburban area will increasingly be replaced by so-called garden or quadrangular apartments or attached, floor-through duplex and triplex homes" (p. 306).

"As cities are gradually reconstructed and their government improved, there will be a gradual return of the middle classes" because, "the city, properly operated, is a more convenient place in which to live..." (p. 307).

"Transportation in the coming supercity will be of the mass variety..." due to "a gradual reduction in per capita car ownership in the U.S." Also, "there will be a great increase in car-rental service for trips outside cities" and, "for distant trips, the airplane will be resorted to increasingly..." (p. 308).

"The future supercity [2110?]...will have no air-pollution problem, thanks to the installatin of prevention devices on buildings and vehicles; will be without slums; will possess more open ground space... will have tree-lined streets (small trees, wide streets); will have no jerry-built structures; will be quite clean, almost noiseless, devoid of billboards.... Manufacturing and storage will be relegated to the fringes..." (pp. 308-09).

It is noteworthy that he did not predict any decline in the size of, or decentralization of activities within, large cities.

11. The Growth of Collectivism and Monopoly

Lundberg used the term <u>collectivism</u> very broadly, i.e., to denote both government activities and private corporate activities. "Most economic activity in the U.S. now, governmental and non-governmental, takes place under large-scale collectivized...auspices" (p. 151). He predicted a great expansion of both public and private collectivized activities. He estimated "governmental economic activity at 20% of U.S. GNP in 1960, and forecast that this ratio would rise to between 35 and 50% in Western Europe and Anglo-America within 150 years. This prediction was largely realized within 20 years in Western Europe, where the ratio is now near 35% if the term <u>economic activity</u> includes all government activity, which is the way Lundberg used it.

He noted that "government radio and television is a reality" in Europe, and forecast that the U.S. government "will also establish its own domestic broadcasting stations" (p. 178).

He forecast that health care will be largely socialized for both technological and social reasons. "What the A.M.A. denounces as 'socialized medicine' will be the inescapable outcome." Such health care may resemble one of our "most completely socialized institutions—education" (pp. 331-32).

He also predicted that "corporation mergers will continue and that fewer and fewer enlarging enterprises in all fields of economic activity will dominate the economic situation...over which the government will have increased regulatory control...dominating if not owning the economic system. Individual or small enterprises will have only an interstitial and marginal role" (p. 152).

He described the past trend toward monopoly, and concluded that, "The future...belongs to collectivist monopoly..." (p. 153). He asked, "What would be the impetus towards" this outcome? and answered, "The same...that has produced the present prevalence of bigness—lower costs, greater efficiency, wide availability, larger volume of business, readier access to capital, and more efficient organization all around" (p. 154).

To ensure that the ever larger corporations become more socially-minded, "it seems likely that all large economic enterprises will...have a wider representation of directors, some representing the point of view of government, some perhaps of labor and some the general public" (p. 161).

12. Centralization of Government

One of Lundberg's most important and most emphasized predictions was that the functions of government would be increasingly and, in time, highly centralized in nearly all countries, especially in the U.S. "The general change...is going to be from federalism to a unitary government, with power that is now local, regional, and particular concentrated increasingly and, finally, definitively in the central government" (p. 167). He noted the well-established past trends in this respect, and projected them into the future. He also argued that such centralization will be needed in order to reduce crime (pp. 171-72, 178-80), regulate private business (pp. 182-84), and protect and aggrandize the U.S. (pp. 185-86). He should have added that only a strong centralized government can assure equal education, health care, pensions, etc., for all citizens.

13. The Rise of Meritocracy

According to Lundberg, the management of economic, social, and political organizations will continue to be transferred from the merely rich and/or shrewd selfmade men to professionally trained administrators and social scientists who will be selected for their ability, not for their wealth or native shrewdness. He predicted that "the man of learning...is going to displace the man of mere shrewdness all along the line in governmental and economic affairs just as the man of shrewdness displaced the muscular wielder of sword, mace and spear" (p. 288), and that "the 21st Century-and beyond—will be the century dominated by the highly cultivated educated man" (p. 286).

I believe that the trend in this direction is already well-established and will long continue, but I doubt that it will move fast enough to make the 21st Century one "dominated by the highly cultivated educated man." Perhpas the 22nd or 23rd Century will be so dominated. Lundberg failed to note that government by experts is incompatible with political democracy, which will probably survive throughout the 21st Century in most advanced countries (see my book, <u>Government by Experts</u>, 1972).

14. On the Effects of Third-World Population Growth

Lundberg devoted a separate chapter to "The Population Problem," and predicted (in 1962) that the continued rapid growth of population in the least developed countries will soon be checked by famine (p. 112). Moreover, he asserted that population growth will long continue to be a powerful brake on economic, social, and political progress in all third-world countries. For instance, he forecast that the governments of nearly all undeveloped countries would continue to be harsh and dictatorial because only such government can restrict population growth and speed up economic progress in these countries (p. 119). However, he claimed that, "What China shows is that communism is not the solution to the problem" in these countries (p. 113). I believe this was a premature judgment, one which he might wish to revise now, twenty years later. And I doubt that population growth will be seriously checked by famine in any country.

15. The Rise of Superstates and World Government

Lundberg predicted that on every continent once-independent countries will increasingly become units of larger federal unions. He forecast that the nations of Western Europe will form their own federal union if they are not absorbed in a communist Europe (pp. 188-90), that Canada will join the U.S. (pp. 218-19), that Latin America will be unified (pp. 203-04), that black Africa will be united (pp. 206-09), and that North Africa and the Arabian Peninsula will be unified (pp. 209-10). He was very vague about the process of political union in Asia but he mentioned a "United Far East" (pp. 210-12). And all this was to happen by 2110 A.D.

As to world government, he expected "eventual rule of most of the world by a federation of the continental regional superstates" described above (p. 220).

16. The Future of Futurism

The last section of this book (2 pages) is entitled "The Future of Prognostics," Lundberg's pedantic and awkward name for futurism. In his opinion, "it is practically a certainty...that it will... become a regular university discipline, replacing much of the present overemphasis upon history," whose study "is itself an oblique invocation of prognostics. For the judgmments of history can be applicable...only to a future. But prognostics itself will be a separate disciplinne..." (p. 351). This prediction has already been partially verified, for a growing number of U.S. universities have introduced courses on futurism since 1963.

He also predicted the U.S. government agencies will hire more and more professionally trained futurists, and prepare more and more studies of future trends, especially in non-economic fields.

17. Comments

Lundberg's outline of the next 150 years is one of the best books on the future published in this century, probably because he was a social scientist and a sane reformer who relied more on the projection of very well established major long-run social trends than on his own personal desires or imagination. His major defect was that he frequently overestimated the speed of social progress. He should have claimed to be covering a much longer future period than 150 years.

ARNOLD TOYNBEE AS A FUTURIST

Arnold Toynbee (1889-1975) was an eminent English historian who eventually began to use his knowledge of history to predict the future. He presented his predictions most fully and definitely in a 239-page book <u>Change and Habit, the Challenge of Our Time</u> (1966), which is the source book for this essay. All page references not otherwise attributed are to this book.

1. The Feasibility of Futurism

The first chapter, "Light from the Past: Its Value and Limits," discusses the degree to which human history can be properly used to predict the future of man. The author reasoned that, "in human affairs, the light thrown on the future by the past is a less trustworthy guide than it is in any of our other fields of action" (p. 5). "In this field, therefore, we cannot make infallible predictions; we can only hazard guesses" (p. 7).

I believe that this reasoning is unsound and misleading. No scientific predictions are infallible, but many predictions about man's future—for instance, the prediction that the population of India will continue to grow rapidly for several more decades-are very likely (95%?) to be verified in the future. Moreover, many predictions made by natural scientists—for instance, most about the weather, earthquakes, and volcanic eruptions—are only slightly probable. But they are more scientific and reliable than mere guesses. The term <u>guess</u> should be restrictd to predictions made without scientific research, and without any evidence. One guesses the turn of a card. One predicts that a well-established social trend will continue. Toynbee's bad logic implies that all of social science, and much of natural and biological science, is pure guesswork because the conclusions are not infallibly true. By this logic, most of his own historical accounts should have been called historical guesses, but he failed to apply this logic to his histories.

Although he believed all futurism to be guesswork, he asserted that "Study does not have to be scientific in order to be illuminating. Where prediction is impossible, guesswork may be valuable so far as it goes— on condition that we recognize the limits...of the light thrown by the past on the future...of human affairs" (p. 8). I simply cannot understand how an unscientific guess about the future can be illuminating, unless it is really a misnamed scientific prediction. And in his many statements about the future, Toynbee rarely used the term *guess*. Therefore, I shall refer to such statements as predictions. Fortunately, he usually offered some scientific reasons for such statements.

2. His Methodology

As a historian, Toynbee naturally used historical trends to predict the future. Moreover, he placed ununusual emphasis on historical analogies. He repeatedly tried to predict the future by comparing the position of advanced societies today with that of advanced societies in some former age, especially in ancient or medieval times. Few other futurists have used such analogies, and none have used them as often as he did.

Toynbee also frequently predicted that men will behave in a certain way because that would be the rational thing to do. On the other hand, he made no use of public opinion trends among laymen or experts. Nor did he explain that the poor will think and act tomorrow the way the rich think and live today.

3. World Government

Toynbee's most significant forecast was his repeated prediction that a world government strong enough to prevent nuclear wars will be created within 100 years. His chief argument for this prediction was rational. "The head therefore sees that, now that it has brought the Atomic Age upon mankind, the institution of war must be abolished, and that this involves also abolishing the institution of local sovereignty, since wars are waged by local sovereign states, and local states are likely to continue to go to war with each other so long a they retain the sovereign right to do so. In the Atomic Age a monopoly of the possession of atomic weapons must be given to a single world authority..." (p. 35).

To further support this prediction, he recounted the long history of ever more successful efforts at political integration which has produced two great superpowers. However, he did not forecast creation of a Russo-American Condominium capable of enforcing world peace. Instead, he forecast the voluntary formation of a world government able to dominate both the U.S. and the U.S.S.R. "We may therefore assuume that the world-state of the future will not have the structure of the would-be world-states of the past, which have been imposed by conquest. It will have the structure of those states, past and present, that have been brought into being by a voluntary union of a number of previously separate and independent smaller units; and the structure of states that have originated in this peaceful way has usually been not unitary, but federal" (p. 140).

He explained that the coming world-state will not be created by conquest because nuclear warfare would cause unbearable losses to both victor and vanquished. "All the would-be world-states of the past...have been established by conquest. ...The literally world-wide world-state that...is the only alternative to mass-suicide can no longer be established in this barbarous and costly traditional way...there would be no surviving victor to clear up the ruins; ..." (pp. 99-100).

Toynbee noted that in 1965 "perhaps 90% of the political and military power in the world was held by the U.S. and the Soviet Union," and that, "when these two powers took identical action," as in the 1956 Suez issue, "the effect was decisive." Moreover, "they have one vital issue in common, namely the preservation of their present virtual monopoly of the atomic weapon" (p.157). In spite of these compelling reasons, he did not predict formation of a U.S.-Soviet Condominium. Instead, he suggested that if the U.S. and the U.S.S.R. knock each other out in a nuclear war, China might "try her hand...at establishing the political world-organization" that is badly needed. Here he seems to imply conquest.

4. The Decline of Nationalism

Toynbee forecast a radical decline in nationalism as a result of improved communication, continued migration, and the creation of a world state. "We can... foresee a world, knit ever more closely together by the continuing advance of technology, in which a human being's local state will have, not the first claim on his loyalty, but the third. This paramount political allegiance will be given to mankind as a whole and to the literally world-wide world-state.... His secondary allegiance will be given to one or more diasporas; some world-wide religious communion, perhaps, and some world-wide professional association..." (p. 87).

Toynbee was probably the first to predict that international "diasporas" or associations will play a major role in facilitating creation of the coming world state. "The most promising of all the portents of reunification is the emergence of a new type of community, the diaspora, which looks as if it may be 'the wave of the future'" (p. 81). Due to the annihilation of distance, "We may expect to see the number, size and importance of the World's diasporas increase as never before. Concomitantly, we may expect to see the hold of the World's local states decrease as the hold of the diasporas increases. We may expect...to see the local states 'de-mytholigized.' Instead of being worshipped as gods, perhaps they will come to be just administered as public utilities...[which] provide those public services that are found...to be still provided most conveniently on a local basis..." (p. 82).

5. Population Growth and Food Supplies

Toynbee described the danger of famine due to the continuing rapid growth of population, which he predicted would result in "the imminent tripling or quadrupling of the size of our planet's population" (p. 210). However, he anticipated that, "since no species ...can increase its numbers to infinity, the current increase in the World's human population will eventually be curbed.... It will be curbed brutally by...famine, pestilence, and war...[or] by voluntary family planning" (p. 37). He failed to mention other probable means, compulsory sterilization and abortion.

He asserted that, "Fortunately, science applied to food production appears to be equal to the task of feeding two or three times as many people as there are to be fed today, and feeding them all on the standard now enjoyed only by an affluant minority....[but] Science can perform these feats...only on one condition...the whole surface of the globe is administered as a single unit both for the production of food and for the distribution of it..." (p. 37). Later he forecast that, "Rather than bring mass-destruction on themselves by allowing two-thirds of the human race to starve, the nations...will agree to transfer sovereign power over the production and distribution of food from their own national governments to another new world authority..." (p. 47).

This prediction is not very plausible because world-government control of agriculture could do little to increase agricultural productivity, which has long been rising rapidly in all advanced, and many backward, countries and because agriculture is most unlikely to be taken over or closely controlled by a federal world government.

Toynbee later predicted that, as a result of his predicted increase in population, "There will be no room left...for agriculture on land; streets and houses will occupy every acre of terra firma. Food production ...will be driven out to sea. We shall exterminate the sharks...and other predatory marine wild life, and shall stock the sea with flocks of herrings and with herds of whales.... Our iron ration will be domestic plankton" (p. 210).

The prediction that the sea will produce far more food than the land is irrational. The share of our total food supply obtained from the sea may increase slightly, but it may also decline, even if many sea mammals become domesticated and herded. Factories producing synthetic food will probably become more important than the sea as a source of additional food. But land will long continue to be the prime source.

6. Transportation and Travel

According to Toynbee, the coming tripling or quadrupling of world population will force radical changes in the means of transport. "We are fast moving into a so far barely imaginable new world in which the largest surviving open spaces will be the airports of supersonic aircraft. There will be no room left for traffic on the surface. Goods that are too heavy to be carried by air will have to be transported underground" (p. 210).

The idea that foreseeable population growth in any country will be so great as to leave no land available for land transport is even more irrational than the idea that it will leave no land available for agriculture. But much long-distance transport may go underground for other, largely technological, reasons.

Toynbee predicted that coming social changes will have important effects on travel. "While travel on business will be on a greater scale than ever before, travel for pleasure will probably tail off. The incentive for sight-seeing will disappear in a standardized world...[and] the public authorities...will be in charge of issuing travel-permits.... Except for strictly necessary business purposes...the inhabitant of megapolis will be more and more rigorously confined within...his own...quarters..." (pp. 210-11). He offered little if any further justification for this very implausible forecast.

I disagree with all the travel forecasts in this quotation. I predict that improved communication and economic reationalization will begin to reduce the relative volume of business travel before 2050 A.D. in all advanced countries, and that pleasure travel will continue to grow faster than GNP in all countries for centuries. I doubt that any permanent increase in the use of travel-permits to limit travel will occur in advanced countries.

7. Urbanization

As stated earlier, Toynbee forecast a long further growth in total world population. He also predicted that nearly all of the additional population will settle down in cities, some of which will become megalopolises. "We can foresee that these new thousands of millions are going to pour into the cities.... In all quarters of the World...the cities are now growing on a scale and at a pace that already foreshadows a future in which the now still separate cities will all have coalesced into one global megalopolis" (p. 203). The prediction of a global megalopolis is irrational both because the continents are separated by oceans and because a large continent can and will support several separate megalopolises quite distant from each other. Moreover, it is likely that all countries will eventually limit the growth of large cities and require wide greenbelts between them.

8. On Nuclear Energy

According to Toynbee, the coming creation of a world government will not only end the danger of nuclear wars but will also permit and favor a far more extensive development of nuclear energy. However, the proper development of nuclear energy will require creation of a world atomic authority because nuclear processes create nuclear poisons which can drift around the world.

He asked, "But would not the abolition of war make the maintenance of a world atomic authority superfluous?" He answered, "The head sees that it would not. It sees that, if mankind does not commit mass-suicide by using atoms for war, it is going to use atoms for peace on a massive scale...[but] the price of harnessing atomic energy...is the production of poisonous atomic waste...[which] can drift round the globe... The problem...can be solved only by action on a worldwide scale...by a world-wide authority..." (p. 35).

9. Technology and Productivity

Toynbee forecast that technological progress will continue indefinitely and will result in affluence and excessive leisure for all. "The accelerating advance of technology is carrying us towards a novel state of society. Everyone is going to find himself in a position that has been enjoyed, hitherto, only by a privileged minority.... We are all going to be paid high wages for working only a few hours in the week on rigidly standardized jobs...[both] in the economically advanced countries...[and eventually] all the rest of of mankind as well."

However, "To extend a privilege to everyone is tantamount to withdrawing it from everyone. When everyone has plenty of money, everyman's money will not be able to buy the amenities that money has bought for the privileged minority in the past. Everyman's money will not even be able to buy necessities; for everyone else will have plenty of money too; so why should anyone any longer be willing to work overtime during the five days of leisure in the week, when the two working days will bring him in more money than he will now be able to use? And what will people do with their five vacation days, when everyone else will be on vacation simultaneously, so that there will be no one left on duty to provide holiday-makers with amusements?" (pp. 218-19).

He also explained that, "We can foresee a time, not far ahead, when not only factories, offices, and post-offices, but restaurants, theatres, cinemas, hotels, banks, stores...will be closed, not just for two days in the week, but for five" (p. 219).

In my opinion, most of the above predictions are so unreasonable and inconsistent that they deserve no serious criticism. Technological progress will certainly continue and result in higher real incomes and more leisure, but the prediction of a two-day work week is implausible, and the prediction that affluence will make it impossible to buy necessities and luxuries is absurd.

10. Leisure and Hobbies

Toynbee predicted that the growth of leisure will induce and permit people to develop hobbies and the fine arts, and do for pleasure many things which have been done for pay or by hired repair men in the past. "'Do it yourself' for your own delectation during your five days a week of leisure...will be the talismanic formula for inspiration. We shall print pictures, chase silver, and carve wood and marble for love, besides mending our own shoes for love and cleaning our own watches for it.... This will redeem our days of leisure from the curse of boredom..." (p. 224).

Toynbee failed to realize that technological progress will continuously reduce the proportion of work which is routine and boring, and will steadily increase the already large portion of work which is non-routine and interesting, like nearly all professional, paraprofessional, and repair work. As a result of this trend, few workers will want five days of leisure a week, even when real wages are more than three times as high as current U.S. wages. Leisure-time hobbies will become more common and time-consuming, but not nearly to the degree predicted here.

11. The Political-Economic Structure

Toynbee predicted further long-continued centralization of control over the economic system. "The scale of operations that our advancing mechanization now demands...are now too great to be within an individual human being's capacity. The Iowa farmer who still manages to own and operate a farm...is doomed to be replaced by an impersonal corporation, and the corporation in its turn is doomed to become first the pensioner, then the creature, and finally one of the departments of...the state" (pp. 213-14).

These plausible and familiar predictions are among the most important in his book, but he did relatively little to justify them.

His use of the term doomed in these predictions is inconsistent with his earlier emphasis on free will and on the need "to guess" rather than "to predict" the future.

12. A World Language

Toynbee discussed the spread of older empire languages—Sumerian, Greek, Latin, Spanish, English—and predicted the general adoption of a world language. He based this prediction largely on the growing ease of travel and communication, not on the policies or influence of the coming world government. He explained that, "the extent of the areas over which some once merely local languages have already been spread by sail and hoof shows that, in the Age of Annihilation of Distance, a world-language is not merely a possibility but is a probability" (p. 81). I agree. I think he could have strengthened his case by noting the rapidly growing use of English as an international scientific language, and the great economic, political, and scientific advantages of the world-wide use of a single language.

13. Religious Trends

According to Toynbee, religion has been declining in the West for over 300 years. "The closing decades of the 17th Century saw the beginning of a recession of Christianity in the West. The tide has gone on ebbing till within our lifetime. The first signs of a possible turn in it did not show themselves till after the end of the Second World War" (p. 110). Any social trend which has continued for over 300 years is highly likely to continue for many decades more, but Toynbee, a very religious person, was most reluctant to make this prediction. The most he was able to concede was that nationalism, communism, and other non-religious ideologies, "will, no doubt, continue to win and retain the allegiance of former adherents of the higher religions unless and until the higher religions recover their previous hold over human hearts" (p. 177). In other words, religion will decline until it stops declining, a remarkably uninformative prediction. Elsewhere he merely said that the future of religion is "uncertain" (p. 27), a superfluous claim since the future of everything is literally uncertain. Scientific futurists believe that all futures are uncertain but that some futures are probable as well as uncertain.

While Toynbee hesitated to predict that religion will revive and grow in influence, he clearly hoped for, and probably expected such a revival. He explained that, in order "to recover," the "higher religions...must once again be true to themselves..." they have to reform their practices in at least three respects. They have to change their attitude and conduct towards each other from hostility and rivalry to love and cooperation; they have to concern themselves, in practical ways, with the crucial issues of the times; and they have to strip off from the permanent essence of their institutions and doctrines and precepts the non-essential accretions with which this essence has been overlaid..." (p. 177).

He went on to assert that all three of these "necessary changes" were already well under way, and thus imply that they would continue. I agree on both points. These trends are almost certain to continue for many decades, probably for centuries, even if religious faith continues its long decline.

Toynbee argued that members of different religions should and will become more tolerant of each other because this would "do more than anything else to win back allegiance to each" religion (p. 178). It seems more likely that religious people have become, and will continue to become, more tolerant of pagans and heretics because their faith in their own dogmas has weakened, and will long continue to weaken.

Toynbee devoted Chapter X to the question of whether the creation of a world state would result in the creation of a new or synthetic world religion. He explained that in the past the rulers of nearly all would-be world states had tried to impose a single religion on their subjects. However, he concluded that, "The historical evidence does not suggest that religious unification is a necessary condition for the maintenance of political unity," and argued for, and implicitly predicted, "religious liberty" in the coming world state (p. 188).

He also predicted that continued growth of religious liberty would result in more and more religious people abandoning the faith of their fathers. "Individual choice at the age of discretion will replace, in more and more cases, the unquestioning and almost automatic inheritance of the religion of one's family and one's homeland; and...there will be a concomitant change in the religious maps of the World. The solid but local blocks of the adherents of this religion and that will dissolve into so many world-wide diasporas, none of which will be in a majority at any point..." (p. 192). I do not believe the resulting new religious minorities should be called "diasporas," but otherwise I think this rare prediction is sound. However, it will take centuries to reduce Christianity to one of several religious minorities in long-Christian countries.

14. Comments

Since the future is always a continuation of the past, the study of the past should be an ideal preparation for the prediction of the future. And Toynbee is one of the very few futurists who have also been historians. Why, then, did he make so many bad predictions?

I think that a futurist needs to be familiar with very recent history, not with ancient and medieval history, the fields to which Toynbee devoted most of his study. Moreover, a futurist needs to be familiar with modern literature on social reform, especially economic reform, because most future social history will consist of social reforms. Toynbee was apparently unfamiliar with most recent trends in and theories of social reform. Finally, he was also apparently unfamiliar with the literature of futurism, which he rarely quoted or cited. Most of his quotations are from the Bible (35%) or even older sources.

STUART CHASE AS A FUTURIST

Stuart Chase (b1888) was a well-known author and social reformer for almost sixty years. He wrote The Tragedy of Waste; Rich Land, Poor Land; The Proper Study of Mankind; and many other popular books and articles. In 1968 he published The Most Probable World. In his words, "It takes a hardheaded look at ten current trends, all deriving from science since Galileo, and then attempts to project them into the next few decades, say to the year 2000" (p. x). In fact, however, he grossly overestimated the speed of social change, so his predictions cover a far longer period.

This essay is entirely based on The Most Probable World because it presumably includes nearly all important predictions made in his earlier books. All page references are to this book.

1. Methodology

Chapter 1, "It Began with Galileo," emphasizes the novelty and importance of the scientific method as a means of creating factual truths, and clearly implies that the author wanted to make verifiable scientific predictions. He distinguished sharply between literary knowledge, including theology and philosophy, and modern science, which involves constant revision of images under the impact of refined observation (p. 4).

For Chase, social change is largely the result of technological progress. "When technology becomes dynamic, people are forced to change their accustomed ways" (p. 5). And technological progress is exponential (p. 16). Therefore, scientific futurists should pay special attention to important technological changes and try to anticipate their effects, both good and bad (p. 13).

Chase discussed very briefly the relationship of science, including scientific futurism, to ethics. He claimed that "science is perhaps the most moral of all man's disciplines" because it openly seeks the truth (p. 9). He evaded the question of whether ethics contains verifiable truths useful to science but not a product of scientific research. I have repeatedly argued that ethical truth claims are senseless and useless (see my book, Religion, Philosophy, and Science).

In Chapter II, "The Limits of Technology," Chase considered the alleged dangers of indefinitely continuing technological progress and the apparently resulting exponential growth of population, fuel consumption, pollution and other products of technological progress. He noted and endorsed John R. Platt's prediction that nearly all major exponential growth curves will soon become S-curves because external factors will slow down the relevant growth rates.

2. Population Growth

The most serious and threatening recent exponential growth curve is that of world population growth. In Chapters III and IV Chase described the reasons for, and the current rate of, this growth, and how this rate differs from country to country. He predicted that, "Long before the end of another century [2067], the S-curve wil take over due to lack of food" or to "birth control" (p. 33). He forecast that the world population total will peak at a level which "could hardly exceed 10 billion" (p. 35). Later he predicted a peak of 7 billion by 2025 (p. 229).

He expected that, "In Asia, Africa, and Latin America, it is [lack of] food which will eventually limit the growth of people" (p. 41). He predicted "dreadful famines" in the 1970s and 1980s. These are very dubious predictions. Since he wrote (1967), birth control has done far more than famine to limit population growth in these regions, and may continue to play this major role.

In his "mind-stretching" epilogue he forecast that the world population annual growth rate will decline to 0.7% by 2000 A.D. because improved methods of birth control will have become "universally available" (p. 229). I believe that this was an over-optimistic prediction.

Chase anticipated that future famines caused by overpopulation would cause "acute political upheavals" in "the Hungry World" (p. 208). Such upheavals are likely whether or not famines occur.

3. Pollution

Chase devoted Chapter 5 to a description of current pollution problems, which he considered to be very serious. He predicted over-optimistically that water pollution will be reduced in some coastal areas "within a decade" by "the coming desalting of sea water by nuclear energy" (pp. 66-67). He asserted that, "In due course industry must include the costs of pollution control" in production costs (p. 68). This implies that unpaid pollution costs will be transformed into paid costs, i.e., taxes, which vary with the pollution caused by production.

In his "mind-stretching" epilogue, he forecast that in the year 2001, the New York sky will be "a deep, unpolluted blue" and there will be no sonic booms, roaring motorcycles, screeching station wagons, or grunting bulldozers." Moreover, daffodils will bloom "by a roadside innocent of beer cans" and "the beaches of Long Island Sound" will be "white and clean, and shore birds...thick in the wide salt marshes," etc. (pp. 226-27). To me, these predictions seem merely over-optimistic as to speed of change, and not at all "mind-stretching." Here, as often elsewhere, Chase was looking forward one or two centuries, not merely three decades, as he claimed.

4. Natural Resources

Chase noted and rejected the pessimistic forecast of "the final exhaustion of natural resources within a century or so." In his opinion, "The probabilities... are strongly against any such trend. For a long time to come, new resources are likely to be developed more rapidly than old resources decline...nuclear power will become dominant.... The prospect of a stripped planet does not seem to be anywhere on the trend curve" (pp. 87-88).

Chase was very confident that nuclear power would largely replace power from other sources by 2000 A.D. "The curve which shows the bulk of inanimate energy coming from atomic power plants by the year 2000—assuming no nuclear war—cannot be seriously doubted" (p. x). Yet now (1983) it seems very unlikely that this confident prediction will be realized in the U.S. or the world by 2000 A.D.

He expected that "nuclear fusion" will soon be achieved; "few [scientists] believe it cannot be done" (p. 89). He predicted that growing use of nuclear energy will "make it possible to put cities anywhere ..." and thus facilitate a more flexible distribution of population, will "solve much of the fresh-water shortage...and even irrigate and reclaim deserts... will give industry lower costs for power...[and] will make practical the exploitation of minerals now buried in the earth's crust and at sea bottom" (p. 97).

Later he anticipated the construction of a "nuclear desalting plant at Greenwich" to supply New York City with fresh water free of chlorine, before 2000 A.D. (p. 226). As a result of such plants, "fear of drought" will by then have "disappeared forever, at least in coastal areas."

Chase forecast that men will learn how to create many scarce raw materials synthetically. "The final solution to raw materials which are growing scarce, and one a good deal more realistic than mining the moon, is to <u>create them synthetically</u>.... Atomic building blocks can be extracted from common materials, such as sand or stone and, with abundant energy, fashioned into any element or compound we desire.... This will not happen tomorrow, but it is on the trend curve" (p. 96).

5. Automation and Unemployment

Chase devoted two chapters (9 and 10) to a discussion of the effect of future mechanization and automation on work and unemployment. He predicted indefinite continued growth in such technologies, and also predicted, less positively, that such growth will not cause excessive unemployment.

"Computers and automatic mechanisms have already taken over a great deal of routine work, such as bank bookkeeping, and they are expected to take over a great deal more. Not only large plants and offices will be computerized, but also small organizations, as the hardware becomes less costly" (p. 136). He forecast that "Computers will soon be at work in the field of preventive medicine, undertaking diagnosis, and saving the time of doctors, technicians and nurses." Moreover, "Middle management seems to be in for a rough future as computers take over the logic of decision making" (p. 130).

Nevertheless, "We are reasonably safe in concluding that there will be enough new fields of work...to keep unemployment in bounds for years to come..." (p. 147). I think he should have been more positive in his prediction that mechanization and automation will not cause net unemployment.

6. Economic Progress

Chase predicted continued rapid economic progress throughout the world, primarily as a result of increased use of nuclear energy. In his opinion, "we can reasonably expect from nuclear energy" that it will "industrialize the low-energy world, two thirds of mankind, and virtually equalize living standards everywhere." Poverty will be "obliterated..." As a result, "every nation will be a Have nation," and "economic rivalries between nations" will be reduced (p. 97). Moreover, by the year 2001 the main human struggle will be "with temptations of material abundance rather than with the deprivations of scarcity." Therefore, economic textbooks will be "rewritten on this principle," presumably as the theory of abundance.

I believe that this economic forecast exaggerates the importance of nuclear energy and grossly overestimates the rate of future economic progress. Moreover, as an economist, I can not understand why the growth of wealth should change the nature of economic theory. In both rich and poor countries economics deals primarily with the allocation of scarce resources and the distribution of scarce income.

Later in his book Chase contradicted his overoptimistic predictions on economic progress by explaining that, "We can be reasonably sure that the years will be rough up to the end of the century; sure that affluent citizens dedicated to having total fun and total comfort will be most uncomfortably disappointed" (p. 200). This is a very vague forecast. Scientific futurists ought to try to make their predictions more precise and, therefore, more easily verifiable.

7. Urban Planning

In Chapter 6, "Megalopolis," Chase described some of the major contemporary urban problems—pollution, congestion, crime, alienation, etc.—and suggested, very hesitantly, that they would be partially solved by substituting electric cars for internal combustion cars, by reducing private car use, by expanding mass transit, and by constructing planned, decentralized new towns and cities. "A number of countertrends [to megalopolization] are already discernible...The major one is the dawning attempt to remove automobiles from all, or part, of the core city...Parallel to this is the 'new towns' movement, whereby brand new satellite communities are built around the core city..." (p. 82). Later he forecast a dozen such satellites around New York City by 2000 A.D. (p. 227).

In his Epilogue he anticipated that by the year 2000 no private automobiles will be permitted in Manhattan. Electric buses, trucks, fuel-cell taxis and bicycles on special paths will then be the sole aboveground vehicles. Moreover, "a good half of New York City's area" will consist of open space, due to "the Great Demolition of the 1980's," and city population will be down to five million (p. 227). Here again he greatly overestimated the speed of social change, but, otherwise, his forecasts were plausible.

8. Economic Structure

In Chapter 8, "The Mixed Economy," Chase explained that all advanced countries have long been moving towards a mixed economy, and predicted that they will continue to do so. Apparently he meant that public and non-profit sectors of the economy would grow faster than the private for-profit sector in capitalist economies, and vice-versa in communist economies. "The trend towards a mixed economy is massive not only in the U.S., but within...Russia. It moves, however, from opposite poles. In the U.S. the public sector is expanding; in the U.S.S.R. it is shrinking" (p. 99).

In the 16 years since Chase wrote these words, there has been a notable expansion of U.S. social security and welfare programs, especially in health care fields, which has already partially confirmed his forecast. I predict a long-continued further expansion of the public sector in advanced capitalist states.

Chase was unusually specific and prescient in his forecast on Chinese economic evolution. "Give China another decade...and her ideological convictions, like those of the Russians, may suffer considerable change" (p. 115). The cultural revolution came to a sudden end about ten years after this forecast was made.

9. Money and Credit

Chase had almost nothing to say about money and banking, but he forecast the creation by 2000 A.D. of a "computerized credit system to which every American citizen belongs" and through which he receives his income and pays all bills without handling money (p.226). He should have explained that this would make the use of paper money and checks unnecessary, but he did not do so. Moreover, he greatly overestimated the speed at which this reform will be achieved.

10. Advertising

In his Epilogue Chase anticipated that by the year 2000 the weight of the New York Times, Sunday edition, will have fallen from eight pounds in 1967 to "just half a pound," due mainly to the drastic reduction of competitive advertising. Moreover, there will be "no commercials on television," which will be supported by taxes debited directly to personal bank accounts (p. 226).

11. The Trend Towards World Government

Chase forecast that the proliferation of nuclear weapons "is likely to speed up as the Hungry World grows more crowded and hungrier...unless halted by a very rugged agreement" (p. 157). However, he was cautiously optimistic about the achievement of such an agreement enforced by a strong world government. He predicted six steps towards this goal. "From nationalism to regionalism, to internationalism, supernationalism the United Nations, the world court, finally to

genuine world government—at least for disarmament...
—this seems to be the political trend, if Armegeddon
does not intervene" (p. 176).

Later, he forecast that, "The most immediate step
would seem to be a firm agreement between the U.S. and
Russia to halt the spread of nuclear weapons. Beyond
that would come action to the same end by all members
of the Nuclear Club" (p. 198). Still later he anticipated that, "As a result of the steady growth of the
mixed economy, the opposing ideologies, of Communism
and the Radical Right [will] have all but withered
away" by 2001 A.D. (p. 228).

He also predicted that "the several military establishments will gradually decline into national
police forces: [because] they no longer have a useful
function against other nations" (p. 179).

In the "mind-stretching" epilogue to his book,
Chase described the United Nations of 2000 A.D. as
follows: "It has a powerful legislative body responsible to no nation but to mankind, and the whole organization is intensively devoted to settling disputes between nations, enforcing disarmament, and balancing
the world economy. Its lordly budget of over $100
billion a year comes from royalties on various supra-
national resources, drawn from the sea, from Antarc-
tica, and from the earth's mantle" (p. 227). This
forecast is very unlikely to come true by the year
2000, but it might come true within another century or
two.

Incidentally, he also predicted a nuclear war in
Southeast Asia in the early 1970's, a forecast which
almost came true.

12. Comment

In this book, Stuart Chase was a cautiously
optimistic futurist, except when estimating the rate
of future social change. He made no bold predictions
about coming economic disaster or utopia, and predicted the continuance of only the most obvious major
social trends. He ignored many social trends he had
discussed in earlier books like The Tragedy of Waste,
The Economy of Abundance, and The Proper Study of
Mankind. The Most Probable World is one of his least
original and stimulating books. Moreover, the title
is misleading because much less than one tenth of the
text is devoted to predictions, the rest being a discussion of current social problems. However, most of
the predictions he made are plausible and reasonable.

DANIEL BELL AS A FUTURIST

Daniel Bell (b1919) a professor of sociology at Harvard (formerly at Columbia) has long been a leader in the development and academic acceptance of the new social science, scientific futurism. He formulated his novel concept of "the post-industrial society" in 1962, and in 1965 was appointed chairman of the Commission on the Year 2000 which produced five volumes of "working papers." He wrote a stimulating "Foreword" to my book, The Next 500 Years (1967).

Bell has been a prolific author. I have made no effort to review all of his writings. This essay is based largely on his influential book, The Coming of Post-Industrial Society, A Venture in Social Forecasting (1973) because I believe it summarizes his previous conclusions on the future. All page references are to this book.

Bell tried to draw a clear distinction between forecasting and prediction. "Though the distinction is arbitrary, it has to be established. Prediction usually deals with events...Forecasting...[with] regularities and recurrences...or...persisting trends..." (pp. 3-4). I have been unable to find a dictionary which makes this distinction. Those I have checked treat forecast as a synonym for predict. It is important to distinguish between predicting events and predicting trends, but not to distinguish between predict and foretell.

Bell asserted then, "Forecasting is possible where there are regularities and recurrences of phenomena (those are rare), or where there are persisting trends.... Necessarily...one deals with probabilities and an array of possible projections...at crucial points these trends become subject to choice (and increasingly...conscious interventions by men with power).... To put it a different way: forecasting is possible only where one can assume a high degree of rationality on the part of men who influence events...What use, then, do forecasts have? Though they cannot predict results, they can specify the constraints, or limits, within which policy decisions can be effective" (p. 4).

Bell described three kinds of social forecasting: "the extrapolation of social trends, the identification of historical 'keys' that turn new levers of social change, and projected changes in major social frameworks" (p. 7). He restricted himself to the latter. "The idea of the post-industrial society, which is the subject of this book, is a social forecast about a change in the social framework of Western society" (p. 9). This restriction explains why he failed to make forecasts in many areas treated by other futurists.

Bell also asserted that, "What a venture in forecasting can do is to pose an agenda of questions, not a panoply of answers" (p. 483), which seems to rule out "social forecast about a change in the social framework of Western society." In fact, nearly all of his 520-page book is devoted to past social trends and to current and future social problems. Less than 2% is devoted to the statement of forecasts about the social framework.

There is a serious fallacy in Bell's implication that it is possible to forecast future new problems without predicting events and/or social trends. New problems will arise only as a result of events and social trends, and one must therefore be able to predict these events and trends in order to predict the resulting new social problems.

One can, of course, assume that nearly all current social problems will remain unsolved, and therefore become future social problems. It is extraordinarily easy to forecast such future problems. I do not believe that Bell meant to make, or state the need for, such easy and almost superfluous forecasts. But if he meant to forecast new social problems without predicting events and trends, he committed the fallacy explained above.

1. The Term Post-Industrial

Daniel Bell was one of the first writers to use the term post-industrial society to denote the stage of social evolution which will follow the industrial society. This term is unsuitable for two reasons. First, it does not tell us much about the society it denotes because it is not descriptive, like the term industrial society. Secondly, it is illogical to use different bases or methods for naming different stages in any series of stages.

If the term industrial society is used because it describes the major form of economic production, then the name of other stages in this series should also describe the major form of economic production in the stages which they denote. To call the stage after industrial society the post-industrial society is as uninformative and illogical as to call the stage after feudalism the post-feudal society, or to call the industrial society the post-agricultural society. Finally, use of the term <u>post-industrial</u> suggests that the stage following it should be called the post-post-industrial society, and so on indefinitely.

Since Bell used the term <u>post-industrial society</u> to denote a society in which more workers are employed in service industries than in agriculture and industry combined, he should have called this society "the service society." For the same reason, he should have called the stage preceding the industrial society "the agricultural society," not the "pre-industrial society."

2. The Rise of the Post-Industrial Society

The most important forecast in this book is about the rise of a new form of society, the post-industrial society, in all advanced countries.

"The thesis advanced in this book is that in the next 30 to 50 years we will see the emergence of...'the post-industrial society'...it will be a major feature of the 21st century, in the social structures of the U.S., Japan, the Soviet Union, and Western Europe" (p. x). He later explained that "1945 to 1950 were the 'birth years,' symbolically, of the post-industrial society" (p. 346). He also noted that, "As a social system, post-industrial society does not 'succeed' capitalism or socialism, but like bureaucratization, cuts across both" (p. 483). In other words, Bell forecast that both capitalist and communist countries will eventually become post-industrial.

Bell offered three different, but partly repetitive, overall outline descriptions of the coming post-industrial society, one in his introduction, one in Chapter 6, and one near the end of his book. All are significant.

In his Introduction (p. 14), Bell specified "five dimensions, or components, of a post-industrial society":

"1. Economic sector: the change from goods-producing to a service economy;

"2. Occupational distribution: the pre-eminence of the professional and technical class;

"3. Axial principle: the centrality of theoretical knowledge as the source of innovation and of policy formulation for the society;

"4. Future orientation: the control of technology and technology assessment;

"5. Decision-making: the creation of a new intellectual technology."

If all advanced countries will move towards the creation or further development of a post-industrial society, as Bell explicitly and repeatedly predicted, it follows that he implied that most or all of these separate trends or events will continue or be fully achieved.

Chapter 6 includes "Table 6-1, Stratification and Power" (p. 359), which shows how Bell believed six major social characteristics change as a society progresses from "pre-industrial," to "industrial," to "post-industrial." The major economic resource changes from land, to machinery, and then to knowledge. The major "social locus" changes from farm, to business firm, to the university and research institute. The "dominant figures" change from landholders and military officers, to business men, and then to scientists. The "means of power" change from force, to politics, to technical-political forces and legal rights. The means of "access" to power change from inheritance and military seizure, to inheritance, patronage, and education; and then to education and co-optation. These assertions too are major long-run social predictions.

At the end of his book, Bell offered another, largely repetitive, overall description of the coming post-industrial society. "In descriptive terms, there are three components: in the economic sector, it is a shift from manufacturing to services; in technology, it is the centrality of the new science-based industries; in sociological terms, it is the rise of new technical elites and the advent of a new principle of stratification...[thus] it means...a changeover from a goods-producing society to an information or knowledge society;...a change...from empiricism...to theoretical knowledge for directing innovation and the formulation of policy" (p. 487).

3. The Growth of a Service Economy

Bell devoted Chapter II (44 pages) to his chief economic forecast. It is entitled "From Goods to Services: The Changing Shape of the Economy."

He noted that growth rates differ from service to service, and that the services rendered by household servants have long been diminishing. He explained that the growth of "health, education, research, and government" will be "decisive" in the creation of the post-industrial society (p.15). He apparently meant that the value or cost of these services will grow much faster than GNP in advanced countries for many decades.

Incidentally, economists define the term economic goods so that it includes economic services; thus Bell's subtitle, "From Goods to Services," is objectionable. He should have written of the shift from tangible goods to services.

Bell noted that "the increasing replacement of men by machines" is continually reducing the relative importance of industrial workers. He suggested that, by 2000 A.D., "the proportion of factory workers in the labor force may be as small as the proportion of farmers today" (p. 125). He had previously reported the proportion of U.S. workers in "agriculture" in 1969 as 5.2%, and the proportion of workers in "industry" as 33.7% (p. 17). Thus his suggested change in the relationship between these proportions seems radical and unrealistic, but he may have meant to include only a minor part of all industrial workers in his class of factory workers.

Bell quoted Victor Fuch's claim that, "For as long as we have records on the industrial distribution of the labor force, we find a secular tendency for the percentage accounted for by the service sector to rise," and said that "it rose from 30% to 60% between 1900 and 1968 (p. 129). He forecast a rise to 70% by 1980. These figures suggest that relatively little further rise is possible, and that therefore this trend will not be very important in the U.S. during the next century or two, but Bell did not note this implication.

The chief reason for this U.S. trend during the past 200 years has been the technological revolution in agriculture which has reduced the percentage of farm workers from over 80% of the work force to about 5%. The continuance of this revolution cannot cause much more shift of labor from agriculture to services.

The introduction of more labor-saving machinery in industries producing tangible goods may shift some labor from such industries to service industries, but this effect will be weakened by the growing mechanization of service industries—computers, electronic payment, new laboratory machines, etc. Moreover, it may be necessary to use a much larger share of the labor force to find and extract oil, coal, and other minerals. Finally, the socialization and/or rationalization of major service industries like trade, insurance, banking, advertising, real estate brokerage, etc., may slow down or end the shift of labor from tangible-good production to service industries. For all of these reasons, I think Bell greatly overestimated the importance of the effect of future relative growth of service industries on the structure of the U.S. economy.

On the other hand, he ignored or seriously underestimated future shifts in workers within the service sector. The proportion of workers employed in education, health care, R and D, and government will probably continue to grow for decades, as he forecast, but most of this shift will probably be from other service industries—trade, finance, etc.—not from tangible-goods industries.

It is noteworthy that some major industries producing nonpersonal services—railroads, airlines, telephone systems, other public utilities, etc.—resemble factories much more than they resemble schools, hospitals, and other industries producing personal services. Therefore, it is misleading to group all service industries together and contrast them with industries producing tangible goods. The growth of giant public utilities is not evidence of the rise of a post-industrial society.

4. The Productivity Trend

According to Bell, "The simple and obvious fact is that productivity and output grow much faster in goods than in services.... Productivity in services, because it is a relation between persons, rather than between man and machine, will inevitably be lower than...in industry. This is true in almost all services" (p. 155). Here we have an implicit forecast that productivity growth in almost all services, and the service sector as a whole, will continue to grow slower than in industry. For reasons previously stated, this prediction is dubious.

Bell explained that, "As a larger portion of the labor force shifts into services, there is inevitably a greater drag on productivity and growth,..." (p. 157). Since the shift from industry to services has long been in progress, this implies that the rate of economic growth has long been declining, in all advanced countries. But in fact growth rates in nearly all such countries have been higher since 1950 than ever before.

5. The International Production Shift

Bell suggested that large multi-national corporations, half of whom are U.S. controlled, will long continue to transfer their manufacturing operations from the U.S. to poorer countries. He explained that "the multi-national corporation not only transfers capital and managerial know-how abroad; it has become an organizational mechanism for the transfer of manufacturing production to low-wage countries and its managerial techniques and technology to the advancing countries while retaining control—and earnings—at both ends.... In the nature of the product cycle, more and more manufacturing of the standardized sort will move to the poorer sections of the world while the post-industrial societies concentrate on knowledge-creating and knowledge-processing industries" (p. 484). Therefore, "as American [manufacturing] management and capital find their most efficient use abroad, and the employment of foreign labor for manufacturing [grows], the U.S. too, as Paul Samuelson points out, might becomed a 'headquarters economy'" (p. 485). This growing division of labor between rich and poor nations will help to make the U.S. economy more of a service economy.

6. The Growth of the Professional and Technical Classes

Chapter III, "The Dimensions of Knowledge and Technology: The New Class Structure of Post-Industrial Society," is devoted to an elaboration of Bell's second major general long-run forecast, namely that the professional and technical classes will long continue to become more numerous and more powerful in all advanced countries.

In his introduction he had previously stated that "the most startling [occupational] change has been the growth of [U.S.] professional and technical employment —jobs that usually require some college education—at a rate twice that of the average. In 1940 there were 3.9 million such persons...by 1964 the number had risen to 8.6 million; and it is estimated that by 1973 there will be 13.2 million..." He added that "the growth rate of the scientists and engineers has been triple that of the working population" (p. 17). These past trends lent strong support to his forecast that they will continue.

The second major reason why the professional and technical classes will long continue to grow in relative numbers and influence is that knowledge will continue to grow. Bell devoted several pages to the "law of exponential increase" of scientific knowledge; and implied that this "law" would long continue to be valid (pp. 177-87).

However, he discussed and rejected the common claim that "we are living in a time of a 'constantly' accelerating rate of technological change,' which is creating new and 'explosive' social problems" (p. 191). He denied that it is possible "to measure" 'the pace of change.' There is no composite index..." (p. 192). I believe he was right on both points.

A third major reason why the professional and technical classes will continue to grow relatively fast is that since 1945 there has been a 300% increase in the proportion of U.S. youth who attend college. Thus, the mere maintenance of recent attendance rates will continuously increase the share of college graduates and alumni in the population for the next 50-60 years. Bell offered detailed figures on this past growth (pp. 121-31), and noted that "we may see a doubling of student enrollments" by 2100 A.D. (p. 246).

He also forecast that the U.S. would then have "about a million persons...holding a Ph.D degree" (p. 242). Finally, he repeated his former forecast that "the university increasingly becomes the primary institution of the post-industrial society" because it "serves as the source for the specialized intellectual personnel needed in government and public organizations;..." (p. 246-47).

7. The Rise of Science

Bell forecast that the coming rise of the professional classes would include an even faster rise of scientists in both numbers and influence. He devoted some 30 pages (378-408) to the past and probable future growth of science. He asserted that, "The roots of post-industrial society lie in the inexorable influence of science on productive methods..." (p. 378), and forecast that "the ethos of science is the emerging ethos of post-industrial society" (p. 386). It will therefore serve the new society as the Protestant ethic served rising capitalism.

He also noted the recent bureaucratization of science, and forecast further bureaucratization. "Given the large-scale growth of science...the enormous amounts of money needed...and its centrality in the post-industrial society, the bureaucratization of science is inevitable" (pp. 404-05). He added that "state intervention" in R and D "is inevitable," for the same reasons (p. 408).

8. Meritocracy and Equality

The Coming of Post-Industrial Society includes a 48-page section entitled "Meritocracy and Equality" in which Bell reviewed and criticized arguments for and against various forms and combinations of meritocracy and equality. While he tried to restrict himself to a statement of problems rather than predictions, he did make two brief forecasts.

First, he explained that, "The post-industrial society, in its initial logic, is a meritocracy. Differential status and differential income are based on technical skills and higher education" (p. 409). Since he had predicted the coming of the post-industrial society, this implies the prediction that society will become much more meritocratic.

Secondly, he rejected the argument for complete equality of results, but forecast the adoption of minimum incomes, i.e., income floors, to make personal incomes less unequal. He explained that income "differences can be tempered" and that "the politics of contemporary society makes this even more likely in the future. Wealth allows a few to enjoy what many cannot have: but this difference can—and will—be mitigated by a social minimum" (p. 455).

He also claimed that, "A striking fact of Western society over the past 200 years has been the steady decrease in the disparity among persons..." (p. 451). But he did not explicitly use this trend to predict the future, as he should have.

9. Health Care Predictions

In addition to forecasting that the health care industry would continue to grow faster than the GNP in all advanced countries, Bell forecast "Within medicine ...the inevitable end of the 'fee-for-service' relationship," which will be "replaced by some kind of insurance-cum-government payment scheme." This means "the end of the doctor as an individual entrepreneur and the increasing centrality of the hospital and group practice" (p. 154). I agree with these forecasts.

10. The Growth of Government

Chapter 4, "The Subordination of the Corporation: ..." explains how and why the profit-seeking activities of private corporations cause external costs and benefits and other social problems which increasingly justify more government control over or operation of economic activities. He asserted that "air pollution... the planning of cities, the control of congestion, the organization of health care, the cleaning up of environmental pollution, the support of education—all these, necessarily, become matters of public policy..." Therefore, "the public sector of the society has to be expanded..." (p. 284).

He also forecast that, "In the post-industrial society, production and business decisions will be subordinated to, or will derive from, other forces in society; the crucial decisions regarding the growth of the economy and its balance will come from government ..." (p. 344).

Much later in the book Bell stressed the supreme importance of this change. "The decisive social change taking place in our time...is the subordination of the economic function to the political order.... The autonomy of the economic order (and the power of the men who run it) is coming to an end..." (p. 373). This is probably both the most important and the most plausible prediction in this book.

My chief criticism of his discussion of this forecast is that he failed to state and develop some major arguments supporting it. For instance, he failed to argue that much more government control over the economy will be needed to achieve: (1) prices equal to marginal costs in decreasing-cost industries, (2) a stable price level, (3) rationalization of inefficient industries, (4) a less unequal distribution of income and wealth, (5) more effective crime prevention and detection, and (6) more freedom of job and career choice.

Furthermore, it is very odd that this predicted "decisive social change" is not listed as a major feature of the coming post-industrial society in any of his summary descriptions of this new social order.

11. Technocrats vs. Politicians

In Chapter 6, "'Who Will Rule?' Politicians and Technocrats in the Post-Industrial Society," Bell reviewed the history of the theory that technocrats will rise to political and industrial power in the new industrial or post-industrial society. He quoted and/or criticized Hegel, Durkheim, Weber, Parsons, Saint-Simon, Marshall, Valery, and Veblen. He concluded that, while technocrats will increase their influence in business and government, they will not rule post-industrial societies. " Though the weights of the class system may shift, the nature of the political system...will not. In the next few decades, the political arena will become more decisive...for the two fundamental reasons I have indicated...crucial decisions...are made by the government, rather than through the market; in addition, we have become a communal society, in which many more groups now seek to establish their social rights...through the political order" (p. 364).

He also asserted that, "It is not the technocrat who ultimately holds power, but the politician" (p. 360). While he used the present tense in this sentence, the context suggests that he was making a forecast. However, he did forecast that, "increasingly, in the post-industrial society, technical skill becomes an overriding condition of competence for place and position" (p. 361).

I believe Bell underestimated the future long-run growth in the economic and political power of social scientists. For reasons explained in my book, <u>Government by Experts</u> (1972), I predict that more and more political decisions will be assigned to social scientists until they become, as a group, much more politically important than mere politicians.

12. Comments

Although Bell's use of the term <u>post-industrial society</u> is questionable, his comprehensive theory of recent and future social evolution is plausible, original, and stimulating. He was perhaps the first to properly stress the growing future importance of the university in society. On the whole, he made a notable contribution to futurism. However, he failed to discuss many major future trends, such as the rise of group child care, birth control, feminism, sexual freedom, civil rights, atheism, free distribution, etc.

R. L. HEILBRONER AS A FUTURIST

Robert L. Heilbroner (b1919) is a distinguished American economist, a professor at the New School, whose first book, The Worldly Philosophers (1953), a lucid history of economic doctrine, became an academic best seller. His third book, The Future as History (1960), was the result of an interest in futurism which has apparently grown steadily since then, and has resulted in three more books on the future, Between Capitalism and Socialism (1970), An Inquiry into the Human Prospect (1974), and Business Civilization in Decline (1976).

In this essay I shall concentrate on the last two books, especially on the last, because they present his latest predictions and because, between them, they restate nearly all of the predictions made in previous books. Both are brief and a pleasure to read, which is one reason I have chosen to review them.

Although Business Civilization in Decline was published in 1976, it consists of essays published between 1965 and 1974, and therefore largely antedates An Inquiry into the Human Prospect. But I shall quote it more frequently because it offers a more systematic and comprehensive body of predictions concerning future social trends. All page references not otherwise attributed are to Business Civilization in Decline.

1. Futurist Methodology

In the Preface to Business Civilization in Decline Heilbroner acknowledged a major indebtedness to Marx and Schumpeter, whose theories of social evolution he repeatedly referred to. "My own assessment," he explained, "draws on both Marxian and Schumpetrian insights, without following either slavishly" (p. 10). He noted that Schumpeter had stressed the Veblenian theory that capitalism creates a "cast of mind" which is "rational, calculating, skeptical" and which,"when turned against the pretensions of property...would reveal them to be as empty as those of nobility" (p. 10).

Heilbroner himself suggested a new or revised theory of social change. He criticized the Marxist theory that economic or technological evolution is the chief cause of social evolution, and claimed that political evolution is an equally important underlying cause of social evolution. He explained that, "the radical view sees the economy as the engine and the government as the caboose in the evolution of capitalism—indeed, perhaps of all socio-economic systems. I believe the process is more accurately likened to a train in which there are two engines, one economic, one political, capable of pulling in different directions a well as coordinating their efforts." He argued that, "Only such a conception...can help us understand the extraordinary variety of institutions ...of countries with private property and market bases" (p. 30).

However, the theory that political evolution is a separate basis of social evolution does not help to explain social evolution unless one has a theory of inevitable or probable political evolution—such as monarchy, democracy, government by experts. Heilbroner offered no such theory of political evolution. He did restate and endorse the idea that economic progress would create a dominant managerial class (p. 56), but this is not a theory of independent political evolution. And in other cases also, as we shall see later, his political forecasts were based on underlying economic forecasts.

Like all scientific futurists, Heilbroner relied heavily on the projection of long-run historical and statistical trends, but, more than any previous futurists except Marx, he called attention to, and based predictions on, probable future conflicts in such trends, for instance, the coming conflict between economic growth and resource exhaustion.

In Business Civilization in Decline Heilbroner divided his predictions into three "stages of change," (1) "the immediate future—the next ten years or so," (2) "the middle distance, say 25 to 50 years ahead," and (3) "the long run" (pp. 11, 32, 41, 101). But, like most futurists, he made short-run predictions which were really long-run predictions. Moreover, it is more convenient to classify his predictions by subject matter, as is done below.

Incidentally, he asserted that it is more difficult to predict middle-distance trends than to predict either immediate-future or long-run trends because we have "an excess of knowledge" about the middle distance, and because "the two most persuasive predictions" for the middle distance—capitalist collapse and successful capitalist reform—"have both been tried and found wanting" (pp. 41-44). I find both of these reasons quite unconvincing.

2. Economic Planning

The author begins Chapter I with these words: "Capitalism is drifting into planning.... The problem is to interpret [this fact].... That is what I seek to do.... It will be my major thesis that the political apparatus within capitalism is steadily growing, enhancing its power, and usurping functions formerly delegated to the economic sphere—not to undo, but to preserve that sphere" (p. 17).

But political expansion and economic planning are two entirely different things. For instance, political expansion and usurpation could continue until an economy is entirely socialist, and all production of vendible goods could still be controlled by profits and losses, without any economic planning of such production, as I explained in <u>Liberal Socialism</u> (1974).

Apparently, he used the term <u>planning</u> to include <u>all</u> "state regulation and control" (p. 35), a definition which makes all advanced capitalist economies planned economies. It also implies that less planning would be needed under socialism than under capitalism because under socialism business managers would have no or less profit incentive to engage in anti-social policies. Economic planning ought to be defined as the substitution of centralized price, wage, output, etc., control for market or profit-loss control, not as mere regulation of markets, hours of labor, safety practices, etc., which has long existed in all capitalist countries.

Economic planning of outputs will continue to increase as the output of free economic goods, those not sold for a price, continues to grow, because the outputs of free goods cannot be governed by profits and losses, but Heilbroner ignored this major valid reason for predicting the growth of economic planning. He even failed to predict a large long-run increase in the relative output of free goods, one of the most likely and most important future long-run social trends (see my book <u>Free Goods</u>, 1976).

Government regulation and control of private industries producing price goods will probably continue to increase as long as private industry survives, but government regulation of industry may well decline after private ownership and competition have been replaced by government monopolies run by professional, socially-minded, salaried managers who will be more aware of social costs and benefits in their industries than their political superiors.

Heilbroner gave three reasons, each a separate prediction, as to why government regulation of private industry is very likely to continue growing in the immediate future: (1) "There is a continued propensity of capitalism to develop generalized disorders that require government intervention," (2) "There is a tendency to develop serious localized disorders," and (3) "There are dangers imposed by a constricting environment" (pp. 32-33). In fact, this is a very vague and incomplete list of the future social trends and events which will require increased government intervention. For instance, it ignores growing needs for safety laws, consumer protection laws, R and D, rationalization of industry, standardization of products, crime prevention, military mobilization of industry, etc. Moreover, the three trends mentioned are long-run, not merely "immediate-future" trends.

3. Government Ownership

Heilbroner predicted that, in certain cases and industries, government control will not suffice to achieve national goals, and, therefore, government ownership will be adopted in the immediate future. He wrote that, "It is evident that railroads, large banks ...cannot go bankrupt without creating a vast wreckage. I therefore suspect that the trend towards government ownership of unprofitable private activities... will increase further..." (p. 33).

Later, still referring to "the immediate future," he suggested that "the most effective means of planning may be mixed productive sectors in which certain units are nationalized to serve as national policy setters ..." (p. 37). But, as previously noted, state enterprises may use profits and losses, not economic planing to control their outputs, and this is true even if they receive large state subsidies. Moreover, I cannot understand how subsidized state firms which practice planning could set feasible policies for competitors who must earn profits. Finally, this prediction is more a "middle distance" or "long-run" forecast than an "immediate future" prediction.

4. Economic Growth

Heilbroner predicted that economic growth in advanced countries would continue through both the immediate future and the middle distance, presumably at decreasing rates, but that it would end "within a century," i.e., before 2076 (pp. 101-2). This is probably both the most important and the most dubious prediction in this book.

To support this prediction, he argued that "industrial growth is an exponential process" and no exponential process can continue indefinitely (p. 102). But overall economic growth has never been exponential for long. Exponential growth in one industry is usually partly offset by growth rate declines in other industries.

Heilbroner also argued that growing depletion of irreplaceable natural resources—coal, oil, iron, etc.—would stop world economic growth before 2076 A.D. (pp. 105-06). But in a book published the same year, The Next 200 Years (1976), Herman Kahn reached the opposite conclusion, and supported his conclusion with far more, and far more persuasive, facts about the probable future supplies of such resources.

Heilbroner himself mentioned several ways in which the exhaustion of irreplaceable resources could be delayed—"the intervention of new extractive technologies, the development of synthetic chemistry, the discovery of means of disposing of vast mountains of tailings and wastes, the extension of capabilities for recycling materials" (p. 104), and this list is very incomplete. Moreover, he called the factors he listed "imponderables," which suggests that he could not give them proper weight in predicting the end of economic growth.

Every increase in the relative real cost of any irreplaceable mineral induces some substitution of other raw materials, some redesign of finished goods to use less of that mineral, and some substitution of less costly finished products for those containing the mineral in question. Moreover, scientists and engineers will continue indefinitely to get more heat out of each unit of coal or oil, and to reduce the need for heat in each manufacturing process. And economists and statesmen will learn how to rationalize our economy in such a way as to make all productive activities ever more efficient, for instance by standardization of products, horizontal and vertical integration, crime reduction, fire and accident prevention, more multi-shift operation, reduction of harmful or useless advertising, etc.

Finally, Heilbroner argued that the growth of pollution, especially heat pollution and the resulting disastrous climate changes, would stop world economic growth within a century or two (p. 105). But so little is known about the degree and effects of future pollution that all predictions about such effects are premature and unjustified, as Kahn explained in his book. Moreover, by the time we learn what such effects can be, we may also have learned how to limit or prevent them.

It may seem that growing use of solar heat could prevent climate changes due to future heat pollution because such use does not cause heat pollution. In The Human Prospect (1976), Heilbroner cited estimates that continued exponential growth of energy use "would reach 100% of the total solar flux" within 250 years

(p. 55n). Hence, maximum use of solar power can merely postpone the heat-pollution-caused end of growth in energy use. In any case, "Difficulties of a much more matter-of-fact kind—resource availability, energy shortages, the pollution resulting from noxious by-products of industrial production—are likely to exert their throttling effect long before a fatal, impassible barrier of irreversible climate damage is reached" (p. 55). Later in this book he forecast that "the citizenries of the wealthy nations will find themselves in a long period of declining physical output per capita...beginning perhaps as soon as the coming decade" (p. 88). This is a very dubious prediction.

5. Domestic Political Authoritarianism

Heilbroner predicted that the near future slowdown in U.S. economic growth would intensify domestic conflicts over the distribution of income. In The Human Prospect (1976) he forecast that these growing conflicts "would bring enormous inflationary pressures ...and would require the imposition of much stronger control measures than any that capitalism has yet succeeded in introducing..." He explained that, "In bluntest terms, the question is whether the Hobbesian struggle...would not impose intolerable strains on the representative democratic political apparatus..." He suggested that "some capitalist nations...may make the necessary structural changes without surrendering their democratic achievements," but, "for the majority...I do not see how one can avoid the conclusion that the required transformation will be likely to exceed the capabilities of representative democracy" (pp. 89-90). This reasoning is unconvincing because the transformation of a rural agricultural society into an urban industrial and service society was much more difficult than any future transformation is likely to be, and democracy grew throughout this difficult transformation.

Later in this book he predicted American social and political changes like those which occurred in China after 1948. "Indeed, I am persuaded that changes of at least this degree of penetration and revolutionary impact will be required within the time span" of 100 years. Moreover, "these behavioral alterations ...will have to allow for, or build on,...the 'hunger' for political authority and the 'fantasy' of political identification," presumably Maoism, which existed in China (p. 122).

6. Religious Change

Heilbroner forecast that "a new religious orientation" will be "a major force for the transformation of business civilization" into a post-capitalist system. This orientation will be "against the canons and precepts of our time," and toward a "wholly different conception of the meaning of life and a mode of social organization congenial to the encouragement of that life" (p. 119).

Since "a high degree of political authority will be inescapable" in this coming society, the new religion will be "nationalist, [and] authoritarian," as in China today (1976). "The deification of the state... seems therefore the most likely replacement for the deification of materialism that is the unacknowledged religion of our business culture.... What is crucial in the statist 'religion,' as I foresee it, is the elevation of the collective and communal destiny of man to the forefront of public consciousness, and the absolute subordination of private interests to public requirements" (pp. 119-120).

Since this prediction does not describe supernatural events, or belief in such events, the term _religious_ is misused. I think he was really predicting a change in popular attitude from self-seeking to benevolence. There is little if any scientific evidence that such a change has begun, will continue, and/ or will begin in the future. Therefore, this prediction seems to be largely or entirely based on wishful thinking.

Of course, as self-seeking men become more educated, they will increasingly recognize that social progress benefits most members of society, and will therefore become more interested in social reform, but this will not constitute a rejection of materialism or the adoption of a new religion.

In _The Human Prospect_ (1976), he restated his "religious" forecast in less theological language. "It is...possible that a post-industrial society would also turn in the direction of many pre-industrial societies —towards the exploration of inner states of experience.... Tradition and ritual...would probably once again assert their ancient claims as the guide to and solace of life" (p. 140). This forecast is implausible in advanced countries because there has been a trend in the opposite direction for centuries.

7. Wars of Redistribution

Since economic growth will cease throughout the world within a century, there will be "an intensification of international rivalry, as the poor nations seek in vain to gain economic parity with the rich ones, while possessing something that resembles parity in their ability to inflict hideous and perhaps irreparable military wounds [with nuclear weapons]." It would be possible to reduce or "avert" this tension by "a redistribution of wealth on a vast scale," but this will not occur. Nor can we look forward to the emergence of a world government capable of appeasing or controlling the poor nations. Therefore, the world will face "terrible threats of 'wars of redistribution'" (pp. 106-07).

In The Human Prospect (1976), Heilbroner gave more space to such possible "blackmail" of the rich nations. He predicted that "some nuclear capability will be in the hands of the major underdeveloped nations within the next few decades, and perhaps much sooner" (p. 42). Moreover, he explained that, "'wars of redistribution' may be the only way by which the poor nations can hope to remedy their condition (italics in original). But such wars are "the worst, not the most likely, possibility" (pp. 42-45).

He optimistically suggested that, "Even if nuclear blackmail is used, it need not lead to a global disaster unless it resulted in...nuclear conflict among the great powers. It is more plausible that a terrorist attack—for example the wiping out of a city in an advanced nation...—would serve as a stimulus to bring a substantial reduction in nuclear armaments coupled with worldwide nuclear inspections, especially in the 'dangerous' underdeveloped countries" (p. 45). This was his only intimation of world government.

8. Conventional Limited Wars

In the books I have read, Heilbroner made no prediction concerning a future nuclear war or wars between advanced countries, but in The Human Prospect (1974), he predicted more than one limited war. "As we have said, the danger of 'limited' war remains, and the probability of such wars is very high. The frequency of 'deadly quarrels' showed no signs of decline over the two centuries before 1940," and there have been over 16 minor wars since 1940. "Very probably wars on this [minor] scale, with this frequency of ocurrence, will continue as long as nation states continue to play their role as the main forms of mass social organization" (pp. 45-46). He did not forecast any solution to this problem, such as peaceful creation of a world government.

9. The End of Capitalism

Partly on the basis of his prediction that economic growth will stop within a century, Heilbroner predicted the demise of capitalism "in all advanced countries" within the long run of a century" (p. 107). In a later book, <u>Beyond Boom and Crash</u> (1978), he reduced this time period to 25 years (p. 88). He offered four specific reasons for this prediction.

First, "the increasingly severe constraints on industrial growth must bring to a halt the consuming passion of a business civilization for private expansion...[and] the end of corporate growth will bring about the progressive elimination of the profits that have been both the means and the end of the accumulation of private property" (p. 108).

This reason is weak because, even in a stable economy, profits can be steadily increased, or at least maintained, by means of cost-cutting innovations in methods of management and operation. Moreover, the author conceded that "a trustified, profitless, bureaucratic 'capitalism' is not unimaginable" (p. 109). Therefore, he offered a second reason, namely, that the coming end to economic growth will greatly intensify the continuing conflict over the distribution of personal income (pp. 109-10). He ignored the fact that it is possible to achieve a radical redistribution of U.S. income distribution under capitalism. Some researchers have reported that the inequality of income in Japan is only half that in the U.S., and inequality in Japan could be further drastically reduced without abandoning capitalism.

His third specific reason was that the previously predicted continuing increase of government control over private business, which he called planning, will gradually extinguish capitalism. He wrote that, "the inescapable rise of planning must also greatly strengthen the power of...technicians, scientists, and planners" and weaken that of capitalists. Thus, "the planification of capitalism...is also a source of its extinction in the long run" (p. 110).

His fourth specific reason for predicting the demise of capitalism within a century was "the prospective erosion of the 'spirit' of capitalism...[especially] a waning belief in the ability of a business civilization to provide social morale" (pp. 113-14). He considered that these factors were "imponderable," but nevertheless gave them weight in his argument.

The most remarkable fact about his prediction of the demise of capitalism is that it ignored nearly all of the economic waste due to capitalist competition, speculation, unemployment, inequality of education, inheritance, and undue limitations of R and D. He overlooked the most important reasons for the probable eventual demise of capitalism.

10. After Capitalism, What?

Near the end of Business Civilization in Decline, the author raised the question, "After Capitalism, What?" and answered, "Not...a 'revolution.' The demise of the business system is likely to proceed by degrees, insensibly altering a civilization that can be called 'capitalist' into one that, whatever its appelation, no longer bears sufficient resemblance to the system we know to enable us to call it by the same name. We project the image of a tightly controlled society where the traditional pillars of capitalism—the legitimacy of private property and the operation of the market system—have been amended beyond recognition, if not wholly superseded by state property and state directives.

"Is such a postcapitalist system to be described as 'fascism?' As 'socialism?' I suspect that these traditional terms have little applicability..." (pp. 117-18). However, in his book An Inquiry into the Human Prospect (1974), Heilbroner predicted "the eventual rise of 'iron' governments, probably of a military-socialist cast" (p. 39).

Unfortunately, he did not limit his prediction of no revolution to democratic advanced countries, where it seems most plausible. The prediction that this social change will occur without revolution in countries like Egypt, Argentina, and India is very implausible.

He also asserted that when "the threats of the environment eventually force a dismantling of large-scale industrial processes...political power is certain to be wielded without regard for any traditional criteria of a business system." Then, "the claims of rents and interests and profits, the play of the market, or the right to conduct 'private' enterprise will appear as archaic as the claims of royalty or nobility in the face of a democratic revolution" (pp. 110-11).

In sharp contrast, I predict that the threats of the environment will not force a dismantling of large-scale processes in the next century, and that the rising managerial class will continue to insist on the use of corrected profits, losses, rent, interest, and equilibrium prices as means of price-goods output and investment control under both capitalism and liberal socialism. Heilbroner seems unaware of the modern welfare economics of an ideal economy. For instance the optimum way to limit pollution is to impose pollution taxes, not to abandon equilibrium prices, profits, interest, etc.

11. Comments

Heilbroner's most stimulating prediction was that political evolution will influence future social trends as much as economic or technological evolution. However, he failed to offer any theory of independent political evolution—such as aristocracy, monarchy, and democracy. Marx and Engels had explained how technological evolution determines social and political evolution. Heilbroner suggested no alternative explanation of the causes of political evolution. But if we do not understand the causes of, and therefore cannot predict the course of, political evolution, the theory that such evolution largely determines social evolution cannot help us to predict social trends.

Heilbroner made several predictions about economic planning, but never defined it. He used it to denote so many different kinds of government behavior that his predictions about it are very ambiguous, and therefore unverifiable and unscientific.

He exaggerated both the short-run and the long-run future effects of natural resource depletion because he underestimated opportunities for material and product substitution, and for technological progress in exploiting oil resources and creating new resources.

HERMAN KAHN AS A FUTURIST

Herman Kahn (1922-83) was one of the most prolific and widely read writers on the future. He was also one of the most optimistic. I largely share his optimistic point of view, expecially on future long-run economic trends.
Herman Kahn was educated as a physicist at UCLA and Cal Tech, and was employed in the Physics Division of the Rand Corporation. The study of physics is not a good preparation for predicting social trends. Kahn's 1961 book, On Thermonuclear War, attracted wide attention. Later he founded and headed the Hudson Institute, a civilian think tank, and wrote several books on the future.
The following essay on Kahn as a futurist is based on two of his recent books, Things to Come and The Next 200 Years because I believe these works give a more comprehensive and up-to-date statement of his views on the future than any other sources. Since these two books cover largely different areas of the future, I shall discuss each of them separately in chronological order.
Both of these books were written by several authors. I credit their conclusions to Kahn because he was the senior author of both books, and presumably agreed with those major conclusions he did not himself formulate.

I. Comments on Things to Come

Things to Come, Thinking about the 70's and 80's (1972), was written by Herman Kahn and B. Bruce-Briggs, with the aid of the staff of the Hudson Institute. The subtitle suggests that this book deals only with short-run social trends, but in fact it discusses many major long-run trends, and I shall devote most of my comments to the latter.

1. The Multifold Trend

Chapter I, "The Multifold Trend in the Seventies and Eighties—The Macro-historical Perspective," deals only with future long-run historical trends. It contains a list of fifteen such trends. In preparing to write my Next 500 Years (1967) I searched the literature for such a list and could find none. And the authors of this list refer to no earlier list. I believe that long-run social trends are extremely important and I cannot understand why social scientists and historians have given them so little attention.

The authors did not call their list a list of long-run social trends. Rather they entitled it "The Long-term Multifold Trend of Western Culture," and wrote of "folds" in this trend. To me the term <u>multifold trend</u> seems meaningless, and the authors did not define it. A statistical trend has fluctuations, but not folds, and it cannot include or combine trends which have no common unit.

The authors explained that, "The long-term multifold trend in Western culture began approximately a thousand years ago, but not all the aspects of it can be traced back that far. Some can be first detected only a few hundred years ago; others go back almost the full millenium." This implies that the multifold trend is separate from and independent of each aspect of it. It also ignores the vital fact that many, perhaps most, of these aspects or trends are much older than a thousand years, which suggests the questions, "Can a multifold trend exist before or after any of its folds?" or, "Can its folds or aspects arise before a multifold trend?" To me, the term <u>multifold trend</u> is literally senseless because it has no observable referrent, and it is therefore impossible to conceive of any way to verify or disprove any statement about it.

It may be objected that this multifold trend is merely an average, or total of the fifteen separate trends he related to it. But an average or total of these trends cannot be prepared because they are not stated in common units (like dollars per person). And even if they were so stated, one would have to assign weights to each trend in order to obtain a significant average or total trend, and Kahn did not assign such weights.

2. Secularization

The fifteen individual continuing, and therefore future, long-run social trends listed under the confusing title, "The Long-term Multifold Trend in Western Culture," are very poorly stated. The first is:
"1. Increasingly sensate (empirical, this worldly, secular, humanistic, pragmatic, manipulative, explicitly rational, utilitarian, contractual, epicurean, hedonistic, etc.) cultures" (p. 8).

A culture is not a trend. And the rise of a culture includes a multitude of different trends. The explanatory adjectives suggest several future trends which are distinct and independent trends. For instance, the growth of utilitarian behavior is quite different from the growth of epicurean behavior, and the growing use of legal contracts is independent of the growth of hedonistic behavior. Moreover, the rise of a sensate culture includes most of the fourteen other long-run social trends in this list, none of which are subordinated to it. But it is illogical and misleading to list subordinate trends as independent, and perhaps equally important, trends.

3. Rise of New Elites

The second future trend in this list is stated as "Bourgeois, bureaucratic and meritocratic elites." But an elite is not a trend, and an elite may rise or fall. Moreover, the rise of a bourgeois elite is a social trend quite distinct from and independent of the rise of either a bureaucratic or a meritocratic elite. China developed an extensive bureaucracy many centuries before a bourgeois elite became powerful, and this bureaucracy continued to grow after the destruction of the bourgeois elite. Moreover, top bureaucrats have for centuries usually been aristocrats, not meritocrats. Meritocracy is incompatible with both feudalism and capitalism. It can develop fully only under socialism. As long as higher education is denied to those who cannot pay for it, meritocracy can be only partially achieved. Thus this second trend really includes three separate major social trends which are at least partly incompatible with each other. Moreover, since they are "rational" and "utilitarian," they are included in the previously listed rise of sensate culture. Finally, the rise of bureaucracy is several thousand years old, while Kahn wrote that his multifold trend, which includes it, is only one thousand years old.

4. Centralization

The third future trend is formulated as "Centralization and concentration of economic and political power." But centralization of economic power is a trend quite distinct from centralization of political power. Thus political power is far more centralized in France than in the U.S., but economic power may be equally decentralized in both countries. Many reforms which centralize or decentralize political power leave economic power unchanged. And a political party may advocate centralization of political power in order to prevent centralization of economic power. For instance, it may urge the passage of laws enabling a strengthened central government to break up trusts and foster competition.

5. Science and Technology

The fourth trend is stated as "Accumulation of scientific and technical knowledge." I have no criticism of this formulation except to note that it is included in the first trend, the rise of sensate cultures. Moreover, this trend, like the previous two, is over five thousand years old, not a mere one thousand years old, as the author implied.

The fifth future trend, "Institutionalization of technological change, especially research, development, innovation, and diffusion," is much less important than the great increase in spending on R and D, which the authors failed to treat as a major social trend. And institutionalization of technological change developed so recently, almost entirely in the last century, that it should not be listed as part of a thousand-year old social trend. However, I believe that it is now well-established and will continue for a very long time. Hence, its use in predicting the future is justified.

The sixth future trend, "increasing military capability," is a technological trend, not a social trend. It may result in significant long-run social trends, such as further concentration of political power, or growing losses from warfare, but, if so, these results, not increasing military capability, should be listed as long-term social trends. Also, it is illogical to list one technological trend and ignore all others, some of which, like the steady improvement of the means of communications and transportation, are much more important as causes of social trends.

6. Westernization

The seventh future trend in this list, "Westernization, modernization, and industrialization," is not a single social trend, but three different ones. Industrialization is only one among many social trends covered by the general term _Westernization_. And most Western countries will experience further industrialization, which will not be Westernization because it will occur in the West. Western countries cannot be Westernized.

The eighth future trend, "Increasing affluence and (recently) leisure," is really two quite separate trends, both a part of Westernization. Affluence may increase while leisure decreases, or vice versa. An increase in affluence usually causes men to choose or demand more leisure, but the cause of a social trend is not a part of the trend, as Kahn here implied.

7. Population Growth and Urbanization

The ninth future trend, "Population growth" is a single social trend, but it is not peculiar to Western culture, nor to the last millenium, as the authors implied. Moreover, in the last two centuries, it has had less effect upon Western culture than the rise of birth control, a major social trend not included in this list.

The tenth trend, "Urbanization, recently suburbanization and 'urban sprawl'—soon the growth of megalopoli," names three quite distinct trends. Urbanization is the concentration of people in towns or cities. Suburbanization is redistribution or relocation of people within a city. And megalopolization is mere growth in the population of very large cities, which may occur without urbanization or suburbanization. It can result from the growth of one city at the expense of other urban areas. Finally, urbanizaton is several thousand years old, and is not confined to Western culture.

8. The Rise of Service Industries

The eleventh trend, "Decreasing importance of primary and (recently) secondary and tertiary occupations; increasing importance of tertiary and (recently) quarteranary occupations," includes several different trends, some of them questionable. I doubt that there has been a recent decline in the proportion of the entire Western work force employed in secondary occupations. Such a decline has occurred in a few very advanced Western coutries, but probably not in the entire area of Western culture, including the USSR, Eastern Europe, Southern Europe, and Latin America. The share of the labor force engaged in secondary industries (manufacturing) has been expanding steadily in these latter very extensive areas, and will continue to do so for many more years.

The twelfth future trend, "Increasing literacy and education and (recently) the 'knowledge industry' and increasing role of intellectuals," names four different and quite independent trends. The growth of literacy is a result of education, a service industry, but it is only one result, and none of the results are part of the growth of education. The growth of the knowledge industries (publishing, communication, research, etc.) is also due in part to the growth of education and literacy but is nevertheless a separate trend or trends. The same reasoning applies to the "increasing role of intellectuals." This is a very significant social trend which deserves separate listing and discussion.

"Growth of the knowledge industries" is far too general a term. As defined in this book it includes the growth of advertising, accounting, and statistics, as well as the growth of publishing and communication. Today most publishing and communication is done for governmental, commercial, religious, and personal purposes, not to create or diffuse knowledge. Most advertising misleads consumers.

9. Social Engineering

The statement of the next future trend is even more complex and more confusing.

"13. Innovative and manipulative social engineering—i.e., rationality increasingly applied to social, political, cultural, and economic worlds, as well as to shaping and exploiting the material world—increasing problem of ritualistic, incomplete, or pseudo rationality" (p. 9).

This is a clumsy summary of most social trends during the last six thousand years, with an eight-word counter trend added to it. It includes most "social, political, cultural, and economic" trends in the East, as well as in the West. The history of man's social progress is a history of ever more rational social behavior. But the authors deny this in their concluding assertion that irrational social behavior is a growing problem. In fact, this problem has been shrinking for thousands of years, as the first part of this awkward and inconsistent trend statement asserts.

10. Universalization of Change

The statement of the fourteenth trend in this list, "Increasing universality of the multifold trends," is fortunately, relatively brief. This trend is a part of the Westernization trend. It is subject to my earlier criticism of the term <u>multifold trend</u>, but it can be translated as the claim that all the component trends are becoming more widespread. This is a dubious claim. For instance, trend 4, "accumulation of...knowledge," was always universal and cannot become more so. It can become more rapid, but this is not what the authors claimed here. The same reasoning applies to part of all of trends 1, 2, 3, 6, 7, 8, 9, 10, 12, 13, and 15.

11. Acceleration of Social Change

The fifteenth trend, "Increasing tempo of change in all the above," is also questionable. For instance, the tempo of population growth has probably already begun to fall in the world, as it certainly has in most advanced Western countries. And the last fact contradicts the previous claim that all trends are becoming more widespread. Even if the tempo of world population growth is still increasing, it will not do so much longer, so this trend is a poor basis for predicting the future.

Many other futurists have predicted increasing tempos of social change. I am convinced that the tempo of social change in the U.S. and other very advanced countries will be much slower during the next 200 years than during the past 200. It is very unlikely that any such future period will see such profound social changes in advanced countries as the spread of literacy, the agricultural revolution, the industrial revolution, urbanization, suburbanization, collectivization, the rise of scientific health care, and other major developments of the past 200 years. Of course, the radical social changes that have already occurred in advanced countries will occur in many backward countries. Some of them will experience an "increasing tempo of change." But Kahn did not limit his prediction to such countries.

The most significant of all social trends is the increase in average real income. In the U.S. and the U.K. the rate of this increase has been almost the same for over 200 years. It is true that some other Western nations have had higher rates of economic progress since 1950 than they had before it, but there has been no "increasing tempo of change" in real wages in these countries since 1960. The sharp post-1950 increase in their rate of economic growth was therefore probably a one-time or rare tempo change. Indeed, the growing scarcity of irreplaceable material resources like petroleum may reduce many economic growth rates during the next century.

It is noteworthy that in his later book, The Next 200 Years (1976), Kahn predicted that the real per capita income growth rate in advanced countries will fall rather than rise in the next 200 years (pp. 49, 56).

12. The Possibility of Prediction

Immediately after listing their 15 future long-run trends, the authors asserted that, "One of the most important assumptions that can be made about the future is that in most countries of the world it looks as if this multifold trend is going to continue, but with important differences in detail in various areas" (p. 9). But if "it looks as if this...trend is going to continue," this justifies a scientific prediction, and such a prediction is not a mere "assumption." Moreover, we do not need "important assumptions" about the future; we need scientific predictions. Yet throughout this book the authors discussed alternative scenarios and assumptions, and usually refrained from making scientific predictions. Apparently they accepted religious or philosophic dogmas concerning freedom of the will or indeterminism which often prevented them from making scientific predictions of future social events and trends. However, they did not discuss such dogmas.

Chapter III is entitled, "A Surprise-Free Projection." I would call this projection a scientific prediction, but the authors explain that it "should not be taken as anything resembling a forecast or a prediction" because, "since surprise will almost certainly occur, a surprisefree projection must be, at least to some extent, wrong" (p. 40). This argument is unsound. Every scientific truth or prediction is to some extent wrong or inaccurate. Only priests and philosophers claim to state absolute truths, and their absolute truths are not scientific truths.

Historians are constantly revising their history books and making their historical conclusions more accurate, but this does not mean that every or any previous conclusion was unscientific. Futurists will certainly revise their scientific predictions repeatedly, but this revision will not imply that previous predictions were unscientific, although, of course, any new or old prediction may be unscientific.

What determines whether any truth claim is scientific or unscientific is the method used to support it, not whether or not it can or will be improved. If the available scientific evidence supports the truth claim at the time it is made, it is a scientific conclusion, regardless of later events or surprises. Hence, a scientific forecast or prediction is possible in spite of the risk of surprise.

Moreover, surprises often offset each other. For instance, if one predicts, on the basis of scientific evidence, that real wage rates in the U.S. will continue to rise for 100 years at an average rate of 1% a year, some surprises may temporarily reduce this annual rate and others may raise it, with no significant effect upon the long-run average rate.

13. Ignored Social Trends

I have been criticizing the authors' statement of individual future long-term social trends in the West. I shall now comment on the structure and coverage of the list as a whole.

First, it includes, "Increasing military capability" but omits increasing agricultural capability, increasing industrial capability, increasing government capability, increasing scientific capability, and so forth. Yet the latter trends are even more important than the former. Of course, results, not capabilities, should be included in a list of major social trends, but if one lists a trend in one kind of capability, one should list several others.

Secondly, this list is stikingly incomplete in its coverage of major political and economic trends. For instance, it ignores the rise of democratic government, the growth of social security, the spread of socialism, the steady increase in the division of labor (including specialization), and the growth of government activities and payrolls. Some of these trends may have been ignored because the authors disaproved of them, but there must be other reasons. Unfortunately, the authors made no effort to explain these and other puzzling omissons.

Thirdly, the authors failed to list several very important trends affecting industrial freedom and legal rights. They ignored the negro liberation movement (including the gradual abolition of slavery), the women's liberation movement (including the long fight for property and voting rights), the rise of birth control (including abortion), the steady liberalization of divorce and remarriage laws, and the democratization of education. Here, as elsewhere, the authors minimized or ignored major long-run liberal social trends.

Finally, the authors revealed a prejudice against intellectuals and liberals. For instance, in discussing item #13 in their list of long-term trends they complained of the "educational incapacity" of many intellectuals. They illustrated this alleged incapacity by asserting that "it is difficult to convince big-city intellectuals that people who own firearms and resist disarmament legislation are not <u>mentally diseased</u> " (my italics, p. 28). Such an extreme and false claim suggests marked bias against liberal intellectuals.

In fact, gun-control laws are supported by the majority of U.S. voters, few of whom are intellectuals. Paradoxically, the authors specifically named Hitler and Goebbels as intellectuals (p. 27), and they surely did not support gun-control laws before they came to power.

The authors' prejudice against liberals may partially explain why they forecast so few coming U.S. liberal reforms like the adoption of health insurance, legalized abortion, equal rights for women, government financing of political campaigns, federalization of unemployment insurance, nationalization of more private industries, the construction of many more planned new towns, and the creation of a world government.

I have criticized the authors' statement of their fifteen long-run social trends in detail because their list of such trends is one of the few that have been published in English and because it contains the most significant and most plausible projections or predictions in Things to Come.

I turn now to criticism of some of the short-run trends or predictions, to which this book is largely devoted. I shall criticize only a few of them because short-run predictions are both less important and less reliable than long-run predictions. They are less reliable because unpredicted, one-time, or irregular events—like wars, crop failures, revolutions, floods, etc.—can distort short-run social trends much more than long-run trends.

14. The Japanese Growth Rate

One of the most important and most carefully discussed short-run predictions in Things to Come was the prediction that the Japanese economic growth rate would continue to be around 10% a year during the 70s and 80s (pp. 47, 232-233). The authors failed to anticipate the effects of the rising world prices of petroleum, soy beans, wheat, and other raw materials and foods upon the growth of the Japanese GNP. From 1974 to 1983 the Japanese GNP growth rate averaged far less than 10%, and this relative decline in the Japanese growth rate will probably be permanent.

The reason for this error in prediction was that Kahn used a short-run trend—Japan's high growth rate from 1950 to 1970—to predict the future. It is usually much safer to base predictions on long-run trends. Over the past one hundred years the Japanese GNP growth rate has averaged much less than 10%.

The authors specifically noted that Japan is "dependent" on foreign raw materials, and asserted that "these are available from a number of sources and it is hard to see how Japan could be put in a situation where it could not fill its requirements" (p. 242) But the vital question is not whether Japan will be able to "fill its requirements," but whether this can be done at prices which permit continued 10% a year economic growth. The latter seems unlikely.

The authors listed fifteen different causes of the high Japanese growth rate since 1950. The first is "High savings and investment rates (almost twice the U.S.)" (p. 233). This factor alone was sufficient to explain most of the Japanese economic miracle. And it in turn was largely due to the forced reduction in Japanese military spending after 1945. The share of U.S. national income spent on defense has averaged higher than the share saved and invested ever since 1945.

Japanese military spending has averaged much less than 1% of GNP, and much less than 5% of national saving and investment. Japan, Germany, and Italy have all had higher postwar growth rates than the U.S. and Great Britain primarily because they were defeated and disarmed in 1945. Since then, only the U.S.S.R. has been able to achieve both a high growth rate and a high rate of defense spending.

Kahn and Bruce-Briggs concluded that "the real 'engine' of rapid growth...is Japanese national character and Japanese leadership..." (p. 234). All such efforts to evaluate national character are very questionable. Are the Germans superior to the British because they have enjoyed a higher growth rate since 1950? I believe it is far more reasonable to explain these growth-rate differences by pointing to differences in saving, defense spending, and other observable events.

15. The 1985 Crisis

Chapter VIII of *Things to Come* is entitled "The 1985 Technological Crisis..." and discusses the social impact of technology. On pages 210-13 the authors listed about 100 possible effects of technological progress, nearly all harmful. They predicted that "some" of these "are likely to occur" (p. 208). They did not identify and explain those that are likely to occur, but they predicted a "1985 technological crisis" (p. 215), which will include three major features: (1) many different technologies will break down or develop out of control simultaneously, (2) the crises will be bigger than past crises, and (3) since pollution and technology grow exponentially, we will have little time to deal with such crises.

These predictions seem extraordinarily vague and unverifiable. So far as I am aware, no technology has ever broken down or developed out of control, but this personal belief may simply mean that I do not understand the terms or claims in question. I doubt that anyone else does. How can one prove that a technology has broken down or that it has developed out of control? The authors did not answer these vital questions, which suggests that the claims may be unverifiable and senseless.

As for crises getting bigger, this too is a vague claim, perhaps unverifiable. Moreover, if our ability to handle crises is growing, larger crises in the future may cause less harm than lesser crises caused in the past.

In discussing the prospect of a coming technological crisis the authors claimed that "a turning away from progress and growth has been heralded for a long time" and has recently become "a strong movement—

perhaps the strongest movement of the last decade" (p. 215). This directly contradicts their previous claim that all social trends are accelerating (pp. 9, 21). There had certainly been no decline in the tempo of social or economic progress in America or in the world as a whole in the years 1945-72. Perhaps the authors here referred to a trend in public opinion, not in social events, but, if so, they did not make this clear. Indeed, throughout this book the authors consistently ignored both public opinion polls and expert opinion polls, which are very useful bases for predicting the short-run future. The index of their book does not mention opinion polls.

It is true of course that the growing scarcity and costs of irreplaceable natural resources may slow down future economic progress, but a shortage of such resources is not a technological crisis. It is also possible that growing expenditures on pollution control will slow down the rate of economic progress, but there is no reason to believe it will cause a technological crisis, whatever that is, in the 1980s. Rather, increased spending on R and D to develop synthetic raw materials and effective pollution control is very likely to promote both technological and economic progress in the long run. Moreover, in The Next 200 Years, published four years later, Kahn failed to repeat this prediction of a 1985 crisis, and, instead, predicted continued rapid economic growth.

II. Comments on The Next 200 Years

In 1976 Herman Kahn and associates (Wm. Brown and Leon Martel) published his ninth book, The Next 200 Years, A Scenario for America and the World. It is one of the best books on future economic trends.

The title is misleading. It suggests that the book deals with most of the principal long-run social and technological trends which will begin or continue during the next 200 years. In fact, it is largely devoted to a refutation of the claim that American and world economic growth will be ended or seriously handicapped by the growth of population and/or by shortages and rising costs in extractive industries-notably those producing food, fuel, and other minerals. Kahn argued that supplies of land and mineral resources are ample to permit a continuing rise in real income per person at near-average 1950-75 rates throughout the next 200 years. He predicted that by the year 2176 world population will be about 15 billion, world per person product (WPPP) about $20,000 (in 1975 dollars), and gross world product (GWP) about $300 trillion. He estimated that in 1976 WPPP was only $1200, and GWP only $5.5 trillion (pp. 6-7). This implies a growth rate in world per capita real income of about 1½% a year.

He also suggested a second perspective or scenario which includes "the eventual establishment of large self-sufficient, autonomous colonies in space" and "substantial migration from earth." He did not try to predict the effects of the latter on population, real incomes, and total output.

Kahn devoted separate chapters of The Next 200 Years to population and real wage growth, energy sources, mineral supplies, food production, pollution, and the problems of transition.

1. Population Growth

In his chapter on population he stressed the claim that the rate of population growth tends to decline as industrialization raises real income and increases urban population. He also properly emphasized that an industrial revolution must be preceded or accompanied by an agricultural revolution which frees labor for urban industry. He was confident that all backward countries are now experiencing both of these revolutions, or soon will experience them. As a result, their real incomes per person will continue to rise steadily and birth rates will therefore begin or continue to fall rapidly. In fact, the world birth rate has probably already begun to fall. Kahn expected world population growth to fall to near zero by 2176 (p. 28), and world population to reach 15 billion (p. 34).

In my book, The Next 500 Years (1967), I predicted a world population of about 8 billion in 2176. Now, in 1983, I still think this prediction is more realistic than Kahn's figure of 15 billion. The recently revealled drastic reduction in the Chinese birth rate, suggested as possible in my 1967 book, supports my prediction that the world birth rate will decline much faster than Kahn expected.

Kahn believed that the rate of growth in real income per capita will be much higher in the now poorest countries, like India, than in the richest countries, like the U.S., during the next 200 years. He predicted that in 200 years the ratio of such real income in the richest countries to like income in the poorest countries will decline from 100 to 1 to 10 or 20 to 1 (p. 49). This is a surprising and dubious prediction because for centuries this ratio has been rising rather than falling. He expected population to continue to grow much faster in poor than in rich countries. If this happens, poor countries will have to grow economically much faster than rich countries in order to equal rich-country real-income-per-person growth rates.

Incidentally, his estimate that real per person income in the richest countries were 100 times as high as such incomes in the poorest countries was far too high. This ratio was probably less than 20 to 1.

2. Per Capita Income Growth Rates

Kahn predicted that real-income-per-person growth rates in advanced countries will decline by over 80% during the next 200 years (pp. 49, 56). He offered several reasons.

First, rising costs of energy and mineral products will reduce growth rates, but will not be the "dominant" factor. Indeed, the chief thesis of his book is that this factor will not prevent continued growth at current rates in the world as a whole. He did not explain why this factor will slow down growth in advanced countries while permitting an increased growth rate in backward countries.

His second reason was "diminishing returns" in extractive industries. This is a restatement of the point just criticized, and is subject to the same criticism.

His third point was that "the marginal utility of wealth and production" declines as real incomes rise (p. 50). But this factor should affect poor countries even more than rich countries. The utility curve declines less rapidly as incomes rise. Moreover, this utility decline has caused no fall in the rate of economic growth in advanced countries during the past 200 years. There must be strong offsetting factors, one of which may be that the real cost of saving declines as real income per person rises. Moreover, the opportunity cost of successful R and D may also decline steadily.

His fourth point is that "vested interests" which oppose growth become stronger as men become richer (p. 51). Yet it has long been claimed that such vested interests are especially strong in backward countries. I think this older orthodox view is much more plausible than Kahn's novel theory. He noted the fact that servants are cheaper in poor than in rich countries as one reason why vested interests in advanced countries will try to slow down growth, but this motive is even stronger in poor countries, where servants are still cheap than in rich countries, where most of the well-to-do have already learned to do without full-time domestic servants.

His fifth and final reason why real-per-capita-income growth "will slow and stabilize" in advanced countries during the next 200 years is "the nature of the growth process itself," by which he meant the growth in the relative importance of services, especially personal services, which are more difficult to mechanize and automate (p. 53). But while it may be harder to cut costs in service industries, it is easy to make services far more productive, as has been done in health-care industries during the past century. An equal improvement in health care may occur in the next 200 years, and in education, law enforcement, and some other service industries also. Moreover, many costly services—advertising, selling, brokerage, etc.—could easily be eliminated.

In summary, his argument that real income per person will rise less and less rapidly during the next 200 years in rich countries, but not in poor countries, seems largely unsound. He ignored the best argument, namely the fact that the demand for leisure increases as incomes rise, but leisure which reduces output and is voluntarily chosen by well-paid workers should really be considered as a part of personal income.

It is noteworthy that in this discussion of future growth rates Kahn ignored, and implicitly contradicted, his 1972 prediction that all long-run social trends are accelerating.

3. The Long-Term Multifold Trend Again

In Chapter VIII, Kahn restated his complex theory of "the basic, long-term multifold trend of western culture" which I criticized in the previous essay. He omitted one previously included fold or trend, added two new ones, revised the wording of restated trends, and radically changed their numerical order, which makes a comparison difficult. However, nearly all of my criticism of the earlier statement still applies.

The omitted trend is "centralization and concentration of economic and political power" (number three), one of the most probable and significant in his previous list. He did not explain the omission. I suspect that he omitted it because he did not approve of it.

4. Superindustrialization

One of his new future trends (#12) was "Recent emergence of superindustrial economy and resulting dominating character of its impact on the social and physical environment" (p. 184). A superindustrial economy is one "where enterprises are extremely large ..." (p. 1). Perhaps this trend is a partial replacement for the much more lucid trend, "centralization and concentration of economic and political power."

If so, the restatement merely confuses the reader. If not, I do not understand it.

5. The Growth of Futurism

His second new trend (#14) was the growth of "future-orientated thinking." I agree that this trend has arisen and will continue, but I doubt that it deserves being included as a separate trend in a list of 16 major social trends, which already include two trends (1 and 3) referring to the "increasing importance" and "the accumulation" and "increasing use" of scientific knowledge, and includes no other trend referring to a single science.

6. The Growth of Group Differentiation

Kahn also amended his formulation of the 14th (old series) trend, "increasing universality of the multifold trend," by adding to it, "an increasingly felt need for national, ethnic, communal or other group differentiation" (p. 184). Here he has again stated two quite distinct, and, in this case, conflicting, social trends as a single major long-run social trend. I would accept the first, "increasing universality," if properly restated, but I reject the second, increasing group differentiation.

The claim that "national, ethnic, communal differentiation" has been growing and/or will continue to is mistaken. Life in North America, South America, Asia, and Africa was far more different from life in Europe 600 years ago than it is today. All of these non-European continents have been continuously Westernized and Europeanized for 100 to 500 years. And this process is certain to continue for centuries in Asia and Africa. For instance, the caste system will weaken and disappear, tribal ties in Africa will weaken, racial miscegenation will continue, American ethnic minorities will be more thoroughly assimilated and Americanized, Europe will continue to be Americanized, national differences in Europe will diminish, and so forth. Cultural homogenization will steadily reduce all national, ethnic, and communal differences.

7. Short-Term Growth Predictions

I turn now to some of Kahn's very short-run forecasts. He predicted in 1976 that U.S. GNP per person would be about 2-1/2 times Soviet GNP per person in 1985 (p. 189). But, the Soviet figure was already over 60% of the U.S. figure in 1975, and, by 1985 should be at least 70% of it.

He predicted that, by 1985, GNP per person would be four times as high in China as in India (about $400 to $100). I doubt that the Chinese figure will be more than twice the Indian figure in 1985 (measured in purchasing power).

Kahn predicted that in 1985 per person GNP would be about 140% higher in France and West Germany than in the United Kingdom (p. 189). I doubt that this difference will exceed 40%. Here, as in other GNP estimates, Kahn seems to have relied unduly on temporary 1975 foreign exchange rates rather than upon differences in the domestic purchasing power of national monies. This inflated his estimates of Japanese, French, and German GNPs.

It is especially remarkable that Kahn predicted that, in 1985, East German GNP per person will be over twice that of the U.K. and over six times that of Brazil (p. 189).

Finally, Kahn predicted in 1976, after the first OPEC oil price increases, that "the period 1976-85 should be characterized by the highest average rate of world economic growth in history, perhaps 6%..." (p. 185). This prediction seems now (1983) to have been far too optimistic.

8. Comments

Kahn's chief contribution in these two books was his persuasive argument that continued world economic growth will not be radically slowed or stopped by increasing shortages of food, energy, and raw materials. His chief fault was his failure to discuss obvious world trends like the rise of support for world government, socialism, social insurance, feminism, and other major social trends of which he apparently disapproved. As a result, his picture of the future is very incomplete.

ALVIN TOFFLER AS A FUTURIST

Like the other authors reviewed in this book, Alvin Toffler (b1928) is not a professional or fulltime futurist. He has written on education and ethical values, as well as on the future. But his 1970 book, Future Shock, was a nonfiction best seller, and immediately established him as one of the best known American futurists. His second book on the future, The Third Wave (1980), covered different ground, and made him still better known as a futurist. As these two books cover quite different subjects, I shall criticize them separately.

I. A Review of Toffler's Future Shock

Toffler claimed that Future Shock provides a "diagnosis" of our social problems, not a "prognosis" of their future, but in fact he stated, or implied, many prognostications. He asserted that, "No serious futurist deals in 'predictions'" (p. 6), which he implied, are precise and certain. In my opinion, the great majority of "serious futurists" have dealt in "predictions," as this term is commonly defined and used.

Toffler advocated greater spending on futurist research (pp. 406-16). And he clearly stated the case for developing and using forecasts which are far from certain. But he refused to call such forecasts predictions. Indeed, he rarely used the term forecast or any synonym. He preferred to speak verbosely of "statements about the future" (p. 7). This vague phrase covers statements of possibilities and dogmatic prophecies, as well as scientific predictions.

1. The Main Future Shock Thesis

As the title implies, the chief thesis of Future Shock concerns future shock, defined as "the shattering stress and disorientation that we induce in individuals by subjecting them to too much change in too short a time." This is "a real sickness from which increasingly large numbers already suffer" (p. 4). "It may well be the most important disease of tomorrow" (p. 13).

Apparently, the term future shock was suggested by the term culture shock. Toffler compared these two shocks and asserted that "culture shock is relatively mild in comparison with the much more serious malady, future shock" (p. 13). He seemed unaware that many culture shocks are also future shocks, notably when people move from very primitive to very advanced societies. And culture shocks can be much more intense than any future shock because they often result from a transition from a stone-age or medieval culture to a modern machine-age culture.

Even within an advanced country a family which moves from a backward rural area to a large city experiences much more change in a much shorter time than do families who remain in the same area and undergo only what Toffler calls a future shock. I do not believe that Americans who continue to live in the areas or communities in which they were raised experience any significant stress or disorientation due to peaceful social change in normal times. Rather, I believe that, for such people, social change reduces boredom, makes life more interesting, improves their living conditions, and slowly—too slowly—increases their real incomes and their personal freedom.

2. The Acceleration of Change

Toffler asserted that "there is widespread agreement...that many social processes are speeding up—strikingly, even spectacularly" (p. 22). This belief is mistaken. Let us consider individually a few of the major social processes or trends of the last century or two.

Perhaps the most significant social trend in advanced countries during the past 200 years has been the long gradual decline in the birth rate. There has been no acceleration in this decline since 1930. In fact the U.S. birth rate was about as low in 1935 as in 1980. It may decline further, but it is extremely unlikely that it will ever decline as much or as rapidly during the future as it did from 1900 to 1940.

The growth of public elementary education has been a major social trend in most countries during the past century, but the rate of growth of such education began to slow down at least fifty years ago in all advanced countries. Public secondary education is expanding faster than public elementary education, but the rate of growth has already begun to decline in the U.S., and will soon do so in most other advanced countries.

To support his claim that social changes are accelerating, which implies that they will continue to do so, Toffler called attention to "the most extensive and rapid urbanization the world has ever seen," namely that since 1850 (p. 23). But the rate of urbanization in the U.S. is much lower now than it was sixty years ago, and urbanization has probably slowed in most other advanced countries. Moreover, he later predicted that this trend will soon reverse itself in advanced countries.

As another illustration of his thesis, Toffler called attention to "the acceleration of economic growth in the nations now racing toward super-industrialism" (p. 24). He noted that for the 21 OECD nations—the "have" states—the average annual real GNP growth rate in 1960-68 was between 4.5 and 5.0%, well above pre-1940 rates, and that such rates double real GNP every fifteen years. "Within a seventy-year lifetime, perhaps five such doublings will take place."

Here Toffler has taken a one-time temporary acceleration in a major social trend and recklessly projected it into the future. Before 1940 the real GNP growth rate had been almost stable in advanced countries for over a hundred years. In fact, GNP growth rates in advanced countries did not accelerate during the 1970s, as Toffler had suggested they would. Instead, they fell sharply.

In Chapter 3, "The Pace of Life," the author asserted that the pace of life is speeding up and will continue to do so. Life is becoming a "rat race." He implied that this will cause future shock in some persons. However, this is the kind of social trend which cannot be scientifically demonstrated. It is not consistent with the long declined in death rates or the shortening of the hours of labor, both of which are demonstrable. And many observers complain about increasing soldiering on the job, long and frequent coffee breaks, failure of workers to report for work on Monday or Friday, and other symptoms of a relaxation of work effort and discipline. Some ambitious executives do voluntarily over-work and participate in a rat race, but there is little evidence that the average American worker is doing so.

3. Shocks due to New Cultural Patterns

In Chapter 4, "Things: the Throw-away Society," Toffler asserted that men discard tangible goods, more and more rapidly. For instance, he noted that, "The average age of dwellings has steadily declined" (p. 50), and that in some cases "it becomes cheaper to tear down ten-year-old buildings than to modify them" (p. 52). However, he did not explain how moving into a new and usually better house causes future shock. I think it is far more likely to cause pleasure.

In Chapter 5, "Places: the New Nomads," the author claimed that Americans move from one place to another more rapidly than ever before, and that this causes future shock. But the shock, if any, caused by leaving one's former home and friends and moving to a new place where everything is strange is not a future shock, it is a culture shock and/or an alienation shock. It is not due to social change, but to personal movement within a society that changes little during this movement.

Chapter 6, "People: the Modular Man," asserts that, due to increasing regional and social mobility and other factors, the average duration of friendship is declining and will continue to do so. The author implied that this causes alienation and future shock. But when one loses a friend, one does not come in contact with the future, because there has been no social change. Hence, any resulting personal shock is not a future shock.

Chapter 7, "Organizations: the Coming Ad-hocracy," asserts that bureaucracy is being, and will continue to be, replaced by ad-hocracy, which requires executives to change their functions and tasks more often. Toffler alleged that this process causes a nervous strain which can result in future shock. "The increased turnover of all these [organizational] relationships places a heavy adaptive burden on individuals reared and educated for life in a slower-paced social system. It is here that the danger of future shock lies" (p. 135). He offered no scientific evidence to support this dubious claim. He overlooked the fact that many, perhaps most, executives welcome most changes in their functions, especially those which lead to or result from promotion. For executives, as for assembly-line workers, the continual performance of unchanging functions is often boring. And even when a change in function is unwanted and/or unpleasant, it is rarely shocking. Finally, any resulting shock is not a future shock, but a shock due to a sudden change in function. It may indeed be a change to an older or more primitive function or method of operation.

Chapter 8: "Information: the Kinetic Image," calls attention to the rapid growth of information in all fields and notes that "the most highly skilled and intelligent...admit difficulty in keeping up with the deluge of new knowledge—even in extremely narrow fields" (p. 140). Toffler implied that this is a new situation. I suspect that it was even more difficult a century ago, when the means of disseminating new knowledge were far less extensive and efficient than they are today. And this problem can always be solved by increasing specialization and by better classification and dissemination of new knowledge.

In more general terms, the author asserted that all new knowledge compels the individual "to relearn his environment.... This...places a new demand on the nervous system" and sets the stage for "that potentially devastating social illness—future shock" (p. 161). But many men fail to relearn very much, and most of those who make a serious effort to relearn and keep up enjoy the intellectual exercise. It makes life more interesting and gives men a satisfying sense of personal achievement. In any case, overstraining to learn or relearn is rarely a confrontation with the future.

Chapters 4-8, discussed above, make up Part Two, entitled "Transience." Part Three (Chapters 9-11) is entitled "Novelty." It predicts many scientific, social, and marital innovations, and suggests that these innovations will help to cause more men to suffer future shock.

4. On Social Revolution

Part Three opens with a number of gross exaggerations about the rate of social change. "We are creating a new society. Not a changed society.... A revolution shatters institutions and power relationships (p. 165), and, he implied, will continue to happen.

The idea that men can quickly create new societies is naive. The Russian communists have probably had more power and made greater efforts to create a new society than any previous political rulers, but they have merely succeeded in speeding up certain major social trends long apparent in old Russia and in other Western countries. All social change is necessarily gradual and, to reformers, discouragingly slow. It is impossible to create a new society except by gradually changing an old one. Revolutions change rulers or ruling classes, but they cannot immediately or rapidly create new societies.

5. Shocks due to Technological Progress

Chapter 9 is devoted to the suggestion, or implicit prediction, of various future scientific and technological advances. The author concluded that "the relentless movement towards transience is reinforced and made more potentially dangerous by a rise in the novelty ratio" (p. 193). In fact, scientific and technological novelties are, on the whole, beneficial and will continue to be so. Toffler offered no persuasive evidence to the contrary. He merely worried, and suggested possible evils. The fact that technological progress is "more potentially dangerous" is not new. Such progress has been ever more potentially dangerous for 10,000 years, but it has also been ever more potentially and actually beneficial.

6. Changes in Economic Theory

Chapter 10, "The Experience Makers," discusses some social innovations which the author claimed will help to cause future shock. The author accused economists of "straight-line" thinking about the future, the mere projection of old social trends. They think in terms of scarcity rather than abundance. He favored more imaginative thinking about an economy in which basic needs have been satisfied. In his opinion, "the super-industrial revolution...will...transform the very purpose of economic activity" (p. 196). It will "psychologize" production, i.e., force producers to meet and cater to the "consumer's subtle, varied, and quite personal needs for beauty, prestige, individuation, and sensory delight" (p. 198). He supported this prediction by citing obvious social trends and applying straight-line social projection of them into the future. He was apparently unaware that economists have long defined economic production as the creation of personal want satisfaction, not as the creation of material objects or unwanted services. He was equally unaware that scarcity, as defined by economists, exists and will continue to exist in all societies, however affluent they may become, because human wants as a whole are insatiable.

7. The Future Growth of Recreational Services

Toffler discussed "certain industries whose sole output consists...of pre-programmed 'experiences'" (p. 200). He noted the past growth of firms providing package holidays, guided tours, tourist ship voyages, health-resort treatments, and other such experiences, and predicted their "revolutionary expansion." Continued expansion is of course inevitable since real income will continue to rise, and every increase in such incomes will permit more people to enjoy what rich men now enjoy, but Toffler did not use this argument. And neither this argument nor straight-line projection supports his prediction of a "revolutionary expansion" in these industries. It is much more likely that the coming expansion will proceed at about the same rate as during the past century.

Of course, the term <u>revolutionary expansion</u> is very vague, and Toffler mentioned no specific rates of change. Over a sufficiently long period of time any gradual rate of change results in a radical or revolutionary change. But here as elsewhere Toffler failed to define his terms and state his predictions so as to facilitate verification of them. He preferred to use sensational terms like <u>revolutionary</u> without explaining precisely what they mean.

8. The Future of the Family

In Chapter 11, "The Fractured Family," Toffler explained that some futurists have predicted that the family will disappear while others have predicted that it will survive and prosper. He thought it "far more likely" that the family will "break up, shatter, only to come together again in weird and novel ways" (pp. 211-12). Among the most probable "weird and novel ways," he discussed trial marriage, temporary marriage, and serial marriage, no one of which is either weird or novel. The further growth of each can be predicted by means of a straight-line projection of one-hundred-year-old secular trends in the U.S. He did discuss several kinds of groups or corporate families, which are weird and relatively novel, but he offered no scientific reason for predicting their long-run increase in importance. Mere conjecture is not scientific prediction.

9. Excess Freedom of Choice

Part Four, "Diversity," includes three chapters written to support the prediction that future increases in human choice among goods and life-styles will create an evil called "overchoice," which will help to cause culture shock.
Chapter 12, "Overchoice," rejects the popular idea that standardization of goods and increasing government regulation will significantly limit human choice (pp. 233-34). Here I agree with Toffler. However, I question his suggestion that "there comes a time when choice...becomes so complex, difficult, and costly that it turns into its opposite...overchoice and...un-freedom" (p. 250). The rich have always enjoyed what he called "overchoice," but do not seem to have suffered future shock as a result.
Chapter 13, "A Surfeit of Subcults," and Chapter 14, "A Diversity of Life Styles," argue that human freedom of choice is increasing because the number of different occupations, vocations, cults, and life styles is steadily increasing. As usual, the author stated his findings in extreme and sensational terms, "Today the hammerblows of the superindustrial revolution are literally splintering the society" (p. 252). He ignored the fact that the data he cited illustrate very old and stable social trends. His great error was his claim that these trends will help to create "an environment so ephemeral, unfamiliar, and complex as to threaten [additional] millions with adaptive breakdown...future shock" (p. 285).

10. Psychological Problems

In Part Five, "The Limits of Adaptability," Toffler finally offered empirical evidence which he believed supports his major thesis. In Chapter 15, "Future Shock: the Physical Dimension," he reviewed evidence which shows that the men who experience the most life changes are most likely to get sick. However, life change include death or illness of a spouse, friend, or relative; harsh treatment by a superior; loss of job, rank, or prestige; and other personal misfortunes which are not social changes. And several of these misfortunes are much more wounding than any social change. Hence, Toffler's claim that this evidence supports his claim that social change causes some form of illness is quite unjustified.

In Chapter 16, "Future Shock: the Psychological Dimension," the author reviewed research data showing that overstimulation of the nervous system can cause mental illness and is growing. However, he noted that understimulation can have the same effect, and he failed to prove that the average level of stimulation is more harmful today than a century or two ago. He offered evidence that the intensity of stimulation has increased, but not that this increase ha been harmful.

Toffler stressed the claim that growing numbers of young people have escaped or retreated from reality, "the rat race," by taking up drugs and entering communes. He ignored the fact that communes in the form of monasteries and convents were far more popular a few hundred years ago than they are today because the real world was much harsher then than it is today.

Until very recently, moreover, the ideal life for most European noblemen and gentlemen was one entirely outside what we call the rat race. They preferred to spend their lives on country estates, hunting, fishing, romancing, dueling, and drinking. One of the distinguishing features of capitalism, especially American capitalism, is that it greatly increased the proportion of upper-class men and women who voluntarily engage in competitive productive labor, often called the rat race, presumably because they enjoy it.

11. The Prevention of Future Shock

Part Six, "Strategies for Survival," the last part of <u>Future Shock</u>, includes four chapters, each devoted to a different class of strategies for avoiding future shock.

Chapter 17, "Coping with Tomorrow," discusses strategies which individuals can use to reduce their personal suffering from changes and new strains in their lives. Here, as elsewhere, the author confused personal problems with social problems, personal changes with social changes, and personal trauma with social shocks. He failed to explain that a vast number of personal shocks can occur in an unchanging society.

The author did suggest certain social reforms to help individuals cope with their personal problems. For instance, he recommended the provision of situational groups, crisis counselors, and half-way houses. But he failed to explain that such agencies deal mostly with personal shocks which are not due to social change.

Chapter 18, "Education in the Future Sense," discusses a variety of educational reforms which Toffler believed would reduce the risk of future shock. As usual, his language is often extreme or sensational-- "education today...is a hopeless anachronism" (p. 353) --but some of the proposed reforms sound promising. My chief criticism is that the sound reforms would be desirable whether or not they could reduce the risk of future shock.

In a section on "The New Educational Revolution," an inflated phrase, Toffler predicted that "Machines will increasingly perform the routine [industrial] tasks; men the intellectual and creative tasks" (p. 356). This trend in the use of machines is centuries old, and its continuance is very unlikely to produce another revolution in industry or education in advanced countries. Moreover, machines are likely to perform much more intellectual and creative work in the future than they did in the past.

12. Concluding Comments on Future Shock

Toffler devoted an entire book to the prediction that future changes will cause increasing numbers of future shocks without ever defining future shock so that statements about it can be understood and proven or disproven. For instance, he did not distinguish it clearly from culture shock and from mental illness. As a result, he failed to prove, or even plausibly argue for, his thesis.

Some of his alleged causes of future shock may have helped to cause or worsen mental illness in persons prone to mental illness for hereditary and/or environmental reasons, but there is no evidence that social progress increases mental illness. And such progress has recently yielded drugs very useful both in preventing and in treating mental illness.

Toffler suggested many possible harmful effects of social change and ignored nearly all the compensating benefits of such change. Thus he could not even begin to argue that the real costs exceed the benefits. And if the average man receives net benefits from social change or progress, it is very unlikely that he will be shocked by such change.

II. A Review of Toffler's The Third Wave

"A new civilization is emerging in our lives, and blind men everywhere are trying to suppress it." This striking opening sentence of Alvin Toffler's 1980 book, The Third Wave, reminds one of the opening sentence of The Communist Manifesto, "A spectre is haunting Europe—the spectre of Communism," but Toffler's book is implicitly an anti-communist manifesto. The "Third Wave," the "new civilization" he predicted, is merely a more advanced stage of inegalitarian, oligopolistic capitalism.

1. The Third Wave Concept

To illustrate how new and important he thought the third wave will be, Toffler placed it on the level of the "First Wave," the introduction of agriculture, and the "Second Wave," the industrial revolution, both of which radically transformed the societies in which they occurred.

However, the Third Wave will not be a general revolution in the method of production, like the first two waves, but a group of many relatively minor, independent changes or trends in different industries and social activities. It will include: (1) the growing use of new sources of energy, (2) the domestication of work, (3) the decline of mass production, (4) the reduction of plant size, (5) the decline of specialization, (6) the decentralization of population, (7) more use of eugenics, (8) the revival of religion, (9) the growth of minority political power, (10) the rise of semi-direct democracy, (11) the relocation of political decision-making, and (12) the disintegration of existing nations. According to Toffler, the creation of this new Third Wave civilization began about 1955, and will be completed within a few decades.

2. Energy Trends

In his discussion of new sources of energy Toffler implied that nuclear reactors will play a very minor role in the production of energy in his new civilization (p. 127). But it is far too soon to form such a judgment. Nuclear technology will continue to improve steadily, and no one can now predict the results of such progress. In 1982, nuclear plants already produced 40% of all electricity used in France.

He also predicted that the production of energy will be decentralized, in spite of a very long past trend towards centralization. The previous criticism applies here too. The growth of solar heating will tend to slow or reverse the long-prevailing centralization trend, but the growth of nuclear power will have the opposite effect, as will the growth of central heating systems. The net effect of these and other factors is still unpredictable.

3. The Domestication of Work

Toffler predicted that, "The most striking change in Third Wave civilization...will probably be the shift of work from both office and factory back into the home." (p. 335). I predict that the centuries-old shift of work from the home to outside places will continue indefinitely, even in the most advanced countries. For instance, the care and education of young children will continue to shift from the home to nursery schools and kindergartens, and the operating hours of elementary schools will lengthen, as more and more mothers go to work outside the home.

He forecast that the development of home computers, two-way cable TV, and other technologies will enable more and more adults to work at home. He overlooked the fact that it is more efficient to install expensive office machines in large offices, where many workers can use the same machines, than to install them in individual homes or offices where only one or two persons can use them. That is one reason why doctors will increasingly choose to practice in clinics rather than in one-doctor offices.

Moreover, the shift of factory work to private homes is even less likely than the shift of office work because most factory machines are large, expensive, and/or noisy, and because the transport of raw materials, components, and finished products to or from millions of private homes would be too costly. Also, many factory materials and supplies are too dangerous and polluting to be used at home. Finally, it will always be cheaper to produce most goods on a scale much larger than that possible in private homes.

Toffler mentioned that men now do some home plumbing, home auto repairs, home building repairs, and a variety of other do-it-yourself domestic jobs. But he ignored more important examples of the decline of domestic production for home consumption. For instance, most American farmers have long been curtailing their production of eggs, milk, butter, and meat for home consumption, and have been steadily increasing their purchase of packaged groceries in town. And urban married women have long been curtailing their home production of cooked food, house-cleaning services, and child care in order to enable them to work outside their homes.

4. The Decline of Mass Production

In a chapter entitled "Beyond Mass Production" Toffler noted that mass production of standardized products has been growing for 200 years in advanced countries, and predicted a sudden and permanent reversal of this trend. Indeed, he claimed, without statistical evidence, that we have already "moved beyond mass production" (p. 169). I doubt both of these last two claims.

The growth of oligopolistic competition has resulted in grossly excessive differentiation of finished consumer goods. Each oligopoly tries to produce unique products, primarily to minimize price competition and provide its salesmen with nonprice selling points. The coming replacement of intra-industry competition by monopoly will result in far more standardization and mass production of products and components. Moreoever, government efforts to standardize nuts, bolts, screws, containers, drugs, tools, etc., in competitive industries will continue to grow and promote mass production of components.

5. The Reduction of Plant Size

Toffler predicted that the average plant will be much smaller in his new civilization. "The traditional Second Wave factory or office, with thousands of people under a single roof, will be a rarity in the high-technology nations" (p. 247). I expect that average plant and office size will continue to increase indefinitely in all nations. Some of the largest plants may be replaced by smaller plants in order to permit intra-city decentralization, but the number of very small plants will decline far more than enough to create a long increase in average unit size.

Toffler cited no statistics to support his prediction on factory and office size. Instead, he referred to Schumacher's book, Small Is Beautiful, and one Australian auto executive. But Schumacher was talking primarily about the problem of backward countries. In advanced countries, auto plants may decline in average size, but plants and offices in most other industries will grow in size as millions of family stores, farms, and offices are merged with, or replaced by, much larger firms. The advantages of large-scale production include greater division of labor among workers and machines, lower raw material costs, lower selling costs, lower building costs, and more continuous use of specialized machines.

6. Despecialization

Toffler stressed the fact that specialization has been growing steadily for over 200 years but intimated that it will soon begin to decline. He wrote of "The revolt against narrow overspecialization" and the rise of academic emphasis on "interdisciplinary thinking" (p. 286). He did not quite dare to predict an actual decline in specialization but he asserted that "straightline extrapolation from Second Wave trends: [like] specialization" yields a "simplistic image" of the future (p. 309). In sharp contrast, I am confident that specialization will continue to grow indefinitely, especially among professional and office workers, because it increases output per worker and also improves the quality of most products.

7. Disurbanization

During the past 200 years there has been a vast and continuous movement of population from farms and farm villages to towns and cities in all advanced countries. Toffler claimed that "this process...has begun to turn around. We see increasing geographical dispersal instead" (p. 248). To support this dubious claim, he later asserted that, "Tokyo, London, Zurich, Glasgow, and dozens of other major cities are all losing population while middle-sized or smaller cities are showing gains" (p. 283) But it is only the core districts of these large metropolitan areas which have been losing population, and losing it to their own suburbs and exurbs. The metropolitan areas themselves have been growing, and are likely to continue growing for several decades, the alleged period of the rise of Third Wave civilization.

8. More Eugenic Progress

Toffler treated eugenics as a major feature of his Third Wave. "Second Wave thinkers conceived of the human species as a culmination of a long evolutionary process; Third Wave thinkers must now face the fact that we are about to become the <u>designers</u> of evolution (p. 278). But the implication that Darwin, Wallace, and Huxley believed that human evolution had ended is entirely unjustified. Animal breeding, the deliberate control of evolution, has been practiced for centuries. And Galton publicized his movement for human eugenics over 100 years ago. The chief opposition to planned eugenic evolution has always come from religious fundamentalists, and Toffler claimed that the Third Wave will include a "wildfire revival of fundamentalist religion" (p. 274).

9. The Revival of Religion

On religion, as on most other issues, Toffler was careful not to make clear, specific, verifiable prediction, but the tone of his book is generally pro-religious and anti-scientific. He forecast the growth of cults and a revival of Christian fundamentalism as features of his Third Wave (pp. 346, 354-55). He suggested that in his new civilization men will be able to "reduce infant mortality and improve the life span, literacy, nutrition, and general quality of life without surrendering...religion or values and necessarily embracing the Western materialism that accompanies the spread of Second Wave civilization" (p. 320). But the growth of materialism, better called positivism, has been caused primarily by the growth of science and education, not by the industrial revolution, and will continue as long as science, and the knowledge of science, grows. There is much reliable statistical evidence that religious faith varies inversely with the amount of education one has received (see my Radical Essays, pp. 163-64).

10. The Rise of Minority Power

Toffler asserted that, "Nowhere...is obsolescence more advanced or more dangerous than in our political life" (p. 418). This claim would have been fully justified if he had been talking about our failure to create a world government powerful enough to enforce world peace, but he claimed that no such government is needed or coming (pp. 309-310). Instead, he advocated other, dubious political reforms.

"The root principles of the Third Wave governments of tomorrow...may well turn out to be minority power... semidirect democracy...[and]decision division" (pp. 398-405). By "minority power" he meant the result of political reforms which will "strengthen the role of diverse minorities, yet permit them to form majorities" (p. 401). This is a very nebulous idea. Toffler suggested several methods of achieving "minority power," including cumulative voting, the creation of "temporary modular parties that service changing configurations of minorities," the appointment of inter-minority diplomats or ambassadors, the formation of more minority alliances, more self-government for individual minorities and the selection of public officials "by drawing lots" (pp. 402-03). He devoted less than two pages to these novel and questionable proposals, and offered no evidence that they have been attracting increasing public support. In the past, most such reforms have been preceded by 50 to 100 years of growing propaganda and public support, but Toffler implied that the achievement of "minority power," like other major Third Wave reforms, will be accomplished within "a few decades" (pp. 4, 8).

11. Semi-direct Democracy

The second "root-principle of...Third World Governments is...semi-direct democracy," which means "a shift from depending on representatives to representing ourselves." The mixture of the two is "semi-direct democracy" (pp. 405-06). Although California and a few other states have made increasing use of the initiative and referendum since 1910, nearly all laws submitted to the voters by initiative and referendum have been far too long and complex for most voters to understand and evaluate them properly. Moreover, it is impractical to require voters to vote on more than 0.1% of all laws submitted to legislators. Hence, it is very unlikely that semi-direct democracy will ever be dominant in advanced countries. It certainly will not help to create a new civilization in "the next few decades."

12. Political Decision Division

The third "root principle" is "decision division," transfering some political decisions from national governments to international agencies, or to local and regional governments. The former process began long ago and has been widely approved. But there is no evidence of growing delegation of political administration and legislation to local and regional governments. Rather, there is convincing evidence that political centralization has been continuing for centuries in nearly all advanced countries. This very important trend will probably continue until supreme political power is centralized in a strong world government.

13. The Breakup of Nations

In a chapter entitled "The Crack-up of the Nation," Toffler predicted that all or nearly all advanced nations will soon break up into smaller parts along racial, language, and even purely regional lines. It is easy to conceive of the Ukraine seceding from the USSR after a Russian defeat in World War III, but he even suggested that the northwest and/or the southwest of the U.S. may secede in peace time, an almost incredible forecast.

Some multi-national and/or multi-language nations—China, India, Pakistan, Belgium, Jugoslavia, Russia, Nigeria, etc.—are likely to disintegrate sometime in the future, but it is very unlikely that France, Italy, Germany, Japan, or the U.S. will do so. In any case, such disintegration would not help to create a new civilization.

14. Internation Relations

The major political problem of our time is how to prevent nuclear wars and create a stable, peaceful world order. Toffler failed to explain how the Third Wave will achieve this goal. He described in illuminating detail the recent rapid growth of international corporations, associations, and government agencies, but he flatly denied that such growth will lead to the creation of a world government able to preserve world peace. Instead, "we are moving toward a world system composed of units densely interrelated like the neutrons in a brain rather than organized like the department of a bureaucracy." (p. 320). Presumably this nebulous "matrix" system will have no department of defense or police able to prevent civil or international wars.

15. General Comments on The Third Wave

Social scientists have identified numerous long-run social trends which began in advanced countries over 100 years ago and are still continuing—population growth, education growth, urbanization, centralization, specialization, democratization, etc. Most of these long-run trends are parts or results of the great agricultural and industrial revolutions which have transformed advanced societies since 1750 A.D. Toffler named the civilization they created the "Second Wave." In order to differentiate his Third Wave civilization from it, he claimed that most of these Second Wave trends have weakened or ended, or even been reversed.

It is relatively plausible to claim that an old and well-established social trend will continue for one or more decades. It is far more risky and far less plausible to claim that a new social trend has been discovered, and then predict that this new trend will continue for decades. I think that most of his old, Second Wave trends will continue indefinitely, and that most of his new, Third Wave trends are imaginary, minor, or temporary.

In many cases where he offered no evidence of a new Third Wave trend, Toffler resorted to pure wishful thinking or conjecture. For instance, after discussing the need to reduce loneliness, he asked, "How might we begin to do this?" (p. 349), and discussed several possible programs. But such conjectures are not a sound basis for predicting the future, especially not for predicting an entire new civilization.

There is an astonishing lack of statistics and references to statistical series and studies in The Third Wave. This is due in part to the author's extensive reliance on wish and conjecture. He also used many anecdotes. He described an individual change in one city, factory, or office and used this case to predict the rapid general adoption of such a change throughout all advanced countries. Such evidence can be suggestive but never convincing.

Since social change is continuous, it is always possible to claim that a new civilization is being created. But Toffler claimed much more than this. He claimed that within a few more decades life in advanced countries will be radically different from what it is today, as radically different as modern city life is from the rural life of 200 years ago. He completely failed to justify this extreme claim.

In many areas of social thought Toffler is a pure reactionary. He urged men to return to the farm or small town, to domestic or individualistic handicraft production, to local self-government, to home care of children, to religion, etc. But he is also a prophet of, or an apologist for, many post-1955 counter culture fads—down with nuclear power, mass production, and economic progress; up with solar power, communes, and handicraft production. There is much overlapping in these viewpoints because many counter-culture ideas are reactionary.

Finally, Toffler failed to predict the continuance of many obvious major social trends, including the rise of feminism, the spread of birth control, the growth of free distribution, the rise of city planning, the growth of preschool child care, the expansion of government control and ownership of industry, the socialization of health care, and the growth of monopoly and oligopoly.

JOHN NAISBITT AS A FUTURIST

John Naisbitt was a business consultant and the publisher of the quarterly TREND REPORT when he published his best-selling book, Megatrends, Ten New Directions Transforming Our Lives, published by Warner Books in 1982. His 290-page book includes an Introduction, a separate chapter on each of his ten megatrends, and a brief Conclusion.

1. Towards an Information Society

Chapter 1 is entitled "From an Industrial Society to an Information Society," which summarizes the first of his ten megatrends. "The information society had its beginnings in 1956 and 1957," but "Now [1982] more than 60% of us work with information as programers, teachers, clerks," and others. In 1950 the corresponding figure was "only about 17%" (pp. 13-14). He failed to explain that, if these figures are even roughly accurate, the trend towards an information society must slow down drastically in the near future because a large part of our workforce will long be needed to produce, transport, and market the food, housing, energy, and clothing we will always need. By his figures, the rise of an information society was a megatrend from 1950 to 1982, but it cannot continue to be a megatrend in the 21st century. Perhaps that is why he did not predict the rate or extent of the future progress of this trend.

Naisbett included in the information sector of society "technicians," who repair many machines not used to transmit information, "nurses," who may spend most of their time making beds, emptying bed pans, etc., and advertising men, who provide much more disinformation than information (pp. 14-15). And it is far from clear whether manufacturers of telephones and computers are in the industrial or the information sector of our economy. His concept of "information" occupations is very vague.

Naisbitt's information sector trend is so general that it obscures and hides several component trends—the growth of education, of health care, of R and D, etc.—each of which may become more important and more enduring than the overall trend from an industrial to an information society.

According to Naisbitt, "We are moving from the specialist who is soon obsolete, to the generalist, who can adapt" (p. 37). I foresee ever greater specialization. The rapid increase of information makes more and more specialization beneficial and inevitable, especially in the professions. Moreover, the mere fact that specialization has been growing for centuries in all advanced countries makes it highly likely that this trend will continue.

2. High Tech/High Touch Technology

Chapter 2 is entitled "From Forced Technology to High Tech/High Touch Technology." Forced technology is that forced upon workers; high touch technology is that which meets "the spiritual demands of our human nature" as revealed by the "human potential movement" (pp. 39-40).

The idea of this second megatrend is far too vague to be useful. Naisbitt offered no statistics on the past or future of this trend. I do not believe it is a measureable trend, and there is little point in making a prediction which cannot be verified.

Naisbitt noted that in 1980 U.S. newspapers printed articles on both increased use of computers and on the revival of the study of ethics in schools. On the basis of this slim evidence, he predicted that, "As computers begin to take over some of the basics of education, schools will more and more be called upon to take responsibility for teaching values and motivation, if not religion" (p. 47). This is not a good method of predicting the future.

3. More International Interdependence

The title of Chapter 3 is "From a National Economy to a World Economy." The author did not state his third megatrend more precisely and explicitly, but he asserted that, "In the new economic era, all... countries... are growing increasingly interdependant... (p. 56), and he may have meant this trend, projected into the future, to be his third megatrend. This trend is centuries old, and has been discussed by innumerable historians and social scientists. It will certainly continue indefinitely. But I doubt that it should be treated as one of the ten most important social trends of our age.

Chapter 3 consists largely of stories of recent developments in business and technology. It also offers much advice; for instance, "The U.S. must also be concerned about real growth, as well as productivity growth" (p. 60), and "We have much to learn from both Japan and West Germany on structural adjustment" (p. 65). It contains few predictions.

He predicted that "Never again will a single country dominate the world the way the U.S. did after World War II" (p. 57). This prediction is highly dubious because the winner of World War III may be even more dominant than was the U.S. in 1950. Moreover, the continued proliferation of nuclear weapons may make world domination by a single nation or alliance necessary and inevitable.

Naisbitt forecast that, "The globalization of the world's automobile industry is inevitable" (p. 64). The meaning of this forecast is not clear, but apparently he referred to growing dominance of the industry by a few giant firms. "The 30... companies now competing on an international scale will, by the end of the 1980s, be reduced to as few as 7 or 8 companies or alliances of companies..." (p. 65). This is a very dubious prediction. By 1990, Korea, China, India, Brazil, Czechoslovakia, East Germany, etc. may all be independent exporters of automobiles.

4. "From Short Term to Long Term"

This is the title of Chapter 4. The fourth megatrend is that U.S. business managers will do more and more long-term planning because they ought to do so. The author reported that several U.S. firms have recently done more long-run planning, but did not claim a long-run past trend in this direction. Thus his grounds for predicting such a future trend are very weak. And, even if it occurs, it will hardly be a megatrend. I suspect that the author has advised many business men to do more long-run planning, and has turned his advice into a prediction.

It would be very difficult to measure any increase in long-term planning. Certainly, no such measurement has been developed and applied. Therefore, we do not know what the current trend is, or how any prediction about it could be verified.

5. Decentralization

Chapter 5 discusses the fifth megatrend, which is that U.S. government, business, and culture are being, and will be, increasingly decentralized. "Centralized structures are crumbling all across America" (p. 97).

To support his unusual claim that government is being decentralized, Naisbitt explained that our state legislatures approve 100 times as many laws each year as Congress. He ignored the vital fact that the net effect of such laws is to centralize political decision making, for instance, by transferring functions from local governments to state governments and/or the federal government. Thus the provision of welfare benefits and social insurance, once local and state functions, have become more and more centralized in Washington. And voters are increasingly demanding more and more federal control over local air and water pollution, pesticide use, automobile safety, food purity, abortion, etc.

To support his claim that business is being decentralized, he explained that McDonalds, a vast new chain of hamburger drive-ins, "no longer builds the exact same restaurant in each new location" (p. 98). But it is the growth of the chain itself that is relevant, and such growth does not constitute decentralization. Moreover, chain organization has been growing among law offices, advertising agencies, accounting firms, real estate offices, banks, and many other classes of firms. And the share of manufacturing controlled by the largest firms has long been growing. Naisbitt failed to quote or refer to any overall statistics which support his claim, and I know of none which do. The great majority of interested observers have deplored, but have not denied, the growth of centralization in U.S. government and business. Naisbitt's prediction suggests pure wishful thinking rather than scientific prediction of the future. As noted previously, he forecast rapid further concentration of the world car manufacturing industry, and he did not explain why the forces causing such concentration would not operate in other manufacturing industries.

6. From Institutional to Self-Help

Chapter 6 is devoted to his sixth new megatrend, an alleged transition from institutional or collective welfare programs to self-help. Like his prediction on decentralization, this sounds more like a plank in the Republican party platform than like a serious, scientific prediction of the future.

To support this rare, if not unique, prediction Naisbitt noted that Americans are smoking less (p. 135). He failed to add that this is the result of advice from government agencies and other institutions. He also asserted that "More than 500 companies... have fitness programs..." which, to me, suggests the growth of institutional help, not of self-help.

He noted that, after a long period of growth, the percent of U.S. births in hospitals had declined from 99.3% in 1973 to 98% in 1978, and implied that this decrease would continue indefinitely (p. 141). But this slight decrease may have been due to statistical errors or to the effects of large-scale immigration, largely illegal.

He reported a few cases of parents who wish to educate their children at home, and implied that the percent of children entirely educated at home would grow indefinitely. "With home computers, home education can increase <u>even more dramatically</u>" (my italics, p. 144). I doubt that there has been or will be any dramatic increase in fulltime home education. Of course, as any society becomes more wealthy and better educated, most parents make greater efforts to supplement their children's formal education, but this is hardly a megatrend, and is probably not what Naisbitt meant to predict.

The most important trends in U.S. education will be the continued growth of formal education for children age 2 to 6 and adults age 20 to 60, and both trends will increase institutional education at the expense of home education and self-help.

According to Naisbitt, "We are shifting from a managerial to an entrepreneurial society" (p. 149). However, he ignored the very plausible arguments of those who support the opposite conclusion. He cited David Birch's finding that between 1969 and 1976 nearly two thirds of all new jobs were created by firms employing less than 21 workers (p. 146), but failed to report how many large firms shifted from entrepreneurial to managerial control during this period. I predict a continuation of the growth of business management by professional managers who are not entrepreneurs.

7. The Rise of Participatory Democracy

Naisbitt's seventh megatrend is the transition from representative democracy to participatory democracy in government, business, and the marketplace. In government this trend takes the form of increasing use of referenda and initiatives (pp. 164-74). He failed to note that this trend is almost 100 years old in the U.S., and therefore is not a "new direction." He also failed to show that it is an international trend. All major social trends go on simultaneously in two or more, usually in most, advanced countries. If the growth of participatory democracy in government is peculiar to the U.S., it is probably not a megatrend.

I believe it is a mistake to predict a transition from representatite to participatory democracy. The use of referenda and initiatives can supplement, but not replace democracy. Only a very small proportion, probably less than 0.1% of all laws is ever likely to be enacted or repealed by referenda and initiatives. Hence, representative democracy will always be the most important means of legislation in democratic countries.

In recent decades there has been a steady growth of the use of public opinion polls to help politicians determine trends in public opinion. They perform this function much more accurately, quickly, and cheaply than do referenda and initiatives, and therefore may soon slow down or end the growth in the use of referenda and initiatives. Naisbitt did not mention the growing use of opinion polls, but he might claim them as evidence of the growth of participatory democracy. I consider them a means of improving representative democracy.

Naisbitt claimed that the growth of participatory democracy in business "permits workers, shareholders, consumers, and community leaders a larger say in determining how corporations will run" (p. 175). He failed to note that the growth of such influence has been largely the result of legislation passed by representative legislative bodies, not the result of direct participatory action on or in business firms by workers, shareholders, consumers, and political leaders. For instance, consumers and workers have induced the U.S. government to increase greatly its control over industrial pollution, industrial accidents, product safety, new drugs, private pension systems, etc. The author's neglect of such consumer influence on government is shown by his remarkable assertion that "consumers... have stopped asking the government for more regulations" (p. 177). I believe that such asking has not stopped, and will long continue to grow.

8. The Rise of Networking

The title of Chapter 8, "From Hierarchies to Networking," summarizes Naisbitt's eighth megatrend, which is the transition from hierarchical to networking forms of organization. "Simply stated, networks are people talking to each other, sharing ideas, information, and resources" (p. 192). I can see no reason why such networks are incompatible with hierarchical management, and I cannot conceive of a governmental or business management structure which is not essentially hierarchical. Naisbitt made no effort to describe a national government or corporate management which has replaced hierarchical administration with networking administration. He merely claimed that more mutual discussion and advice would be useful within hierarchical organizations. It is very difficult to determine whether such discussion and advice is actually growing. Even if it is growing, it is not a major social trend, let alone a megatrend.

9. "From North to South"

This is the title of Chapter 9. Naisbitt's ninth megatrend is that "a massive shift... in population... wealth and economic activity from North to South" is occurring, and, presumably, will continue (pp. 207-08). In fact, the centuries-old U.S. population megatrend is the movement of population and industry from the East to the West, not from the North to the South, and I predict this movement to the West will continue to be larger than any North-South movement. Texas is really more western than southern. Florida is the only southern state which has recently grown rapidly as a result of North-South migration. Moreover, much of the growth of Florida and Texas has resulted from migration from the South (Latin America) to the North.

Naisbitt himself conceded that "The North-South shift is really a shift to the West, the Southwest, and Florida" (p. 210). If so, why call it a North-South shift?

10. More Options

The tenth and last chapter is devoted to Naisbitt's tenth megatrend, namely the growth in the number and variety of choices Americans can make in life styles, occupations, consumers' goods, religion, etc. "In a relatively short time, the unified mass society has fractionalized into many diverse groups with a wide array of differing tastes and values..." (p. 232).

There are two chief objections to this thesis. First, there was no "unified mass society" with common tastes and values in the early decades of this century. For instance, the percentage of foreign-born U.S. residents declined steadily from 13.2% in 1920 to 4.7% in 1970. And differences in the life styles and values of immigrants and natives, of the rich and the poor, and of whites and negroes were much greater in 1900 than in 1980. The long-run trend has been increasing assimilation of immigrants and negroes, and increasing homogenization of life styles and consumption patterns.

Secondly, every increase in average real income per person gives men greater freedom of choice among life styles, occupations, and consumer goods, and such income has risen almost steadily in the U.S. for over 200 years. Thus the growth of such freedom of choice is not a new trend which has transformed our society "in a relatively short time," specifically, since 1956. Freedom of choice will of course continue to grow indefinitely as real incomes rise. It is noteworthy that Naisbitt failed to note this trend in personal real income, a trend far more important than any of his ten megatrends.

According to Naisbitt, "The U.S. is today undergoing a revival of religious belief and church attendance" (p. 239). In fact, there is a great preponderance of evidence that such belief and attendance have long been declining. For instance, Gallup polls report that the percent of U.S. adults who claim they attended church during the previous week declined from 49% in 1955 to 40% in 1980. And the World Christian Encyclopaedia (1981), edited by the Rev. Dr. D. B. Barrett and published by the Oxford University Press, reports that the number of "nonreligious" persons rose from 1.3% of U.S. population in 1900 to 6.7% in 1980, with the most rapid increase (50%) occurring between 1970 and 1980. Barrett predicted another 50% increase in the number of nonreligious persons in the U.S. by 2000 A.D.

11. General Comments

As the full title of his book makes clear, Naisbitt concentrated his attention on "new directions" or trends. But a trend which is new today, i.e., which is not well and long established, may disappear or reverse itself tomorrow. It should not be called a megatrend until it has become obvious and well established. The term "new megatrend" is almost self-contradictory.

It is very significant that Naisbitt never explained how long a future he was covering. He talked mostly about social changes now in process, without venturing to predict their long continuance, perhaps because he was aware that a new trend may disappear or reverse itself tomorrow.

Very little of this book is devoted to the author's explicit predictions. It consists largely of anecdotes and of advice to business managers and politicians. The author long served as a business consultant, and much of this book is a summary of the advice he had given.

Naisbitt largely limited his discussion to social trends in the U.S. But only trends common to most or all advanced countries are significant enough to be called megatrends.

He phrased most of his megatrends in such a way that it will be difficult if not impossible to verify their existence, and never noted the statistical series which could be used to verify them.

He failed to include in his list of ten megatrends many trends more important than any in his list—for instance, the growth of population, of abortion, of preschool education, of real personal income, of the scale of management, of government ownership, of social insurance, of nuclear armament, of civil rights for negroes, etc. On the whole, he contributed very little to the science of futurism or to our knowledge of the future.

GERARD O'NEILL AS A FUTURIST

Gerard K. O'Neill is a professor of physics at Princeton University, originator of the space-colony concept, and author of the best-selling book, The High Frontier. In his new 1981 book, 2081, published by Simon and Schuster, he forecast many features of human life as of the year 2081.

1. Method of Prediction

In his stimulating first chapter, "The Art of Prophecy" (pp. 18-38), O'Neill briefly reviewed and evaluated some of the major predictions and methods of fifteen earlier prophets, utopian and science fiction authors, and futurists - More, Verne, Wells, Kipling, Haldane, Clarke, George Darwin, George Thomson, Bernal, Tsiolkovski, Orwell, Bellamy, Aldous Huxley, Zamiatin, McGeorge Bundy, the Club of Rome, and Heilbroner. As the chapter title and contents suggest, the author made little effort to distinguish futurism from its prescientific predecessors. And he never explicitly limited 2081 to scientific futurism. However, he relied primarily upon scientific methods of prediction, including projection of well-established trends. The major exception was a brief reference to "my own value judgements," including placing a higher value on "the freedom of the individual" than on world peace (p. 19).

His review of the literature led O'Neill to conclude that, "most prophets overestimated how much the world would be transformed by social and political change and underestimated the forces of technological change" (p. 20). One reason for this dubious conclusion may be that he reviewed the work of too many novelists and too few scientific futurists. However, many science fiction authors have grossly overestimated the speed and extent of future technological change, and I shall argue that O'Neill has done the same.

Although he claimed that most futurists have overestimated the speed of social change, he charged that some, including Bellamy, had predicted the development of a "static society" (pp. 28, 31). In fact, after describing a celebration of the year 2000 in Looking Backward, Bellamy had written glowingly of "the further progress that shall be made, ever onward and upward, till the race shall achieve its ineffable destiny" (p. vi). In this and other ways his review of the literature distorted or ignored the views of futurists who predicted continuing social change.

Like Karl Marx, whose name is not mentioned, O'Neill claimed that technological progress is the chief cause of social change. He devoted chapters II to VI to the major classes of technological change—computers, automation, space colonies, energy, and communications—which he forecast would be the major causes of near-future social change, "the drivers of change," from 1982 to 2081. He largely ignored non-technological factors such as the spread of education, the advance of social science, and the growth of social reform movements.

He consistently minimized or ignored the importance of well-established social trends. For instance, he asserted that, "Irreversible change is confined... to a single area: technology and its consequences" (p. 33). He also mistakenly claimed that "All our present political forms—dictatorship, democracy, and their variants—have been with us in some form for millenia." (p. 32). This implies that the rise of modern democratic government is an imaginary or unimportant political trend, which may be the reason he did not forecast the continuance or spread of this trend.

Moreover, his claim that the technological change is irreversible implies that men will never abandon the use of nuclear power or weapons. Yet he himself predicted that bicycles would partially replace automobiles in many urban areas (pp. 140, 223), and that the use of nuclear fission power may be limited or ended for political reasons (p. 24).

O'Neill stressed the sound idea that it is possible to make many valid predictions by determining the probable evolution and growing effects of recent technological advances. "The future," he wrote, "is likely to be shaped far more by the evolution of technologies we already understand than by the effects of scientific breakthroughs that we do not even suspect" (p. 36). Many of his predictions were based upon his projection of such technological evolution. He used this method of prediction much more than most other futurists have used it.

O'Neill suggested that, in predicting the future, "we must also take into account the well-known phenomenon of growth called the 'S-curve', "—slow growth, rapid growth, slow growth—(p. 37), but, in predicting individual trends, he never referred to this curve, or used it to support his predictions.

Finally, he based many of his forecasts partly upon an explanation of the benefits that would result from the forecast trend or event, but he did not list or discuss this method of prediction.

2. Population

According to O'Neill, the Earth's population "will exceed 6 billion before the year 2000" (p. 26). By 2081 it will have risen to 10 billion (p. 76), the natural annual rate of growth due to births will be 1%, and "off-Earth emigration will be higher than that. As a result, Earth's population will continue declining after 2081 until in 2131 it will be lower than it had been for over a century" (p. 186), i.e., less than 9 billion.

3. Agriculture

O'Neill forecast that agriculture will soon experience a radical revolution. Closed-cycle (greenhouse) agriculture will largely replace open-field dirt farming because it will reduce water consumption and pollution, exclude bugs and blights physically rather than chemically, reduce land use and permit reforestation, produce superior products, and help to preserve small, one-family farms. "As it gradually takes over during the next century...it will have an enormous positive effect on reducing the pollution of our lakes and streams, increasing the purity of our foods, and permitting the reforestation of our landscape" (pp. 23839). He should have added that it would increase oxygen and decrease carbon dioxide in the atmosphere, and thus delay or prevent a harmful rise in Earth's average temperature.

Nevertheless, these predictions are very dubious because of the high capital costs of greenhouses. They may prove economic for some plants in some areas, but probably not for maize, wheat, soy beans, sugar cane, potatoes, rice, etc.

4. Automated Factories

By 2081, factories will be "largely automated" and "usually located underground with trees and flowers growing above them" (p. 209). In advanced countries the assembly line and material handling and processing will be automated. Moreover, nearly all maintenance and repair work will be done by mobile robots. And many robots will be able to reproduce themselves. Only the invention and design of new plants, factory tools and machines, and finished products will require human labor, "because machines can't dream" (pp. 56-57).

I believe there will be a strong factory-automation trend during the next 100 years, but I predict the trend will be much less rapid than O'Neill predicted. I doubt that much maintenance and repair work will be done by robots before 2081, and the prediction that some machines and/or factories will be able to reproduce themselves (p. 58) seems quite unreasonable.

5. Working at Home

O'Neill forecast that continuous future improvement and cheapening of the means of communication will greatly increase the proportion of people who work at home for an outside employer. This trend will be so substantial that "it will ease the congestion of the morning and evening rush hours" (p. 99). Later, he explained that while top executives "will probably continue to work in city skyscrapers...the clerical work of 2081, most of it done through computer consoles, will occupy employees in their homes, far away from their company's headquarters" (p. 200). I explained earlier why such predictions are unjustified.

6. Hours of Labor

According to O'Neill, U.S. workers will labor for pay only about eight hours a day, three days in a week in 2081 (p. 165). He did not discuss the lengths of paid summer or winter vacations, but implied that they would be more liberal than today.

I expect that the median hours of labor will still be longer than 24 hours a week in 2081, and that men will work for at least four days a week. A five-day, thirty-hour week seems most likely. It is the last hours of labor each day which are the most tiring and the least productive.

O'Neill also predicted a great increase in the use of flextime, flexible hours of labor. I agree that many workers will be given more and more freedom to alter the scheduling or performance of their regular hours of labor.

7. Health Care

O'Neill predicted the adoption of "a complete system of national health insurance in the U.S. ...many decades" before 2081. He also forecast that surgery will be automated, performed in "automatic operating rooms...fully controlled by computerized machinery and supervised by expert surgeons." They will "virtually eliminate the possibility of error" (p. 198).

He explained that the costs of malpractice insurance will remain high for doctors on Earth, but predicted that that doctors in "most orbited hospitals" will not experience such costs because their colonies will adopt no-fault insurance laws (p. 198). Moreover, so far as "medicine is socialized, malpractice suits will disappear because the government will refuse to submit to them" (p. 203).

He asserted that, "As computers are further miniaturized and automation reduces the cost of complex mechanisms, we can expect also that surgical implants [of miniature computers] will substitute for the use of drugs" to control physiological processes like the flow of blood and ovulation (p. 203). And "the doctors may be assisted in diagnosis" by computers (p. 204).

I agree that the adoption of national health insurance in the U.S. is very probable, and that computer diagnosis will become more common, but his prediction of automated surgery by the year 2081 seems very unrealistic.

8. Abundant Cheap Energy

O'Neill predicted that energy will become increasingly abundant throughout the next hundred years. As a result of this trend and of economic growth, "In 2081... most advanced countries may be using energy at six times the present North American per capita rates" (p.83), "the world average per capita use...is likely to equal present North American levels" (p. 80), which implies unrealistically rapid growth rates in nearly all countries. The author had explained that living standards vary directly and proportionately with per capita energy use, that in 1981 India had a standard only "a fiftieth" of the U.S. level (p. 76), and that energy will be put to use much more efficiently everywhere in 2081 (p. 94).

According to O'Neill, "all the methods for generating energy that are now in use will still be operating in 2081" (p. 85). But, "We'll probably shift during the next century from a fossil-dominated energy economy to a healthier reliance on long-term resources. In my guess, from 50...to 95% of the energy used on Earth in 2081 will be from self-renewing or near infinite resources...nuclear fission and fusion...perhaps thermal power...satellite solar power," but not much from ground-based solar power because it will remain too costly and environmentally harmful (p. 86).

"My own favorite energy source, not only for 2081 but for the 1980's, is Satellite Solar Power (SPS)" obtained from "a large array of solar cells or of turbogenerators, located in synchronous...orbit above a point on the equator" from which low-density microwaves are relayed to ground station (pp. 91-92). SPS would be relatively benign environmentally because it would heat the atmosphere only half as much as other energy-generating methods (p. 93). These predictions concerning SPS seem quite unrealistic.

9. The Real Income Trend

O'Neill forecast that average annual per person real income in the U.S. will rise fairly steadily from about $16,000 for a family of four in 1980 to about $200,000 in 2081 (in 1980 dollars). He claimed that the same rate of growth, 2.5% per year, existed from 1880 to 1980, and therefore is likely to continue for another hundred years (p. 156).

In fact, such personal incomes rose at much less than 2.5% from 1880 to 1980. The rate was only about 1.6% a year, which, if projected to 2081, would yield a relevant family income of only about $80,000 (in 1980 dollars). Moreover, due to continuing depletion of natural resources, high military spending, low savings rates, reductions in the hours of labor, etc., American real personal incomes are likely to grow less rapidly in the next hundred years than in the last.

Although he predicted continued rapid economic progress in the U.S., and presumably in other advanced countries, he forecast that, "Twenty years from now our world will be poorer and hungrier than it is today" (p. 76). This implies a marked decline in real personal incomes in "the other four fifths of humanity." This decline is very unlikely because in recent decades economic growth in backward countries like India, Mexico, and Brazil has been more rapid than in the U.S.

10. Identification Anklets

O'Neill forecast that by 2081 almost all persons on Earth will wear identification anklets which will not only serve like universal credit cards but will enable everyone to "receive phone calls anywhere" and "pick up merchandise in a store and walk out with it, free of the delay of waiting in a check-out line" (p. 117). Moreover, the location of each anklet wearer will be repeatedly detected by local sensors and reported to central computers, which can be used for police purposes (pp. 152, 158).

I believe that a universal identification credit card is far more likely than such an anklet to be widely used in 2081, and I doubt that any device will, by 2081, permit most people to receive phone calls anywhere.

Although he had explained that identification anklets could serve as substitutes for a credit card, O'Neill later forecast that credit cards would still be used in 2081, and even that most people would need "three or four major credit cards." He attributed this continuing irrationality to "competition and antitrust laws" (p. 171). As usual, he did not hesitate to predict radical technological advances, like the use of identification anklets, but was unwilling to predict economic reforms, like the rationalization of the credit card industry.

11. Money and Crime

If people carry less money, and banks, offices and homes contain less money, burglary and the theft of money will obviously decrease. "Money robberies are likely to decrease because money transactions will evolve to exchange of coded information between computers. Instead we will see an increase in...the counterfeiting of credit cards and the manipulation of monetary credit" (p. 201).

These are very conservative predictions. If the use of tangible money for payments over $10 were abolished, and if all bank statements were subject to inspection by police, it would be possible to prevent or detect nearly all crime, including computer and credit card crimes, for all suspiciously large personal expenditures would be disclosed to the police. The adoption of this easy method of crime prevention and detection is much more likely than the general use of identification anklets by 2081.

According to O'Neill, "The most frightening development in crime will be...terrorist assaults," including those "carried out with nuclear weapons." The rise of electronic fund transfer will do less to restrict such crime than to restrict other crime (p. 202). I agree on the growing danger of nuclear terrorism, but I believe that police surveillance of bank statements could be very effective against such terrorism in a largely cash-less economy.

12. Household Robots

O'Neill forecast that by 2081 most U.S. homes would enjoy the services of a general purpose, talking, household robot capable of performing most of the tasks now performed by a well-trained butler, cook or gardner. It will be able to respond to most requests, answer the doorbell, serve drinks and meals, weed the garden, cook food, etc. (pp. 150-151, 154-163).

I doubt that there will be any robots capable of performing so many tasks by 2081. And if there are some, they will be far too costly for use by an average American family. Robots will play an ever-growing role in industry and commerce, perhaps even in homes, but they will not perform most housekeeping chores by 2081.

13. Shopping

In 2081, home computers will reorder staples whenever stocks run low (p. 141), but personal shopping for other goods, especially shopping goods, will be practiced more than ever because real family incomes will be over ten times their 1981 level and most people will greatly enjoy shopping for luxuries (p. 159). Both credit cards and identification anklets will be used to facilitate payment by direct electronic debits to personal bank accounts (p. 171), and nearly all purchases will be delivered to homes by underground parcel transport systems. Some items ordered by phone or computer will be delivered "in less than one minute" (p. 162). The last, unrealistic prediction is typical of O'Neill.

14. Books and Magazines

By 2081 books will be available "in the form of a small square wafer about as big as my thumbnail and not much thicker." They will be magnified and displayed for reading on thin "flexible slates, each the size of a standard sheet of typewriter paper." Portable "composition machines," i.e., improved typewriters, will be about the same size, and will store typed material (p. 171).

However, "for high-quality, glossy reproduction of colors, as in art books, maps, and slick-paper magazines...the printing of ink onto paper" will still be best (p. 237). There will be a great many more "magazines specializing in luxury, cuisine, fashion, or the collection of beautiful or rare books" because real family incomes will be far higher (p. 159). The last two predictions are very plausible, but the others are dubious.

15. Driverless Cars

By 2081 all country highways and city streets will be equipped with electronic devices which guide and space autos so that passengers need make no effort to drive their suitably equipped cars. They will merely instruct their car computers where they wish to go, and the car will take them there. Moreover, before a passenger sets out, his car will bring itself to his front door and, after his arrival, will park itself or return to its garage automatically, on voice commands (pp. 135-138).

The development of driverless cars will permit the movement of freight in unmanned trucks and the use of unmanned taxicabs in cities. Also, parents will be able to send their children to school in unmanned private cars, which will perform as vocally instructed by the parents (p. 236). He also explained that, "Once driving is automated, we can expect an enormous saving in human life" due to the prevention of highway accidents.

These predictions seem very unrealistic, primarily because the installation of such electronic equipment on all or most streets and highways would require enormous capital investments to achieve relatively small economic benefits. I predict that more profitable investments will be available. It is not economic to do everything which is technologically possible. Moreover, vandalism could easily sabotage electronic highway controls and cause many accidents.

16. Private Airplane Use

O'Neill predicted that by 2081 "private aircraft... will be as common...as is the family car today." They will be "quiet and fuel efficient [and] will fly at half the speed of sound, entirely under the control of a central air-traffic computer" (p. 192). He even offered a picture of such a plane. Control of flight by central computers will greatly reduce the danger of collisions and other accidents.

He based this daring prediction partly on his forecast that "the average family in 2081 will be about twelve times as wealthy, in real...currency, as a similar family today" (p. 190). I have already argued that this is a gross overestimate.

Furthermore, I doubt that private airplane use on the predicted scale will be anywhere near reasonably safe in 2081. I predict that less than one in ten U.S. families will own a private airplane by 2081, and that few if any private planes will be unpiloted.

17. Underground Transport

By 2081 nearly all large cities less than 500 miles apart will be connected by six-foot-diameter tunnels through which "vehicles running in vacuum and supported only by magnetic fields" move at speeds up to 2000 miles per hour (pp. 131, 215). It will be possible to travel from New York to Washington in such a tunnel in "only fourteen minutes—at a cost of less than four dollars..." (p. 134).

Moreover, every U.S. city wll have a similarly operated tunnel system which permits home delivery of all small retail purchases. And package loading and unloading at each terminal will be automated (p. 176). I strongly doubt that these predictions will be fully or largely verified by 2081, primarily because of the immense capital investments required.

18. Covered Cities

By 2081, O'Neill predicted, most Americans in severe climates will live in new covered garden towns. A typical covered town or city unit will be a mile square, house 10,000 persons, and have a three-layer roof covering the entire city. The outer layer will consist of several meters of metal frame and insulation "topped by a sheet of bright, reflecting aluminum" It will be divided into sections which can be rolled to one side of the town. The middle layer will consist of glass, similarly movable. The inner layer will be a screen to keep out insects. When the outer cover excludes light, the town will be lighted by high pressure sodium lamps. In winter, snow plows will sweep snow off the largely flat outer cover (pp. 144-45). The use of such a town cover will permit the year-round maintenance of a near-ideal climate and semi-tropical trees and gardens within a town, and may even reduce heating and cooling costs.

"Despite all the disadvantages that big cities now face...they will survive and will be healthier in some respects by 2081" because their blighted areas will be replaced by parks, greenbelts, and new covered towns, and their desirable areas will be renovated and covered over (pp. 200-01).

I believe that the kind of three-layer city roofs predicted above will be much too expensive to be economic in 2081, though one or two experimental covered towns may exist then.

19. Russia

In 2081 Russia will still be a dictatorship with a "state-centralized economic system, low productivity, and a powerful secret service." But emigration will be permitted, and the average Russian will be "wealthier than his ancestors" and own a private car. Tourists will still be warned against the purchse of black market rubles, and "a great many Russians" will still be "obviously apprehensive about being seen talking to...a foreigner." However, centralized, planned control of state enterprises will have been slightly relaxed (pp. 211-12).

O'Neill was almost as pessimistic about the future of Russia as he was overoptimistic about the future of America. He implied that the gap in living standards will become far larger. Since this gap has long been declining, this prediction seems very questionable.

20. Africa

O'Neill anticipated that in 2081 Africa will remain the most backward and unstable continent in the world. Many African nations will be ruled by military dictators. "After 150 years of civil war and revolution, every village" will be "stuffed with weapons" (p. 205). These predictions seem contradictory, for few dictators allow subject villages to be stuffed with weapons.

On the other hand, by 2081 some relatively successful African nations will be "well on the way to universal education, thanks to direct broadcast satellites, and economic prosperity..." This is one of his few forecasts that seem cautious and conservative to me.

By 2081 "every African nation, no matter how small" will be armed with nuclear weapons, and the evidence of past nuclear wars and acts of terrorism will be obvious (p. 206). Such wars and acts will be the results of African disputes, not of the cold war or other outside interference. I believe they are more likely to be a part of the cold war.

21. Space Colonies

By far the most important and unusual prediction in 2081 is the startling forecast that, "Well before 2081 a substantial fraction of the human population may be living in space colonies" (p. 66). Indeed, "By 2081 there may be more Americans in space colonies than...in the U.S." (p. 71). The context makes clear that the author meant to state probabilities, not mere possibilities.

"A space colony would be an Earthlike habitat outside Earth's shadow, growing its own food and deriving all its energy from the sun" (p. 61). "A metal shell can hold the atmospheric pressure we need for breathing. Water once introduced...will remain, circling through a closed ecological cycle. The effect of Earth's gravity can be duplicated by rotation.... Lunar soil can rest on the interior of a metal shell to form land area.... In space...grain...flowers, trees, and grass can flourish" (p. 64).

O'Neill even forecast that as early as 2023 it will be possible for a group of 20,000 families to buy a fleet of second-hand space ships capable of carrying and housing them, and all tools and machines needed to construct immense space colonies from asteroid materials, on a five-year trip to the area where the space colonies will be built (pp. 106-07). Such a forecast is utterly fantastic! I doubt that such a colonization project will become feasible in a thousand years.

The most startling feature of this prediction is the size of the predicted mass emigration to space colonies. It is plausible to predict the creation of a single permanent residential space colony before 2081, but O'Neill forecast that "by the year 2010...there will be many space colonies..." (p. 105). Here he used will, not may.

I expect that there will be several small scientific and/or military space stations in operation by 2010, but the prediction that there will be many permanent space colonies by that year, or many thousands by 2081, seems completely unreasonable to me. A space station is unlikely to house more than 20 men before 2010. O'Neill suggested that a typical space colony would house 10,000 persons (p. 107).

There are several reaons why mass emigration to space colonies before 208 is very unlikely.

First, great social changes cannot occur that fast, except perhaps as a result of devastating nuclear warfare. Social inertia is too real and powerful to permit immense and rapid emigration to space colonies before 2081.

Secondly, I doubt that it will be technologically possible to house and feed many thousands of families in space colonies by 2010, or many millions by 2081. O'Neill suggested that the raw materials for constructing space colonies will come from the moon and from asteroids (pp. 64-65), but such materials will have to be mined, refined, and fabricated into building materials and components before they can be assembled into space colonies. No methods for such processing on a mass scale in the very harsh moon or space environment are likely to be developed before 2010, or even 2081.

Thirdly, life in a pressurized space colony will always be much less safe than life on earth because any failure of the space structure due to accident, meteors, fires, sabotage, terrorism, or military attack will rapidly depressurize the space colony in the same way that a hole in a high-flying airplane depressurizes it. Moreover, for these and other reasons, travel to and from space colonies will always be much more dangerous than travel on Earth.

O'Neill predicted that many people will emigrate to distant space colonies in order to escape the risks due to continuing intermittent warfare on Earth (p. 243). But space colonies, however distant, would be extraordinarily vulnerable to military attack or terrorist sabotage. The shell of a space colony could be easily ruptured by a minor military attack or by a terrorist bomb, and any such rupture would result in rapid depressurization of the colony and death for nearly all of its inhabitants, who would rarely wear costly and cumbersome astronaut suits.

Finally, I am convinced that even if large-scale emigration to space colonies becomes technologically feasible, it will not become economic, i.e., economically sound. O'Neill suggested that by 2023 it will cost only "several billion (1981) dollars" to house 80,000 persons in eight space colonies (pp. 106-07). But it cost over $30 billion to put a few men on the moon for a few hours only.

O'Neill assumed that there will be rapid technological progress and great cost reduction in space travel and construction. He ignored the vital point that continued technological progress and cost reduction in travel and construction on earth will help to preserve an enormous cost difference between activities in space and on earth. I doubt that it will ever be economic to house millions of people in space.

Today it would cost far more to build a complete, self-sufficient new colony in space than to build one in any one of many empty and desolate areas on earth —the Sahara Desert, Northern Canada, etc. And the situation will be similar in 2010 or 2081. Moreover, there is still ample space for building new towns in most states within the U.S. What is relatively scarce is not land, but capital for investment in new towns and colonies on earth. And there is no good reason to believe that space colonization will increase such capital or make it more productive.

According to O'Neill, "the fundamental transformation that space colonies will bring about is from an economics of scarcity—the 'zero-sum game' that we are forced to play on Earth—to an economics of abundance" (p. 62). This is a naive and senseless prediction! All economic progress makes most goods less scarce. But there is no scientific way of determining when an economy of scarcity turns into one of abundance. For economists, economic goods are scarce by definition, and the term <u>economy of abundance</u> is self-contradictory. For laymen the term is meaningless because no statement containing it can be verified, in theory or in practice.

22. Space Travel

O'Neill anticipated, by 2081, 100-ton space ships large enough to carry a score or more or passengers for months or years in great comfort at incredible speeds. Each such ship "will have to produce an amount of power equal to about one-fifth of the installed electric generator capacity" in the U.S. today (p. 120). It will fly between space colonies and orbital stations and will not land on the Earth. Orbital shuttles will carry people and cargo between the Earth and orbital stations. Spaceports, located on the equator, will be as large and crowded as big-city airports on Earth are now, serving 500 million passengers a year (p. 186). He went into much interesting detail as to the technologies involved. All of this is fascinating but unbelievable, science fiction not scientific futurism.

23. International Language

O'Neill suggested that by the year 2081 a new international language, Common Basic, would be used as the chief international language. It will not be "as logical as...Esperanto or Interlingua," but will be "more politically acceptable," because it will employ "words from every major language grouping on Earth." But "only 1% of the people on Earth" will speak it at home (p. 115).

I doubt that such a language will be created and widely used before 2081. I predict that English will still be the most widely used international language. It already contains words from all major languages.

O'Neill also forecast the use by 2081 of "slim pocket model" electronic trnslators each of which will contain "a few thousand words of vocabulary of each of 300 languages" and "ample vocabularies and grammars of almost literary quality" for every "important world language." To use it, one "simple holds the device midway between" the speaker and the auditor so it can "relay spoken sentences in either direction" (p. 172).

Here again, I believe, O'Neill has grossly overestimated the speed of technological progress. Large machines which can roughly translate one language into another will probably be in use by 2081, but not "slim pocket models" which can translate many languages almost perfectly.

24. International Relations

In 2081 the Earth will have no world government, empire, or condominium able to preserve peace. Rather, most nations will not only have more powerful nuclear weapons but other new and old weapons as well. O'Neill predicted that, "the political world of 2081 will still be fragmented into nations...still...heavily armed" (p. 32). War will be about as frequent as in the past. He failed to say how many of these wars, if any, would be fought with nuclear weapons, but he wrote, "There is reason to hope that nuclear war...will not escalate to the point of total destruction." However, "continuing peace seems equally remote as long as the power of the nation-states remains" (p. 243).

Although he did not explicitly predict the social and economic costs of the wars he expected, he did predict a tenfold increase in world wealth, which implies that these economic costs will be negligible.

While he minimized the future losses from nuclear warfare, he stressed the magnitude of coming losses from nuclear terrorism. He explained that, during the 21st Century in Africa, "every now and then one of their capitals went sky-high when the local out-party managed to smuggle in a nuke" (p. 206). He also forecast that during the next 100 years Japan will "suffer more through terrorist bombs than through all the wars of the past century" (p. 218).

25. Comments

In this essay I have ignored many technological predictions, especially those which have no obvious and significant social consequences. As a natural scientist and engineer, O'Neill featured technological, not social, progress throughout his book, while I, a social scientist, am concerned chiefly with future social trends. Since I am not an engineer, I have been reluctant to criticize his individual technological predictions on technological grounds, but most of them seem unrealistic to me both because they predict very rapid technological progress and because they would require a very great increase in the rate of national saving and investment.

O'Neill consistently minimized the need for and probability of social change, and equally maximized the probability of radical technological change. He had little if anything to say about the future growth of birth control, feminism, nursery schools, euthanasia, negro liberation, free legal services, rationalization of industry, etc., but a great deal to say about space colonies, interstellar flight, domestic robots, antimatter, etc. And when he wrote about social change, he usually revealed strong conservative views, for instance on eugenics (p. 24).

ADRIAN BERRY AS A FUTURIST

Adrian Berry was a science writer for the London Sunday Telegraph in 1974 when his book, The Next Ten Thousand Years, A Vision of Man's Future in the Universe, was published by the New American Library. It is largely devoted to predictions concerning space travel and colonization.

This book opens with a brief laudatory account of the rise of modern science and Francis Bacon's brilliant attack upon all philosophic reasoning. This rejection of philosophy implied that the author was devoted to scientific futurism, but he did not make this vital point explicit, as he should have. In his final chapter, "The God of Spinoza," he did engage in unproductive philosophic reasoning, but this did not affect his predictions.

1. His Thesis in Brief

According to Berry, "The thesis of this book is that economic progress and [progress in] technology are going to continue, not merely for decades, not even for centuries, but for millenia. Earth cannot provide the living space and the raw materials for such colossal geometric progression; space itself will be exploited. The planets around the sum will be inhabited and industrialized. Jupiter, the largest of these planets, will be dismantled and its fragments displaced to capture the sun's radiation more efficiently. But even these great projects will be a mere beginning. Men will also explore and colonize the planets of other suns" (pp. 24-25).

2. His Answer to Pessimists

To prepare the way for his optimistic predictions, Berry devoted Chapter 2, "No Limits to Growth," to a brief but strong criticism of both the claim that economic growth will be strictly limited by the exhaustion of natural resources and/or by dangerous pollution and the claim that population growth will limit growth in real per capita incomes.

Among the pessimists, Berry gave special attention to the Club of Rome, whose best-selling book, The Limits of Growth (1972), he wrote, had predicted "the collapse of civilization before the year 2100" if present trends in population, food supplies, pollution and raw material use continued (p. 28). Berry claimed that much had already been done to reduce pollution, and that more could and would be done. He also noted the continuing discovery and creation of new raw materials and fuels. He quoted, with approval the World Bank economists' conclusions that many of the assumptions fed into the Club of Rome economic models were "extremely pessimistic" and "not scientifically established," and that the use of data was often "careless and casual" (pp. 29-31).

Berry discussed the threat of nuclear wars and endorsed Herman Kahn's 1961 estimate that even after a disastrous nuclear war it would take no more than forty years for the U.S. to regain its previous economic condition (p. 34).

He then noted the predictions of near-future famine in the third world by Wm. and Paul Paddock and by Paul Ehrlich. "Their statistics," he claimed, like those of the Club of Rome, are based on wrong assumptions; facts that contradict their theses have been ignored" (p. 36). He explained that birth rates are falling in many developing countries, and predicted that it is "very unlikely that the 2% growth rate of [world] population will be maintained for the rest of this century." He noted and endorsed the prediction of experts that "during the next century [world] population will stabilize at about 10 billion" (p.39).

3. On Long-Run Economic Growth

After his plausible criticism of the pessimists, Berry described and predicted the enormous economic growth which will occur if the U.S. GNP continues to grow at 3% a year, thereby doubling every 23 years, for centuries. He estimated that by 2200 it will be 868 times as large as it was in 1971 (p. 47), and in 10,000 years it will repeat this incredible growth more than 60 times, eventually becoming "10 billion" times the 1971 level. He made these predictions in order to convince the reader that the U.S. and other countries will eventually have ample resources to finance space flights and projects which will each cost far more than total world GNP today.

In spite of these optimistic predictions about incredible coming wealth, Berry repeatedly claimed, later in his book, that overpopulation, pollution, and war on earth will be reasons for the future colonization of the moon, Venus, and other extraterrestrial sites (pp. 81-82, 97). To me it seems that a land where everyone is a millionaire is not seriously overpopulated and can easily afford to eliminate nearly all pollution. Moreover, an earth devastated by

repeated nuclear wars is unlikely to be able to pay
for the colonization of Venus.

Berry explained that his prediction of long-continued exponential economic growth rested on three assumptions:

"1. That there will be no substantial change in the sun's radiation.

2. That the solar system will not be invaded by a hostile or a meddlesome alien technology.

3. That there will be no fundamental change in human nature—or, more precisely, that the human reaction to stimuli will remain constant" (p. 49).

He then devoted three pages to a justification of these assumptions, and concluded that they could be restated as sound scientific predictions.

His third assumption, the most dubious one, clearly implies that mankind will not be greatly improved by eugenic measures during the next 10,000 years. Berry argued that such measures are unlikely to be adopted because most men now disapprove of them as limitations on human freedom (p. 52). In my opinion, this is an extraordinary weak and naive argument. Nearly all great social reforms were long unpopular before they were finally adopted.

Berry's list of three necessary assumptions omits the most important, for instance, the assumptions that: (1) adequate fuel and raw materials will be available, (2) nuclear warfare will not prevent the needed GNP growth and (3) population growth will not invalidate his predictions. As noted above, he did discuss these points briefly in his criticism of the pessimists, but his discussion will satisfy few critical readers. Later, he asserted that, "Even if the earth's resources prove ultimately to be finite, those of the solar system and of the great galaxy beyond are...infinite" (p. 53). Yes, but the critical question is whether earth's finite resources are sufficient to allow men to reach and exploit the planets and our galaxy. The history of the last 200 years may well justify a prediction that world economic growth will continue for another century or two at 1 to 2% a year, but not the prediction that it will continue for 10,000 years at 3%, or even 1%, a year.

4. Colonization of the Moon

According to Berry, the next major advance in space will be the colonization of the moon. "The moon ...will provide men with the land and the environment to achieve one of his greatest advances in technical and industrial growth" (p. 58). He did not predict when this colonization will begin, but he forecast that "lunarians" will number "some hundreds of thousands" before the year 2050 (p. 78).

To make his prediction seem plausible, he explained how large supplies of water could be provided on the moon by digging wells or by importing liquid hydrogen, which is 100 times lighter per cubic inch than water. He also explained how electricity could be produced cheaply by using the full solar heat of the lunar day (pp. 61-63).

Berry claimed that both optical and radar telescopes on the moon could be far larger, because of lower gravity, and far more useful, because of clear days, than on the earth, and therefore predicted their construction on the moon (pp. 67-74). He forecast that some industrial processes—like the production of vacuum-cast alloys—will be shifted to the moon because the moon environment favors them (pp. 74-75). He even suggested that certain human diseases and ailments—cancer, arthritis, old age, etc.—could receive better care in moon hospitals and rest homes than on the earth because of the lower gravity there (pp. 75-76). He predicted that "lunarians will live underground in subsurface cities" (p. 78). Surface agriculture will be carried on "under the protection of a transparent dome." Eventually, "the moon will attract so many thousands of immigrants that ultimately even the environment of this planet, with a surface area the size of Africa, will begin to deteriorate" (p. 79).

Since man has repeatedly landed on the moon, the prediction that some men will in time live on the moon is plausible. But Berry's prediction that the moon will have a population of some hundreds of thousands by 2050 is incredible. I predict that such a total will not be achieved in the next 1000 years, and probably never, for two main reasons.

First, life on the moon will always be dull and unattractive, as Berry conceded (pp. 80-81). "The environment will be dull, and the discipline will be wearisome.... A man will be unable to leave his base unless he is wearing the most ridiculous clothes, in which the slightest tear could bring an unpleasant death." I expect that men will endure such conditions temporarily in order to engage in scientific research and extraordinarily profitable activities, but will never choose them as a family living environment.

Secondly, the immense investments required to colonize the moon would yield an economic return far less than would an equal investment on earth. The vital question is not whether colonization of the moon will ever be possible, but rather whether it will ever be econonic. There is now no evidence that it ever will be economic, except as a means of scientific research, and such limited-purpose colonies are not the kind that Berry predicted.

There is still a vast amount of unused waste land on earth. Making such land habitable and fruitful will always cost far less per acre than the development and colonization of land on the moon. The continued progress of science and technology, which will make trips to the moon ever cheaper in real terms, will have a similar effect on all methods of improving life on earth. It may eventually become economic to obtain certain fuels and raw materials from the moon, but it is highly unlikely that life on the moon will ever become cheaper and more attractive than life on earth.

5. Flying City States

According to Berry, the creation and occupation of ever larger flying city states, immense space stations, will take place almost simultaneously with the near-future colonization of the moon. "Under the constant threat on earth of overcrowding, civil strife and nuclear warfare, and, above all, because of the commercial need for space manufacturing in solar-orbiting factories, the 1990's are likely to see the beginning of the construction of flying cities, which will ultimately expand to many miles in diameter, and provide permanent homes for hundreds of thousands of people" (p. 163).

To create artificial gravity, these cities will spin on an axis. There will be "great fields of agriculture or hydroponic farms beneath transparent domes" and "really sophisticated advances in weightless manufacturing will be achieved" (pp. 164-65).

Such cities will receive most of their raw materials from the moon because rocket takeoff from the low-gravity moon requires far less power than rocket takeoff from the earth. Industrial wastes will be ejected into space and propelled towards the sun. Their basic electric power source will be the sun. And "as the cities become more complex...they are likely to follow their own orbits around the solar system.... By the 23rd century, a region approximating to the earth's orbit around the sun will be a seemingly endless stream of massive residential and industrial hardware" in the form of flying city states (pp. 166-67).

Such predictions are fascinating but implausible. Men will probably build ever larger space stations for scientific, military, and, perhaps, industrial use, but they are very unlikely to build residential flying cities in the foreseeable future.

6. The Colonization of Venus

According to Berry, the present environment of Venus "is totally unfavorable to human life." For instance, 90% of the atmosphere "consists of the unbreathable gas, carbon dioxide" and "the temperature at the surface...is approximately 900° Fahrenheit" (p. 83). Nevertheless, Berry confidently predicted an immense human colonization of Venus.

To prepare for the colonization of Venus, man will have to radically alter its climate. Since this climate resembles that of the earth before life appeared, it will be necessary to repeat artificially some of the evolution which occurred naturally on earth. Microorganisms—like those which appeared spontaneously on the earth, gradually consumed vast quantities of carbon dioxide, and liberated the oxygen—will be scattered over and through the atmosphere of Venus. Blue-green algae, the first genuine life form on earth, may be the most suitable. According to Berry, this simple and relatively inexpensive procedure will suffice to create a livable environment on Venus (pp. 90-94).

"Living on Venus will have its inconveniences... the plant rotates extremely slowly, so...that...each day and each night lasts about 60 earth days. The two-month nights...will resemble arctic winters." Nevertheless, "adventurous farmer colonists and others determined to be independent...and to escape...from the earthly dangers of pollution, overpopulation, and war" will colonize Venus and multiply until Venus has about as large a population and as many social problems as the earth (pp. 96-98).

Berry did not predict how long this process of reconditioning and colonizing Venus will take, but the title of his book and his predictions of later events suggest that it should take far less than 10,000 years. I think it is more likely to require at least a billion years because it took natural evolution on earth that long to produce a livable environment on earth. Moreover, I doubt that men will ever leave a super-affluent and well-governed earth to live through 60-day arctic nights on Venus, except for scientific research.

Berry predicted the colonization of other planets after the colonization of Venus. He explicitly excluded only Mercury because it is too close to the sun (p. 175). But he made no effort to explain how these other planets could be made habitable. Instead, after discussing the colonization of Venus, he next predicted the creation of the first great Dyson sphere.

7. "Building the First Great Sphere"

This is the title of Chapter 13, in which Berry made his most daring predictions. The great sphere, really a large part of a sphere, "will comprise tens of millions of [artificially created] loose-flying objects, ranging from several hundred earth-sized [colonized] worlds to countless smaller industrial planetoids," all circling the sun in synchronous orbits like that of the earth (p. 176). They will be so numerous that they will absorb "at least half" of the sun's radiation (p. 178).

This sphere—called a Dyson sphere after Freeman Dyson, who first suggested it—will be created out of material obtained by disintegrating the planet Jupiter, whose "mass is more than twice that of all the other eight planets put together." Berry discussed three possible ways to disintegrate Jupiter, and forecast the use of "fusion reactors...placed in suborbits inside Jupiter's atmosphere, flying above the slushy surface. They would "suck in the gaseous hydrogen and convert it steadily by fusion into heavy elements such as iron," which would be moved to the desired new orbits by means of "rocket motors or more probably magnetic fields..." (p. 174). I omit most of the technical explanation here because I think few readers would understand it, and I am not competent to criticize it.

"The huge population centers of a completed Dyson sphere would consist of millions of different-sized worlds. To an inhabitant of any one of these worlds the daytime sky will seem much like that of today. The sun will be roughly the same size distance from him as it is from us.... The night sky will be brilliant from the glare of the reflected sunlight of countless [new, Dyson sphere] celestial objects" (p. 177).

8. Interstellar Travel and Colonization

Berry predicted that construction and colonization of such a Dyson sphere around the sun will be followed by human trips to and colonization of planets revolving around other suns or stars, and eventually the construction of Dyson spheres around many of these stars. "The" human exploration and colonization of this almost unbounded expanse of suns with their accompanying planets represent the true future activity of man" (p. 25).

Since the orthodox current interpretation of physical laws suggest that it will always be very difficult, if not impossible, for man to travel the vast interstellar distances, Berry offered a new interpretation of these laws. He predicted that men will learn how to travel to the stars by slipping out of space into "superspace," more specifically, into "the inner hole of superspace" (p. 115).

"Worm-holes are the entrance to superspace and the exits from it...a spaceship could pass through a worm-hole, enter superspace, and then emerge from superspace through another worm-hole into another part of our own universe...inside superspace time does not exist, and a journey through any part of it would therefore be instantaneous..." (p. 122). Thus instantaneous interstellar travel by human colonists will eventually be possible.

Moreover, Berry predicted that even if this unorthodox method of space travel does not work, men will develop "engines that will accelerate a starship to nearly 670 million mph, which will permit starships to reach the nearest stars in a reasonable time. The passengers will age so slowly, due to their speed of travel, that they will require only three weeks' food and water for a nine-year (by earth time) trip (p. 125).

Berry asserted that "there are likely to be hundreds of millions of worlds in the [our] galaxy fit for human occupation" and that, "Multitudes of colonial expeditions will set out" and find "suitable planets." In time "Dyson spheres are likely to become as relatively commonplace in the galaxy as expressways have become in modern industrial countries" (p. 178).

Berry did not predict near-future interstellar trips, "But by the year 2100 it will be a very different matter. If the growth of technology, science and wealth sustain anything like the [recent] rate... the first tentative moves to colonize our local [extra-solar] sector of the galaxy will by then have begun" (p. 140). This is a wild prediction! I strongly doubt that such colonization efforts will begin in the next 1000 years.

9. Peace on Earth

Berry repeatedly predicted that warfare on earth will continue long enough to be a major cause of emigration from the earth to the moon, Venus, and other extraterrestrial sites (pp. 81, 97). These forecasts imply that earth-dwellers will be unable to create a world government strong enough to prevent nuclear wars on earth.

Moreover, he went on confidently to predict warfare not only on a colonized Venus (p. 98) but also between various planets colonized by humans and between such planets and those inhabited by other higher forms of life (p. 141). "The bloody histories of colonial conquests on earth will probably be repeated. Alien communities...will perhaps be destroyed so that adventurers from earth can fill the holds of their ships with some precious commodity" (p. 140).

In sharp contrast, I am confident that a world government able to prevent nuclear warfare will be created before 2100 A.D.

10. Comments

The Next 10,000 Years is as interesting and stimulating as the best science fiction, but is not much more scientific. Few if any physicists believe in superspace and worm-holes in space. Moreover, in his most plausible predictions Berry ignored or minimized the basic economic problems. Men will not colonize the moon or Venus, or build flying cities, unless it is economic as well as technologically feasible. And the progress of technology will create unlimited new opportunities for profitable investment on the earth, as well as lower the real costs of space travel and colonization.

MAJOR U.S. SOCIAL TRENDS, 1984-2100

Having recently read or reread and criticized the predictions of scores of futurists, including many not reviewed here, I now wish to revise, restate, and summarize my own predictions on major social trends in the United States during the next 116 years.

The trends discussed fall into three classes: social, economic, and political, which will be treated in this order. The discussion of each trend will be very brief. Most of them have been discussed more fully in my book, <u>The Next 500 Years</u> (1967), which includes several hundred other predictions.

In this essay I assume that there will be no nuclear war harmful enough to seriously slow or distort normal social evolution in the U.S.

In all cases the prediction concerning the direction of the trend is much more likely to be verified than that concerning the amount of change.

I. Social Trends

1. Population Growth and Change

The population of the U.S. will continue to grow throughout the next century, primarily because of continued immigration, but the rate of growth will decline almost steadily, from about 10% a decade to less than 2%. This rate will decline because the American people will become increasingly aware of the harmful effects of immigration and overpopulation. By 2100 A.D. the U.S. population will be between 400 and 500 million.

As a result of continuing relatively high immigration of brown, yellow, and black immigrants, and of relatively high birth rates among brown, yellow, and black residents, the skin color of the typical or median U.S. resident will become darker and darker throughout the next century.

Whenever two or more races live in the same area, some miscegenation is inevitable. The less it is restricted by laws and customs, the more rapidly it proceeds. Nearly all laws against miscegenation have been replaced in the U.S., and all forms of discrimination against minorities and those who practice miscegenation will continue to decline indefinitely. Therefore, miscegenation in the U.S., where several races live side by side, is certain to continue and increase for centuries. It will result in continued racial homogenization.

2. Increase of Knowledge

The most fundamental and influential U.S. social trend will be the continuous growth of knowledge, due largely and increasingly to organized scientific research and development (R and D) in specialized R and D institutes and university laboratories. Spending on such organized R and D will grow from about 2% of U.S. GNP in 1980 to between 4 and 6% by the year 2100 because men will become ever more aware of the large social gains from R and D, and ever more able to finance increased spending on R and D.

Since most of the benefits of R and D cannot be appropriated by private investors, the share of R and D financed by government will continue to increase, rising from about 50% in 1980 to over 80% in 2100 A.D.

3. More Spending on Education

Another fundamental U.S. social trend during the next century will be an almost steady increase in the share of GNP invested or re-invested in education. I expect this share, now about 10%, to rise to about 15% by 2100 A.D., in spite of a long decline in the proportion of children in the total U.S. population.

Relative spending on education will continue its long rise because Americans will become richer and because the amount of useful knowledge will continue to grow, due to continued spending on R and D. Moreover, R and D on methods of education will develop new and ever more effective methods of education, especially for infants and mature adults.

The year at which formal education for children begins will be gradually reduced from 5 or 6 to 2 or 3. The number of school days in the year will rise by over 10%, and the average number of hours of education per school day for children 6 to 18 will rise by over 10%. The size of the average school class will fall almost continuously, reaching 20 students per teacher before 2100. Relative public spending on adult classroom education will rise by over 100%, and perhaps much more. Per capita real spending on libraries will probably grow over twice as fast as real GNP. Such spending on educational broadcasting will grow over five times as fast as real GNP.

4. Continued Technological Progress

The continued growth of investment in R and D and education in the U.S. and other countries will result in continuous and multifarious technological progress in all industries and activities. Many new synthetic foods and raw materials will be developed. New, less costly sources of energy will be created. New methods of construction and building prefabrication will be invented. New methods of reshaping the landscape and digging tunnels and canals will become known. New and more efficient methods of political decision-making and government administration and control will be developed and used.

5. More Relative Spending on Health Care

The share of U.S. GNP spent on health care, now about 10%, will continue to rise steadily, reaching a level between 14 and 18% by 2100 A.D. The chief causes of this rise will be: (1) a continuous increase in the share of aged persons in the U.S. population, (2) a continuous increase in the number and average real cost of effective health-care treatments, (3) a large further increase in average real incomes, i.e., ability to pay, and (4) a great increase in the free provision of health-care services.

6. More Socialization of Health Care

The proportion of health care costs financed by private persons and firms will decline steadily, and that financed by taxes will rise steadily. By the year 2100 over 90% of such costs will be collectively financed. The figure is now only 50%. Moreover, over 90% of health care personnel will work for salaries, not for fees. And nearly all such personnel will work in clinics or hospitals, not in separate private offices. These trends will continue because they will permit more specialization among doctors and nurses, will decrease the proportion of unneeded treatments, and will increase the consumption of needed health services.

7. More Group Child Care

The proportion of young children who spend some of the day in group care institutions—nurseries, nursery schools, kindergartens, etc.—has long been growing, and will continue to grow for many decades. The chief reasons for this growth will continue to be growing recognition of: (1) the benefits to children from social contacts and group learning, (2) the need to provide more care for the children of working mothers, and (3) the reduction in child-care costs made possible by group child care. Also, new and ever more effective methods of teaching very young children will be developed, which will make preschool group child care ever more beneficial.

8. More Female Workers and Executives

The proportion of female workers in the U.S. work force will continue to rise for many decades, but at slow and steadily falling rates of increase, because the figure is already above 40% and is unlikely to ever rise above 50%. However, the proportions of women who are senior business and government executives, doctors, lawyers, scientists, legislators, etc., will continue to rise rapidly and indefinitely. By 2100 over 35% of such positions and professions will be occupied by women. The current figure is less than 10%.

This further growth and elevation of the female work force will be largely due to: (1) a great relative increase in the proportion of women who are well-educated, (2) a great increase in the provision of child-care facilities for working mothers, (3) a gradual reduction in the length of the average working day, (4) a continued fall in the proportion of women who have more than two children, and (5) a further long decline in male discrimination against female job and promotion seekers.

9. More and Better Broadcasting

Since the average American spends over three hours a day listening to radio and TV programs, trends in radio and TV broadcasting can be major social trends. During the next 116 years, the number of radio and TV channels and programs available to the average American will grow by more than 500%. Moreover, the quality of these programs will improve steadily and considerably, chiefly because commercials will be increasingly restricted, and eventually eliminated, and because the library of fine old programs will grow steadily.

10. Declining Religious Faith and Behavior

The centuries-old decline in religious faith will continue. The proportion of Americans who report belief in each religious dogma will decline slowly but almost continuously. This trend will become more and more obvious as public opinion polls on religious faith become more numerous and more reliable.

The income of religious organizations will decline as a share in GNP, slowly but almost continually.

A similar decline in church attendance will become more obvious as statistics on attendance become more complete and reliable. Between 1980 and 2100 A.D. the proportion of Americans who attend church each month will fall by over 40%. The proportion who pray each week will fall even faster.

The chief causes of this continued decline in religious faith and behavior will be: (1) the recent and future growth of higher education, (2) the growth of knowledge, (3) wider acceptance of the scientific point of view, and (4) the growth of personal security and welfare.

11. More Artificial Insemination

The proportion of total births which results from artificial insemination will increase almost continuously during the next 116 years, both because such insemination permits infertile couples to have children and because more and more fertile couples will use it for eugenic reasons. By 2100 A.D. over 25% of all births in advanced countries will result from artificial insemination.

The continuous further growth of knowledge concerning the congenital causes of human defects and abilities will result in ever-growing use of artificial insemination with sperm from superior donors in order to assure parents that their children will be superior physically, mentally, and emotionally.

12. More Human Sterilization

The proportion of both men and women who voluntarily have themselves sterilized will increase almost continuously in all advanced countries. Sterilization will be increasingly used, both as a means of effective birth control and as a means of eugenic progress.

Moreover, compulsory sterilization will also grow. Well before 2100 A.D., nearly all advanced countries will begin to use, or increase the use of, sterilization as a means of preventing the insane, the feebleminded, chronic criminals, and chronic welfare mothers from having more children.

Religious and moral opposition to sterilization and artificial insemination will decline steadily for many decades because religious faith will weaken and religious people will become more liberal and tolerant,

13. Less Crime

Some time during the next 40 years serious crime rates will reach a peak. They will then begin a long decline in all advanced western countries because:

(1) unemployment rates will begin or continue a long decline, (2) welfare and social insurance will become more comprehensive and more generous, (3) the use of cash will be radically restricted, (4) the distribution of income will become much less unequal, (5) laws against some "immoral" sexual acts will be repealed, and (6) more and more drug addicts will be provided with cheap maintenance doses.

14. More Suicides

The percentage of old people who die by suicide will soon begin to increase because: (1) religious prejudice against suicide will weaken, (2) laws against aiding suicide by the dying will be weakened, and eventually repealed, (3) juries will increasingly refuse to convict violators of such laws, and (4) more and more old people will desire a dignified, painless, and economical death. By 1200 A.D., over 10% of all deaths will be due to socially approved suicide. Today only 1.2% of U.S. deaths are reported as suicides.

II. Economic Trends

1. Reduction in the Hours of Labor

The average hours of paid labor per week will continue to decline irregularly, to a level of about 32 hours by 2100 A.D. Vacations will become longer, and the average hours per year for full-time workers will fall from about 2000 to about 1400 hours. The chief reason for this decline will be the continued rise in average real wage rates per hour of labor.

2. Rising Real Wages

U.S. real wage rates per hour and per year will continue to rise throughout the next 116 years, at about the same average rate they have risen during the past 100 years. The chief causes of this further rise will be largely the same causes active during the last 100 years, namely: technological progress, better education of workers, improved health care, additional saving and investment, and better business organization and management.

Because of the future decline in the hours of labor per day, week, and year, average real wage income per year will not rise nearly as fast as real wage rates per hour.

3. Falling Unemployment

U.S. unemployment rates will decline. By 2100 A.D. the rate will be below 2%, and nearly all unemployment will be short term, i.e., less than three months. All school leavers will be assured employment within a short period.

A variety of measures will be adopted to reduce unemployment: (1) provision of more vocational training for youth, (2) payment of subsidies to employers of school leavers, (3) government employment, at below market wages, for those unable to secure regular public or private jobs, (4) the adoption of compulsory simultaneous hiring programs, and, finally, (5) granting all qualified job seekers the right to demand suitable employment where and when they want it.

4. More Capital per Worker

The real value of the capital goods used by the average worker will continue to rise steadily during the next 116 years, because of increased mechanization and automation. Many new, improved, and more costly machines and tools will be invented and increasingly used. Offices, as well as factories, will use more and more new machines. As real wages continue to rise, the use of both new and old machines will become ever more economic. By 2100 A.D. average real investment in tangible capital goods per worker will probably be over ten times the 1980 level, and may be much higher.

5. Increased Plant Size

The average size of the local business unit--store, farm, factory, office, etc.--will continue to grow almost continuously in nearly all U.S. industries because an increase in size reduces internal operating costs and usually improves the products. An increase in plant size normally permits an increased division of labor, the use of larger and/or more specialized machines, more conservation of energy and raw materials, lower inventory/sales ratios, lower building costs per unit of output, and many other economies. An increase in the division of labor and in the use of larger and more specialized machines also improves the quality of most products. By the year 2100 A.D. the average local business unit will be over six times as large as the average 1982 unit.

6. Growth in Average Firm Size

The predicted growth in average unit or plant size will help to increase firm size, and other business trends will have the same effect. The continued relative growth of systems of chain stores, chain banks, chain restaurants, chain hotels, etc., will tend to increase average firm size. And the integration of more and more manufacturing firms with one or more of their major raw material suppliers and/or wholesalers and retailers will have the same effect. Finally, the continued growth of conglomerates with subsidiaries in two or more different industries will tend to increase average firm size. In sum, horizontal integration, vertical integration, and conglomerate diversification will all reinforce or supplement the effect of growth in average plant size. By 2100 A.D., the number of independent business firms will be less than 20% of the 1984 figure.

7. More Specialization

The continued growth of population, knowledge, plant size, and firm size will result in ever-growing specialization among farm workers, skilled workers, office workers, and professionals. The trend towards increased specialization among workers is very old and obvious, and nearly all the past reasons for it will continue to operate indefinitely. Only among some assembly-line workers and machine operators has specialization reached or exceeded its optimum limits.

8. Rationalization of Insurance

I use the term insurance here to include the services of all public and private agencies which protect people against loss of property or income and pay financial benefits—welfare, social security, private property insurance, etc.

All people need insurance against all possible major losses. But the competitive selling of separate insurance policies to millions of persons is very costly and wasteful. Therefore, all economically justified personal insurance will eventually become universal, comprehensive, and compulsory, and will be provided by a single national agency financed by taxes. This should happen in many advanced countries, including the U.S., before 2100 A.D.

9. The Growth of Monopoly

During the next 116 years monopoly will grow at the expense of business competition. Public utilities, which are natural monopolies, will grow faster than other industries. Most old public utilities will continue to grow relatively fast, and some major new public utilities—cable TV, cable computer service, central heating, etc.—will be created and/or will grow even faster. Moreover, some U.S. industries which are still at least partly competitive--airlines, railroads, general hospitals, automobile manufacturing, airplane manufacturing, etc.—will be reorganized as monopolies in order to reduce costs and/or improve their products and services. By the year 2100, over half of all U.S. workers will work for private or public monopolies, including government agencies.

10. Less Advertising

The growth of monopoly will make advertising less profitable. Moreover, the governments of all advanced noncommunist countries will take steps to reduce advertising expenditures per sales dollar before 2100 A.D. This is very likely because most advertising expenditures are socially wasteful (they increase total costs, not total national output), because they usually mislead consumers, and because they reduce the quality and utility to consumers of nearly all periodicals and broadcasts which contain advertisements. By 2100 A.D. the share of U.S. GNP devoted to advertising will have fallen by 50 to 75%. However, this share may continue to grow for several more decades before it starts a long decline.

11. The Elimination of Commercial Banking

Commercial banking is the loaning and reloaning of reserves behind demand deposits. This results in the creation of new purchasing power, which tends to cause inflation. Commercial banking decentralizes control over the quantity of money (broadly defined) and, therefore, over the price level. That is one reason why such banking will be increasingly controlled, restricted, and eventually eliminated during the next century in all advanced countries.

Another reason is that the profits from the creation of new money should accrue to society, not to private bankers and their customers. The creation of new money by bankers is almost as anti-social as the creation of new money by thrifty counterfeiters.

The best way to restrict, and eventually end, commercial banking is to gradually raise cash reserve requirements to 100%, and this is the way most likely to be used. The most probable alternative is for the government to print enough paper money to permit commercial banks to achieve 100% cash reserves at a single step. The new money could be loaned or given to the banks.

12. Restricting the Use of Cash

For over 100 years an ever larger share of all payments in the U.S. have been made by check or check substitute rather than by cash. This trend will continue indefinitely because payment by check is safer and more convenient. Checks can be sent through the mail more easily, serve as receipts when returned and, when stolen, cannot be easily cashed or spent.

Moreover, payment by check or check substitute leaves bank records which can easily be inspected and used by governments to reduce crime. Therefore, the U.S. government will gradually restrict, and eventually prohibit, the use of cash to make substantial payments, and will end the printing and use of paper money. It will also require, before 2100, that all persons receive all personal income and pay all substantial personal living costs through a single personal checking account. This will permit the police to easily detect nearly all illegal payments and income, and to enforce payment of nearly all taxes and legal debts. Politicians and business men will be unable to collect or spend large cash bribes. Bank robberies will cease because banks will have little cash, and stolen cash will be hard to spend. In other words, virtual elimination of the use of cash is highly likely because it would drastically reduce crime, corruption, and tax evasion.

13. Rationalization of Check Handling

In order to minimize the real costs of handling bank checks and check substitutes, most of which must now pass through two or more banks and a clearing house, the U.S. government will, before 2100 A.D., require that all demand bank accounts—those transferable by check—and all check handling be concentrated in a single national chain banking system. This reform will greatly simplify, cheapen, and speed up the handling of all bank checks and substitutes because no check will thereafter have to pass through more than one banking firm, and most will pass through only one local branch bank because no city will need more than one local check handling bank.

In the period preceding the achievement of this inevitable reform, chain banking will become national, and chain banks will handle an ever larger proportion of all checks, partly because they can handle checks more cheaply.

The substitution of electronic fund transfers for bank checks will continue to grow throughout most or all of the next 116 years. By 2100 A.D. the percentage of fund transfers made electronically, now less than 1.0%, will rise above 50%. By then most personal income payments will be deposited directly and electronically in bank accounts, and most bills will be similarly debited to personal bank accounts in order to reduce payment and billing costs and speed up payments.

14. Rationalization of Transportation

During the next 116 years the number of independent competing transport firms in the U.S. will decline almost steadily. All railroad systems will eventually be merged in a single system, and airlines will be similarly consolidated. Then, if not before, all transport industries will be united under a single national firm, probably state-owned. This unification will occur because it will permit nation-wide standardization of equipment, rationalization of freight rates, coordination of operating schedules, shipment by most economic means and rates, an ideal division of transport functions among different means of transport, an optimum scale of purchasing supplies, and other economies of monopoly.

15. Rationalization of Water Supply

The demand for water is growing so fast, and private competitive depletion and allocation of water is now so wasteful, that a radical rationalization of water allocation is inevitable in all advanced countries before 2100 A.D. Governments will assume ever-increasing control and ownership over all ground and underground water supplies. They will eventually require that all water users pay a price for all water used, including well-water, and prices will be adjusted so as to end depletion of underground supplies, balance supply and demand for water in each river basin, and assure that all water is sold to the highest bidders and used in the most productive ways. All private water rights in the U.S. will be abolished or bought by the government before 2100 A.D.

III. Political Trends

1. More Government Control Over Business

Government control over private business firms has been growing continuously in all advanced countries for over 100 years, and will continue to grow during the next 116 years. As in the past, it will take a great many different forms. Nearly all of the old forms will become more comprehensive and effective. Among the major new or greatly expanded forms of control will be: (1) general price and wage control, (2) compulsory hiring measures, (3) compulsory savings laws, (4) compulsory cartelization, (5) creation of export and import monopolies, (6) regulation of advertising, (7) standardization of products, (8) drastic limitation of the use of harmful raw materials, (9) standardization of accounting methods, and (10) general control of private investment.

2. More Government Control over Harmful Consumption

During the next 116 years the amount and the effect of government control over the consumption of harmful goods—narcotics, handguns, hard liquor, tobacco, gambling, etc.—will increase steadily. As a result, per person consumption of each of these classes of goods will probably fall by over 50%, and, in some cases, much more. The U.S. government will increasingly restrict advertising and sales effort for such goods, carry on relevant anti-consumption advertising and education, limit the places and hours of sale, prohibit the sale of the most harmful goods, and enforce the relevant laws more and more effectively.

3. More Free Distribution

In 1980 about 20% of all U.S. consumers' goods were distributed free of charge. Such free goods include free education, free health care, free highway use, free police protection, free national defense, etc. The share of U.S. consumers' goods provided free of charge will rise almost continuously during the next century and will probably be above 40% by 2100 A.D. The largest increases will be in free provision of health care, child care, preschool education, legal services, and educational broadcasting. Free health care alone--dental, psychiatric, medical, public, etc. —will amount to more than 15% of GNP. For an elaboration of this prediction, see my book Free Goods (1976).

4. More Government Capital Creation

During the next 40 years the federal government will adopt and maintain the policy of raising taxes enough to balance the federal budget and will also increase spending on social problems. Soon thereafter it will begin to pay off the federal debt, and will eliminate this debt before 2100. It will then use the continuing surplus to make large purchases of private securities and mortgages in order to maintain the higher national net savings rate created by its previous tax and debt-retirement policies. The net effect of these policies will be a 50 to 100% increase in the U.S. net savings rate before 2100 A.D.

These predictions on capital formation are not projections of past social trends. They are based on welfare economic theory. In other words, I believe these predictions will be verified because the predicted trends would markedly increase economic growth and welfare.

5. Higher Taxes

In order to provide more free goods and pay off the national debts, all capitalist countries will raise their taxes considerably. In the U.S., taxes now amount to about 32% of GNP. This share will rise above 50% by the year 2100. This rise will be achieved principally by increasing personal income, inheritance, and poll taxes. Taxes on business will decline radically because such taxes are uneconomic. They fall unequally on different products and methods of production, and thereby distort both consumption and methods of production.

6. More Public Ownership

Government ownership of the means of production has been growing for over 100 years in all advanced countries, and will continue to grow for many decades. The continued growth of oligopoly and monopoly will result in more and more government regulation, and the problems of regulation will result in ever-growing demands for public ownership. By the year 2100 nearly all U.S. railroads, pipe lines, public utilities, hospitals, clinics, banks, forests, farm land, oil fields, mines, and large multi-family housing projects will be largely or completely government owned. As a result, the share of total U.S. real estate owned by government and non-profit agencies, now about one third, will rise above two thirds.

7. More Centralization of Government

The governments of all advanced countries which have semi-autonomous provincial and/or local governments will continue to become ever more centralized. More and more of the functions of local governments--education, health care, welfare, air and water protection, etc.--will be transferred to provincial and/or national governments. And many provincial government functions will be transferred to national governments. Moreover, national governments will almost continuously increase their control over the performance of those functions which remain in provincial and local government hands.

This centralization is highly likely because it is needed: (1) to improve the performance of most functions now performed by provincial and local governments, and (2) to assure that all citizens secure equal amounts of free public services. For instance, there is no good reason why children in one area should receive better education or health care than children in any other area in the same country.

Moreover, the vast progress in transportation and communication since 1789 has brought most Americans closer to their national capital than they then were to their county center. They now receive much more and much more accurate information about their national government than about their county or city government.

8. More Public Opinion Polling

The use of scientific public opinion polling to determine public attitudes on political questions of wide public interest will grow almost steadily throughout the next century because such polling can reveal public preferences much more quickly, cheaply, and accurately than elections. Increased use of public opinion polls will reduce the need for elections for legislative offices, which, for this and other reasons, will become much less frequent. For instance, the term of office for members of the U.S. House of Representatives will be increased from two to four or more years before 2100 A.D. By that year the Congress will spend over $100 million a year on public opinion polling, which will save several times that sum in election costs and committee hearing costs.

9. More Government by Experts

Throughout the next century the functions of government will be increasingly delegated to experts, especially to highly educated social scientists and professional public administrators, because proper performance of ever more numerous and complex public functions will require more and more professional education. Universities, therefore, will devote an ever-growing share of their facilities and staff to the graduate education of social scientists and public administrators.

In the U.S. this growth of government by experts will occur at all levels of government. The Congress will steadily expand the size and raise the educational level of its committee staffs. The permanent civil service will employ more professional staff and assume higher administrative functions. A growing proportion of judges will be appointed. Similar changes will occur in each state government. More and more counties and cities will employ professional county and city managers as senior local administrators. The spoils system will continue to weaken, and civil service will grow and improve at all levels of government.

However, no country is likely to adopt complete government by experts—election of senior executives and legislators by fellow experts—before 2100 A.D. As explained in my book <u>Government by Experts</u> (1972), this evolution will probably require at least two centuries.

10. More Public Financing of Elections

The recent adoption of public financing of a major part of the costs of presidential campaigns will be followed by a series of federal, state, and local laws providing for more and more public financing of federal, state, and local political campaigns. The percentage of total campaign costs so financed will rise in almost every decade, until it exceeds 70% by 2100 A.D. Moreover, the relevant laws will be increasingly designed so as to make spending per candidate more equal. This will result in more and more restrictions on large private campaign gifts.

11. More One-House Legislatures

The movement for more democratic and efficient one-house legislatures will continue to grow until all state senates and the U.S. Senate have been abolished, but these goals will probably not be fully achieved by 2100, and the U.S. Senate may be reformed by basing its membership per state on population.

12. Formation of an English-Speaking Union

Cooperation between the U.S. and other major white English-speaking nations--the U.K., Canada, Australia, and New Zealand--has long been growing, and will continue to grow indefinitely. It will probably result in the formation of a formal military alliance before 2050 A.D., and the creation of a federation, a complete political union, before 2100. The role of each nation within this union will closely resemble that of each state within the United States.

The creation of such a union is probable because it will permit free movement of people, goods, capital funds, and armed forces between all parts of the new union, and because it will increase the world-wide influence of the U.S. and its English-speaking allies.

13. A Russo-American Condominium

The greatest threat facing civilization is the threat of one or more nuclear wars between the two superpowers or their successors. The ideal way to prevent such wars is to form a world government strong enough to disarm all individual nations and enforce world peace. Unfortunately, it is very unlikely that such a world government will be created before 2100 A.D. It is far more likely that the U.S. and the U.S.S.R. will gradually become more cooperative, and will eventually create a Russo-American Condominium which will act effectively to prevent nuclear wars. This will probably occur before the year 2100.

It is easier to predict the formation of this Condominium than to predict any particular events in its creation or operation. However, one major feature of the Condominium Agreements will be a division of most or all of the world into two zones of control--an American Zone including Western Europe, both Americas, Australasia, etc. and a Soviet Zone including Eastern Europe and nearly all of Asia.

The two superpowers will agree not to wage war on each other, and to come to the aid of the other power whenever such aid is requested. They will act jointly, first to prevent any further production of nuclear weapons by other powers, and, secondly, to compel all other nuclear powers to surrender their nuclear weapons. Then they will drastically reduce their own military spending.

After this Condominium has existed for many decades, it will very gradually surrender more and more of its international peace-preservation functions to a reformed and strengthened UN or its successor, which will long be dominated by the two superpowers. They will never surrender their supreme power to a world government dominated by backward countries, but advanced nations other than the U.S. and the U.S.S.R. will gradually acquire more and more influence in this undemocratic world government.

ANNOTATED BIBLIOGRAPHY

(*designates most important)

Adams, Henry, The Degradation of the Democratic Dogma (1919) 317 pages. Like his brother, Brooks, Henry Adams, the descendant of two U.S. presidents, predicted that a continued concentration of capital in advanced countries would destroy democracy, and that competition between great capitalists and capitalist countries would result in a great economic "smashup," to be followed by socialism. He also claimed that historians should try to develop scientific historical theories which permit the prediction of the future (see his "Letter to American Teachers of History"). Adams anticipated the continued biological and intellectual degeneration of the human race. He forecast that a new ice age would cause enormous human suffering and death (pp. 176-77).

Ayres, Robert U., Uncertain Futures, Challenges For Decision Makers. 1979. 400 pages. In addition to discussing such challenges, Ayres offers a wide variety of forecasts for many major countries--both developed and undeveloped--over the next 50 years, with special attention to those most likely to affect U.S. business men.

Beckwith, B. P., Beyond Tomorrow, A Rational Utopia. 1986. 200 pages. This book describes the world of 2500 A.D. and social trends from 1986 to 2500.

Baade, Fritz, The Race to the Year 2000, Our Future, A Paradise or the Suicide of Mankind. 1962. 70,000 wds. Baade is a German agricultural economist and a Social Democrat leader. The first half of his book is largely devoted to the race between population and food output. He concluded that by 2,000 A.D. China will have 1.5 billion people, with ample food produced by a mere 100 million farm workers. The Chinese non-farm labor force will be five times that of the U.S. The second half is largely devoted to the growth of world energy and steel output. Baade predicted that by 2000 A.D. communist workers (including Chinese) will be "as well provided with energy and capital goods...as the smaller labor reserves of the capitalist world" (p. 218).

*Bacon, Francis, New Atlantis. 1529. Many editions. Although this book is a utopia, Bacon clearly expected that many of his proposals would soon be adopted. He was probably the first to implicity forecast the creation of large industrial research institutes which would continuously develop new artificial raw materials, breeds of animals, medicines, plants, fertilizers, machines, scientific instruments, manufactured products, etc. He even foresaw the creation of machines for "some degree of flying in the air" and submarines. He did not discuss the resulting social trends.

Barney, Gerald B., Study Director, The Global 2000 Report to the President Entering the Twenty-First Century. 1982. 766 pages. "If present trends continue, the world in 2000 will be more crowded, more polluted, less stable ecologically, and more vulnerable to disruption than the world we live in now" (p. 1). This authoritative study contains a mass of statistics to support these conservative forecasts.

*Bentham, Jeremy, An Introduction to the Principles of Morals and Legislation. 1780. 335 pages. In this and other works Bentham advocated and predicted, explicitly or implicitly, many of the chief social reforms and trends of the next 200 years, including prison reform, political democratization, reform of criminal laws, growth of free public education, decline of religious faith, and the independence of all colonies.

Bird, Arthur, Looking Forward, a Dream of the United Americas in 1999. (1899) reprinted in 1971. 234 pages. This crude, jingoistic, and bigoted dream of the future is note-worthy only because it was one of the first American books devoted to a nonfictional forecast of the long-range future social trends. The author predicted a merger of all American states, English rule of all Africa, German rule over France, general U.S. use of cremation, pneumatic-tube mail delivery, "aerial navigation" and air wars, the general use of horseless vehicles, paved highways everywhere, electric farm tractors, and control of all infectious diseases.

Bird, Caroline, The Good Years, Your Life in the 21st Century. 1963. 254 pages. Bird discussed recent and prospective changes in life style due to aging of U.S. population and a predicted decline in U.S. economic growth rate. Life will become "more communal, more equal, less competitive" (p. 48). "Most work will eventually be done in places that don't look like offices at all" (p. 115). More people will continue working after age 65, in more interesting jobs (p. 117). Old women "will be sexually more venturesome" (p. 155).

*Birkenhead, The Earl of, The World in 2030 A.D., 1930. This important but largely forgotten book was one of the first to offer predictions in a wide variety of fields for the next 100 years. The author, a lawyer and politician, predicted the use of ectogenetic or test-tube births for eugenic purposes, adoption of a ten-hour work day, large-scale replacement of farm products by synthetic foods, cheap atomic energy, the use of wind and tidal power, colour TV in every home, university education for all, the elimination of poverty, trips to Mars, irrigation of the Sahara, etc. Unfortunately, he wishfully predicted that Britain would still rule India in 2030 A.D.

Boulding, Kenneth E., The Meaning of the Twentieth Century, The Great Transition. 1964. 208 pages. Boulding, a religious economist, forecast a "great transtion...from civilization to post-civiliation." This vague concept seems to include all progressive social changes now occurring in advanced countries. It is based on the growth of science. Boulding discussed "The War Trap," "The Difficult Takeoff," and "The Population Trap" separately in 3 chapters which make up 1/3 of his book. He predicts that social scientists will largely determine the shape of the coming "post-civilization." He made few if any more specific verifiable predictions.

Bryson, Lyman, editor. Facing the Future's Risks. 1953. 318 pages. The future in physics, chemistry, biology, economics, politics, crime, population, etc., is predicted by 13 experts.

Brzezinski, Zbigniew, Between Two Ages: America's Role in the Techtronic Age. 1968. 334 pages. He predicted that American individual and social life will be radically transformed by technology and electronics (p. 16). The U.S. will move from the industrial to the technetronic age. A "meritocratic elite" will rise to power, and will plan social change so as to make it rapid and smooth (pp. 18, 22). Business men will lose power, and intellectual institutions will gain power. The third world will lag further behind advanced states and this will strengthen "an ideology of rejection of the developed world"

(p. 24). The government may "impose well nigh total political surveillance on every citizen" (pp. 17, 21).

Burckhardt, Jacob, Force and Freedom: Reflections on History. 1943. 382 pages. In a 1944 letter, Burckhardt wrote "I have no hope at all for the future." He forecast an "era of wars" which will bring about the militarization and regimentation of life. "The military state must become one great factory," and there will be a "general leveling down" to a standard of personal and cultural mediocrity (pp. 47, 345). A new race of tyrants will appear. "Long voluntary subjection under individual Fuhrers and usurpers is in prospect" (pp. 41, 345). These tyrants will recognize no limits to their arbitrary power, and will rule "absolutely brutally." Liberal Protestantism will "scatter like dust" and be replaced by dogmatic fundamentalism.

*Carr, Edward H. The New Society. 1960. 118 pages. A brilliant historian explains why "Modern history begins when history becomes concerned with the future as well as with the past." He expects the social trends advanced by the French, American, Russian, and Industrial Revolutions to continue for centuries.

Cetron, M. J., and Thomas O'Toole, Encounters with the Future, A Forecast of Life into the 21st Century. 1982. 308 pages. Cetron, CEO of Forecasting International, and O'Toole, a Washington Post science reporter, offer a wide variety of predictions, many unrealistic, mostly for the years 1982-2000. Progress in health care "will lift life spans to 200 years" before 2200 A.D. (pp. 70-75). The U.S. will adopt national public health insurance before 2000 A.D. (p. 25). Nevertheless, the number of doctors will fall (p. 255). Increased use of robots (100,000 by the year 2000) will help to reduce the average weekly hours of labor to 32 by 1990, and to 25 by 2000 A.D. (pp. 33, 242-43). In 2000 A.D. Americans will use wristwatch radios to phone Tokyo for 25 cents a call.

Clarke, Arthur C., Profiles of the Future, an Inquiry Into the Limits of the Possible. 1962. 234 pages. Clarke has published 17 novels, chiefly science fiction, and several books on missiles and space. He has predicted contact by radio with extraterrestrials by 2040, and meetings by 2100. On p. 232 there is a table listing some 40 equally unrealistic predictions, including anti-gravity devices, replicators (which convert water or air into any desired good), planetary engineering, intelligent animals, immortality, world brain, climate control, etc., all by 2100 A.D. This book is highly readable and contains some plausible predictions, but nearly all concern technology. Very little is said about social trends.

Clarke, I. F., The Pattern of Expectation 1644-2001. 1979. 335 pages. This scholarly book by a University of Strathclyde don "surveys the three main stages in the course of futuristic literature," beginning with L'An 2440 (about 1775) by Mercier, and coming down to the predictions by modern futurists. Unfortunately, less than 2% of this book is devoted to scientific futurism, the rest being devoted to utopian literature and science fiction.

Clarkson, Stephen, editor, Vision 2020. 1970. 200 pages. This offers the ideas of over 50 Canadian writers on the Canada of 2020. Contains many plausible, verifiable predictions, including forecast by Robert Fultard that dignified suicide will become a common, legal method of death by 2020 (p. 87).

Cornish, Edward, editor, The Great Transformation, Alternative Futures for Global Society. 1983. 160 pages. This anthology reprints articles by 17 Futurist contributors— W.W. Harman, A. Brown, M. Mead, J. PLatt, G.T.L. Land, F. Capra, B.M. Hubbard, B.P. Beckwith, R. Dreikurs, J.C. Glenn, H. Myers, M.A.G. Michaud, L.A. Zuircher, C.W. Graves, R. Larson, J. Fowles, Estandiary, and M. Delianova.

Darwin, Charles Galton, The Next Million Years. 1953. 210 pages. Throughout most of the next million years, population in most areas "will tend to multiply until...[it] is limited by the means of subsistence," which will cause starvation among the poorest classes (pp. 170-71). Therefore, "there will have to be a revision of the doctrine of the sanctity of the individual human life." Our coal and oil resources will soon be exhausted, and water power will become the chief source of energy (pp. 186-87). Hence, "mountaineers...will tend to rule the world..." (p. 188), and "there will always be rich and poor" (P. 189). In advanced countries "the standard of living" of the poor will be lower than it now is (p. 189). "Man will become cleverer" (p. 98), i.e., his native intelligence will rise, but he will not otherwise change biologically (p. 206). Human slavery will reappear (p. 190). Fanatical superstitious religion will survive indefinitely and exercise great influence (p. 202), but "will hardly be held by the highly intelligent" (p. 203), who will retain their confidence in scientific thinking (p. 204). A world government will "occasionally" be created and survive" for a period" (p. 203).

Dickson, Paul, The Future File. 1977. 260 pages. This book has three main parts: (1) The State of the Future" includes a history of futurism, a classification and description of futurists, and a summary of 10 SRI scenarios; (2) a 37-page collection of plausible predictions by other futurists, and (3) an "Almanac and Directory" of futurist research organizations, and an 8-page list of notoriously bad predictions.

Dietz, David, Atomic Energy in the Coming Era. 1945. 184 pages. Dietz, a science professor, predicted the creation in the near future of atomic planes which would carry several thousand passengers and cars which "will travel for a year on a pellet of atomic energy the size of a vitamin pill."

*Eldredge, H. Wentworth, The Second American Revolution. 1964. 403 pages. This book is an argument for, more than a prediction of, (1) a greater concentration of power in the U.S. president, and (2) the development of a true political meritocracy. Eldredge is a liberal political scientist and is strong for political centralization. "State governments and city governments have nearly reached functional death...State governments especially are the dying gasp of provincialism" (p. 359). He condemned bicameral legislatures, committee seniority systems, rotten buroughs, etc.

*Ellul, Jacques, The Technological Society. 1964. 449 pages. According to this sociologist, there is one best technological solution for every problem, and every society will eventually adopt all such best solutions. Therefore, all societies will become more and more alike. Thus it is possible to predict the future by discovering the ideal solutions to social problems. Nuclear wars are inevitable because atom bombs are ideal weapons. All countries will become totalitarian because totalitarianism is most efficient. In sum, "everything which is technique is necessarily used as soon as it is available....This is the principal law of our age."

Evans, Christopher R., The Micro Millenium. 1980. A computer scientist predicts a future that includes the collapse of the work ethic, a cashless society, sweeping social and psychological changes, and much more.

Ferguson, Marilyn, <u>The Acquarian Conspiracy</u>. 1980. 448 pages. She claims that the world will continue to experience a "great shuddering, irrevocable shift...deeper than revolution...the ascendancy of a startling world view" promoted by the Acquarian Conspirators who have been greatly influenced by Eastern spiritual traditions. The eventual result will be world-wide anarchism, decentralized government by self-selecting, autonomous leaders of local co-operative societies.

Ferkiss, Victor C., <u>The Future of Technological Civilization</u>. 1974. 369 pages. Ferkiss explained what he wants to happen, not what will happen. He assumed that most major social trends will continue, but he disapproved of most of them.

Foreign Policy Associastion editors, <u>Toward the Year 2018</u>. 1968. 177 pages. This book contains original essays on weaponry, space, transport, communication, weather, educational technology, behavioral technology,, computer technology, energy, food, population, economics, and oceanography by 13 different experts. The aim of the writers was "to set the technological context of social and international policy over the next 50 years" (1969-2018). They make many verifiable predictions; for instance, N. E. Halaby predicted use of an international identity card to facilitate control of travelers, and I. de S. Pool predicted greatly increased use of social "indicators."

Fowles, Jib, <u>Mass Advertising as Social Forecast, A Method for Futures Research</u>. 1976. 153 pages. This is a well-written scholarly book on the rise of futurism and the methods used by futurists. Fowles urged use of advertisements because they reveal the human needs which will most influence the future. His argument is original but unpersuasive. He includes a bibliography of 300 items, mostly journal articles not listed in my bibliography.

Fuller, R. Buckminister, <u>Critical Path</u>. 1981. 471 pages. In this book Fuller used his religious metaphysics as the basis for a "normative futurism"--what ought to be rather than what might be. He urged intelligent cooperation with the will of God. He implied, for instance, that God wants development of an "omni-world-integrating electrical energy network grid" because this will "realistically put all humanity on the same economic accounting system and will integrate the world's economic interests and value systems and lead...to the...elimination of the 150 sovereign-nation system." He optimistically predicted further technological progress in all human activities. He minimized the role of government and social reform in future progress.

——. *Utopia or Oblivion, the Prospects for Humanity.* 1969. 366 pages. "Geodesic-dome Fuller was a prolific and popular futurist, but he did not write lucidly. This book is a collection of 12 uncoordinated and often repetitive essays and speeches (1964-69). He predicted that "we will always have war" until abundance prevails everywhere (p. 151), which implies oblivion, not utopia, but he also forecast a world government. He predicted that the growth of multinationals will equalize wage rates throughout the world by 1975 (p. 191), that progress will provide "enough for all" everywhere by 2000 A.D. (p. 311), that China, India, Africa, and Latin America "will achieve full industrialization" by 1980 (pp. 202, 222), that U.S. cities would soon be covered by vast geodesic domes, that one-mile high buildings will be built, that some cities will float on the sea, that factory-built skyscrapers will be flown to construction sites on detachable wings (p. 351), and that some new cities will float in the air (pp. 356-57).

Gabor, Dennis, *Inventing the Future.* 1964. 237 pages. Although he claimed to be merely suggesting one possible future, Gabor made several major predictions. For instance, he forecast both that ever more labor will be needed to produce ever scarcer minerals, and that technological progess will soon eliminate most work and create an "Age of Leisure [four-hour work days]...within one generation" (pp. 4-6). These predictions seem to conflict. He expected that Russians and Americans will become more prosperous and less ideological. In time, "the tension will subside, as it did in Western Europe, though only after many centuries of war" (p. 19). He stressed the evil effects of overpopulation, and predicted that religious leaders in all countries will cease to oppose birth control. He forecast that technological progress will create "social uselessness of a large fraction of humanity in the long run" (p. 125). He expected a rapid transition from the use of fossil fuels to the use of nuclear power. In 1967 he claimed that "In Britain probably the last coal-burning plant ever to be built is now on order."

*Galbraith, John K., The New Industrial State. 1967. 425 pages. In this lucid and witty book the author described some recent social trends and projected them into the future. He predicted that: (1) control over large U.S. corporations will continue to shift from stockholders to professional managers (pp. 87-89), (2) political power will pass from capitalists to such managers and to social scientists (pp. 386, 406), (3) the influence of intellectuals will continue to expand (p. 466), (4) they will favor arms control and appeasement (pp. 325-26), (5) mature corporations will gradually become "part of... the state" (pp. 392-93), (6) U.S. and U.S.S.R. social trends will increasingly converge (pp. 389-91),(7) governments will increase their efforts to stabilize aggregate demand (p. 327) and price levels, (8) U.S. antitrust laws will be reformed to permit collusive price control by oligopolists (p. 197), (9) the adoption of "a system of wage and price restraint is inevitable" (p. 259), and (1) the adoption of strong and comprehensive metropolitan-area planning is likely (pp. 360-61).

Gershuny, Jonathan, After Industrial Society? The Emerging Self-Service Economy. 1978. 181 pages. The author claims that advanced nations have moved, and will move, towards self-service economies, not towards service economies, as argued by Bell and Galbraith. The manufacture of capital goods for use in the home will continue to grow, which will reduce the relative importance of service industries. The washing machine industry will grow, and the purchase of commercial laundry services will decline.

Godwin, William, Enquiry Concerning Political Justice. 1793. Godwin was one of the first writers to predict the great political, social, and economic progess which would occur in Europe in the next 200 years. He was less realistic and more utopian than Condorcet, but he correctly forecast great progress in popular education, in workers' living standards, in length of life, in technology, in political justice, in the arts etc. He even persuaded Malthus to revise the dire predictions in the first edition of his essay on population and concede that moral restraint might make possible great social progress. For more on Godwin, see entry for Holcroft, Thomas, below.

Gordon, T.J. and R.H. Ament, <u>Forecasts of some Technological and Scientific Developments and their Societal Consequences</u>. 1969. The authors polled many experts on their forecasts on the timing and results of 83 possible future technological advances. The results revealed that nearly all experts had grossly overestimated the future speed of technological and social change. For instance, the experts predicted that weather control would be possible and economical by 1982, that human clones would be created by 1985, and that control of the behavior of some people in society by radio stimulation would be possible by 1985.

Gribbon, John, <u>Future Worlds</u>. 1981. Gribbon, an astrophysicist, condemned as "nonsense" all efforts to predict the future (pp. 11-12), but he forecast that U.S. economic growth would continue (p. 17), that "the vast majority of the world's population will still be living on the Earth's surface for our lifetimes," that "the world's population will continue to grow" (p. 20), and that recent "economic trends will <u>not</u> proceed more or less smoothly through the next 30 years and beyond," as Kahn had predicted (p. 28). He condemned "neo-Malthusian gloommongers" (pp. 26, 77-80) which implies he believed that he could predict the future. He forecast "a leveling off of [world] population...between 6,000 and 10,000 million" (p. 96). He asserted that electricity demand will soon stop growing (pp. 115-16). He expected "that the '1974 poor countries' will be industrialized by 2050 A.D. (p. 119). He forecast that nuclear power will <u>not</u> become more important than either oil or natural gas as a share of world energy output in the year 2050 (p. 123). He expected that world spending on "the war machine will be over 13 times the 1968 level in the year 2000" (p. 51).

Harman, Willis, <u>An Incomplete Guide to the Future</u>. 1976. 160 pages. The author, a Stanford professor of electrical engineering, predicted that a major, spiritually motivated, social transformation will occur. He asserted that the projection of past trends is a poor basis for predicting the future. He forecast a decline in emphasis on scientific thinking and research, and an increase in emphasis on transcendental, wholistic, ethical, and metaphysical reasoning. Unfortunately, his metascientific analysis yields few if any verifiable scientific predictions. He wrote much more about his spiritual longings than about about the probable future.

Hawken, Paul, The Next Economy. 1983. 215 pages. Hawken is a tool manufacturer and econmics editor of Co-Evolution Quarterly. His main thesis is that the U.S. is in transition from a "mass economy" to a radically different "informative economy." The age of the mass economy was marked by economic expansion, mass production, degradation of the environment, technological innovation, the growth of consumption and affluence, rising real wages, increasing specialization and division of labor, a decline in the durability of goods, and the professionalization of services (pp. 8-9). Nearly all these trends will slow down, reverse themselves, or disappear in the coming "informative economy," due chiefly to higher relative costs for fuel and capital. "Oil will become increasingly expensive" (p. 35). He predicted a long growth of barter and cash transactions among Americans (pp. 115-16). He expected that U.S. farms will become smaller and less mechanized (p. 102). He predicted that U.S. real wages will continue to fall indefinitely (pp. 86-87).

Henderson, Hazel, Creating Alternative Futures, the End of Economics. 1978. Henderson is a self-educated economist who rejects most orthdox capitalist and socialist economic theory. Her book includes 23 diverse and uncoordinated essays (1970-71). For her, every inventor and social reformer is a futurist. Like Shumacher, she advocated and forecast radical decentralization of industry and government (pp. 187-88), a handicraft revival, agrarianism, etc. She claimed that "we are in the throes of a great economic transition—from a society which maximizes production [and] consumption...to a society which minimizes production..." (p. 147). She predicted the end of economic growth in advanced countries (pp. 357, 381), and a long-continuing shift of the U.S. labor force from capital-intensive to labor-intensive industries (pp. 160-64), 181-87). Most economists predict an opposite trend.

Heppenheimer, T.A., The Red Future. 1983. 295 pages. The author, an aerospace engineer, concentrated on technology and had little to say about social trends. He predicted that most current trends will continue at recent rates of change. "Overall, the year 2000 will be amazingly like 1980" (p. 231). A nuclear war is unlikely "before the year 2050," will be strictly limited, and "will be a naval war fought for control of the seas"

(p. 189). Although the author had published books entitled <u>Colonies in Space</u> and <u>Towards Distant Suns</u>, his chief comment about these subjects here is that "it would be the height of folly to assert we will never build space colonies or send ships to the stars" (p. 118). His forecast is that CO_2-induced warming of the earth will raise sea levels by 16-20 feet before 2100 A.D., and by 200 feet "over thousands of years" (pp. 50-51).

Holcroft, Thomas, <u>Memoirs</u>. 1816, 1926.
"His vision of the future is the same as Godwin's: family affections are to be submerged in universal benevolence; gratitude is to disappear as all become unselfish benefactors; promises will be unnecessary; laws and punishments will disappear with crime; property distinctions will vanish as all work cheerfully for the common good; division of labor will give everyone leisure to cultivate the arts and sciences. All this is to be accomplished, as in Godwin, not by sudden revolution, but by slow and continuous (and continuously accelerating) progress over an almost infinite period of time" F.E.L. Priestly, editor, <u>Enquiry</u>...by Wm. Goodwin. 1946 reprint, Vol. III, p. 48.

*Huxley, Aldous, <u>Brave New World</u>. 1932. 175 pages. In this lucid and brilliant dystopia Huxley identified, lamented, and ridiculed some major contemporary and future social trends—growth of population, centralization of government, expansion of government functions, growth in the scale of production and business management, growth of scientific research and knowledge, decline of religious faith, growth of large cities, the rise of social engineering, the spread of collectivism, etc. In <u>Brave New World Revisted</u> (1958) he re-asserted many of these ideas, and claimed that "the probability of over population leading...to dictatorship becomes a virtual certainty...20 years from now all the world's over-populated and underdeveloped countries will be under some form of totalitarian rule—probably by the Communist party" (p. 11). He also anticipated a radical growth in the use of scientific propaganda and brainwashing.

*Jones, Thomas E., <u>Options for the Future. A Comparative Analysis of Policy-Oriented Forecasts</u>. 1980. 350 pages. This book is largely devoted to summaries and criticism of six major groups of predictions concerning major social trends; those by Delphi panelists, by Brzezinski, by

Kahn and Wiener, by Bell, by Harman, and by Meadows. Excellent bibliography lists some 420 items.

*Kahn, Herman, World Economic Development: 1979 and Beyond. 1979. 542 pages. Contains very plausible optimistic predictions of major world economic trends to year 2200. World population will stabilize at 10 billion in 21st Century, when average world per capital income will be $20,000 in 1979 dollars. This will mean worldwide abolition of most absolute poverty.

Kostelanetz, Richard, ed., Social Speculations, Visions for Our Time. 1971. 307 pages. This is a collection of long quotations from the recent futurist writings of 33 modern futurists, grouped under the categories of history, technologies, environments and cities.

―――. Human Alternatives, Visions for Us Now. 1971. 300 pages. This is a similar collection, but few of the 34 quoted futurists were represented in Social Speculations. The new categories are knowledge, organisms, economics, politics, education, and planning. Both books include bibliographies (4 and 7 pages).

Laue, Theodore H. von, The Global City: Freedom, Power, and Necessity in the Age of World Revolution. 1969. The chief thesis is that the entire non-Anglo world has long been undergoing a complex process of economic, political, and cultural Anglo-Americanization, a process which will continue until world cultural homogenization and world peace have been achieved. This process will provoke repeated third-world resistance and rebellion because most nations are unprepared for industrialism and democracy. Many will adopt totalitarianism as a means of speeding up their Westernization.

Leontief, Wassily, The Future of the World Economy: A UN Study. 1977. 110 pages. Economist Leontief, a NObel Prize winner, led a team of scholars making a study of the world economy for the United Nations. The study employed input-output analysts, the econometric technique pioneered by Leontief. The researchers reached optimistic conclusions about the physical and environmental potential for economic growth and concluded that the limits to growth are not physical but rather political, social, and institutional in character.

*Malthus, Thomas Robert, An Essay on the Principal of Population as it Affects the Future Improvement of Society,...1798. Many editions and reprints.

As its title makes explicit, this classic was written to reveal the future of mankind, and was accepted by many readers as a great contribution to scientific futurism. It popularized a new method of predicting the future. According to his "principle", every increase in the means of life, especially food, permits, and is normally followed by, an equal increase in population, so no enduring rise in the standard of living occurs. Thus, neither social reform nor technological progress can enable mankind to enjoy a better life.

This is a harsh version of his theory of population. In subsequent editions of his book he increasingly qualified his theory until it lost most of its original force as a means of predicting the future.

He noted and rejected Condorcet's percipient prediction of the rise of social insurance. He also repeated Condorcet's prediction that birth control would solve the population problem.

*Manuel, Frank E., and Fritzie,P. Manuel, Utopian Thought in the Western World. 1979. 900 pages. This fascinating treatise is the most complete and authoritative survey of Utopian literature. Utopian writers were the first to anticipate many future social trends and events. F.E. Manuel taught history at Harvard.

Martin, James, The Wired Society, A Challenge for Tomorrow. 1978. 300 pages. "The use of telecommunications described in this book will change work patterns, leisure time, education, health care, and industry. The news media, the processes of government, and the workings of democracy could be fundamentally improved" (p. 5). Among the results will be a vast movement of business and population from U.S. cities to "country villages" (pp. 11-12), and rapid achievement of a $3\frac{1}{2}$ day work week (p. 9). Martin described a city "10-20 years in the future, ...where the air is crystal clear and most cars are kept in large parking lots on the outskirts" (p. 8). Much office work will have been transferred from offices to homes (pp. 184-86). Most news will be "delivered electronically to printers in the home" (p. 69). Doctors will examine patients electronically in their homes (p. 10).

*Meadows, D.H., D.L. Meadows, J. Randers, and W.W. Behrens III, The Limits to Growth. 1972. 205 pages. This is a report for the Club of Rome's Project on the Predicament of Mankind. The authors explain that, if the major social and economic world trends which prevailed from 1900 to 1970 continue unchanged, world population will soar to about 12 billion by the year 2050, and then fall rapidly to about 6 billion by 2100, due chiefly to starvation. Their estimates do not allow for raw material, process, and product substitution, for social and economic reform, for technological progress, for new discoveries of mineral resources, or for a nuclear war.

Mercier, Louis Sebastian, <u>L'An 2440</u>. Paris, 1771. Mercier was one of the first utopian authors to predict social conditions in the future rather than describe them as existing in the past or the present. He predicted streets brilliantly illuminated and empty of prostitutes, more orderly street and sidewalk traffic, more social politeness, comfortable hospitals, great advances in science and the arts, general social welfare, inextinguishable lamps, motion pictures, and many other inventions and social reforms.

Nietzsche, Frederich W., <u>The Philosophy of Nietsche</u>. 1927. Nietzsche (1844-1900) asserted that "the future of German culture rests with the sons of the Prussian officers" because "the manliest men shall rule" (p. 803). He despised "universal suffrage" and predicted the rule of brave, strong, pitiless supermen (p. 801). He forecast the creation of a "United Europe" dominated by Germans, which would then "enter into battle for the mastery of the world with good prospects of victory." England will not be able to continue to play its leading role because its democratic government will allow too many common men to have power (pp. 803-04).

O'Leary, Brian, <u>The Fertile Stars</u>. 1981. 132 pages. O'Leary predicts the creation of solar power collectors in space, retrieval of raw materials from asteroids, the settlement of space colonies, and the colonization of the stars. He has little to say about future social trends on Earth.

O'Neill, John J., <u>Almighty Atom</u>. 1945. Science writer O'Neill forecast that atomic power would enable engineers to connect all major U.S. cities with "vacuum tubes," in which trains will travel up to 10,000 miles an hour. "The travel time from Boston to New York," he estimated, "would be 10 minutes."

Ortego y Gasset, Ortega, <u>The Revolt of the Masses.</u> 1930. 196 pages. The author offered possibilities, not predictions. Under liberal democracy there has been an era of great social and political progress for the masses, but they are ungrateful and may destroy the rules and institutions responsible for this progress (pp. 11, 52-60). "If that human type [the masses] continues to be master in Europe, 30 years will suffice to send our continent back to barbarism. Legislative and industrial technique will disappear...." (p. 52). European world rule may be ending (p. 181), and no new world ruler is in sight. Neither Russia nor the U.S. will become superpowers (pp. 138-39). Europe will be united in a single state (pp. 171, 179).

*Owens, Robert, The Revolution in the Mind and Practice of the Human Race; or the Coming Change From Irrationality to Rationality. London, 1849. In this and other books, Robert Owen confidently predicted the gradual peaceful rise and worldwide spread of free education, feminism, free thought, humane treatment of the criminal and insane, full employment, producers' cooperatives, communism, sexual liberation, sobriety, thrift, and humanitarianism. He was an ardent prophet of the rise and universal application of psychological behaviorism. He foresaw the coming decline in the corporal punishment of children, wives, and criminals, and in sectarian religious faith.

*Place, Francis, Illustrations and Proofs of the Principles of Population. 1822. Place, the radical tailor of Charing Cross, was an ardent disciple of Bentham. and shared most of his views about the future. He forecast universal acceptance of birth control and a radical decline in birth rates. He also foresaw the rise of strong labor unions, political democracy, and feminism.

Platt, John R., The Step to Man. 1966. 216 pages. This is a collection of 12 essays on ways to increase human intelligence and scientific knowledge. The first discusses microprint books. Platt was a Christian physicist (Un. of Chicago), and one of his essays is a plea for Christian self-reform. He predicted that most exponential social trends will soon slow down, and that society will experience a crisis in the years 1966-86. If we survive, we will achieve "a wealthy...powerful and coordinated world society reaching across the solar system;..." He made no important original predictions, and the crisis he predicted did not appear.

Polak, Fred, The Image of the Future. 1973. 320 pages. This is as translation of a book written about 1953 by a Dutch Jew. It contains a sophisticated history of thought about the future from Plato to Toynbee, and a few predictions. Religious faith will continue its long decline. Science is still in its dawn, and will grow indefinitely. The trend towards socialism will continue.

―――. Prognostics, A Science in the Making. 1971. 453 pages. This is an excessively erudite and confusing review of ideas which the author believes are relevant to a study of the nature, methods, and prospects of futurism. The author predicted a rapid further development of this study. It maks no other predictions.

*Richardo, David, Principles of Political Economy. 1817. He created the modern theory of land rent, and used it to predict that future increases in population would prevent any rise in real wages. He forecast that both food prices and land rents would rise indefinitely. He also advocated and predicted more government control over paper money and banking, and the adoption of universal suffrage.

Shelp, Ronald K., Beyond Industrialization, Ascendancy of the Global Service Economy. 1981. 243 pages. He predicts "a continued acceleration of service expansion" (p. 21). "Both economic history and empirical evidence suggest that services will become a more important component of the world economy" (p. 68). The growth rates will be much higher in backward than in advanced countries (p. 69). The rise of services in advanced countries will displace more and more manufacturing to less advanced countries (p. 4), which will import ever more services.

Sorokin, Pitirim A., The Basic Trends of our Times. 1964. 206 pages. Sorokin, a Harvard professor of sociology discusses three basic social trends: (1) a shift of creative leadership from the West to Asia and Africa, (2) a continued disintegration of the hitherto predominant "sensate" or materialistic culture, and (3) the rise of an "integral culture" much more like the religious culture of the middle ages. But pages 78-130 (Ch. 3) are devoted to an excellent statement of the doctrine that the U.S. and the U.S.S.R. have been growing more and more alike for 50 years, and are now very much alike in all essential features—education, religion, ethics, econ. life, etc.

There is a 30-page chapter on religious polarization which argues that mankind is

dividing increasingly into two groups, fervent
atheists or fervent believers.
Spengler, Oswald, <u>The Decline of the West</u>, 2 Vols.
1926-28. Spengler rejected the idea of progress
and confidently predicted that the 20th Century
would be an era of tyranny, imperialism, and
almost constant warfare. Warfare will become
wars between the personal followings of born
leaders—the new Caesars—rather than wars between national armies. Parliamentary democracy
will soon be abolished (II, 172, 368). The
Germans will be the eventual military "victors"
(II, 430-32). They will establish a universal
imperium under a new Caesar. "Blood" will
regain its rights. The masses, a shiftless mob,
will live poorly in giant "barrack-cities."
They will return to religion as a solace for
their miseries.
*Stableford, Brian, and David Langford, <u>The Third
Millenium; A History of the World: AD 2000-3000</u>.
1985. 224 large pages. This is perhaps the most
comprehensive, detailed, and sophisticated futurist book since 1960. It features technological
rather than social trends. It predicts that a
U.S.-U.S.S.R. condomium will prevent major
nuclear wars until a strong world government is
created, about 2500. It forecasts an average
lifespan of over 200 years, general use of ecto-
genisis, rigid birth control, a 50% decline in
world population, creation of three new human
species for colonizing the seas and space, the
colonization of space, interstellar travel,
contact with alien starmen, etc.
Stine, G. Harry, <u>The Hopeful Future</u>. 1983. 238
pages. This book features the rapid growth of
space factories, power plants, and colonies
during the 21st Century. In advanced countries
most basic industries, except agriculture, will
be located in space by the year 2100. The
average length of life will be about 200 years.
On earth, most workers will work at home.
Religion will become more popular and will
"demolish" materialism.
Teich, Albert H., editor, <u>Technology and Man's
Future</u>, 3rd ed., 1981. 430 pages. This is a
collection of 22 article and book excerpts pub-
lished in the years 1966-81 by R.S. Morison, Hal
Hellman, A.W. Weinberg, J. Ellul, R.B. Fuller,
R.M. Pirsig, E.G. Mesthene, J. McDermott, T.J.
Gordon, and R.H. Ament, D.H. Meadows <u>et al</u>,
C. Freeman, J.F. Coates, P.F. Drucker, E. Weak,
Jr., D. Nelkin,H. Brooks, E.F. Schumacher,

P. Goodman, John Todd, L. Winner, and Colin Norman. These readings feature the effect of technological progress on society.

Thomson, George, The Foreseeable Future. rev. ed., 1960. 40,000 wds. Academic in literary style, and conservative in conclusions, this little book deals almost entirely with technological trends. Its nine chapters discuss energy and power, materials, transport and communications, meteorology (weather), food, biology, "some social consequences" (5,000 wds.), and "thought." It predicts stronger materials, synthetic animal feed, development of more intelligent animals, rapid cultural homogenization (p. 126), and better methods of education.

Toffler, Alvin, ed., The Futurists. 1972. 322 pages. This anthology reprints 22 article. and book sections on futurism and the future by Toffler, Paul Ehrlich, M. Mead, J. McHale, M. McLuhan, R. Jungk, A.I. Waskow, A.C. Clarke, O. Helmer, H. Kahn, T.J. Gordon, M.S. Iyengar, I. Bestuzhev-Lada, G.R. Urban, K.E. Boulding, Y. Hayashi, D. Bell, G. Flechtheim, B. de Jouvenal, F.L. Polak, J. Wren-Lewis, and R. Buckminster Fuller. It contains much discussion of futurism and futurists, but few quantified verifiable predictions.

*Wells, H. G., The Shape of Things to Come. 1933. 431 pages. This was written as "a Short History of the World for about the next century and a half" (p. 4). Old and discouraged, writing during the Great Depression, Wells predicted that another world war, beginning in 1940, would result in a long period of social, economic, and political disorganization, disease, and disorder.

INDEX

Advertising, 79, 137, 197, 291, 296, 299
Agriculture, 15, 68, 78, 90, 99, 110, 113, 116, 123, 149, 158, 185, 189, 194, 203, 248, 266.
Airplanes, 78, 93, 106, 178, 272
Automation, 62, 176, 195, 266-7, 270-2
Automobiles, 78, 85-7, 116, 147, 154, 178, 196, 257, 271
Banking and credit, 68, 80, 95, 97, 150, 161, 169, 197, 260-1, 296-7
Birth control, 15-6, 55-6, 90, 97, 140, 148, 154, 172, 176, 185, 193, 292
Bureaucracy, 141-3, 223, 241, 261
Capitalism, 117, 119, 123-4, 134-9, 189, 211, 217-8
Centralization, of government, 41, 43, 132, 155, 163, 179, 189, 223, 235, 252, 258, 300
Colonialism, 17, 49, 122-3, 130, 160, 168
Communication, 46, 147, 155-6, 184-5, 269
Communism, 72, 75, 103-4, 119-20, 124, 127, 168
Concentration of capital, 35, 63, 179, 257, 294; of power, 25, 41, 179-80, 223, 235, 252, 303
Condorcet, 1-21, 28, 30, 33, 38, 51, 106, 172
Cooperatives, 42, 55, 58, 68, 184
Democracy, political, 17, 24, 37, 39-40, 44, 56-7, 65-9, 127-34, 144, 164, 167, 215, 259; social, 39-41, 47-8, 56-7
Division of labor, 26, 35, 36, 204-5
Domestic production, 149, 248-9, 267
Economic crises, 123, 128, 160, 169, 213, 231
Economic planning, 126-8, 162-4, 169, 195, 212-3, 218
Economic progress, 35, 45, 53-4, 70, 98-9, 108, 136, 145, 147, 165, 176, 195, 204, 213-4, 218, 227, 230, 234, 240, 269, 279-80
Education, 13-4, 26, 34, 46, 115, 138, 151-2, 159-60, 174-5, 201-2, 205, 225, 259; adult, 14, 77, 152, 174, 259, 301; free public, 58, 64, 66-8, 76-7, 174
Energy, 78, 99, 109, 117, 147, 172, 187, 194, 214-5, 234, 247-8, 268
Equality, 39-40, 44, 47-8, 56-7, 97, 118, 160-1, 164, 166, 177, 206, 224
Ethics, 22-3, 29, 35, 53, 89, 103-4, 112, 154, 192, 256
Eugenics, 16, 89, 97, 110-1, 115, 176, 250, 259, 278, 281, 292
Exponential growth, 192-3, 205, 213-4, 226, 232, 281
Family, 38, 60, 89, 97, 118, 141, 151, 175, 235, 244, 291
Feminism, 16, 38, 48, 55, 59, 75, 89, 99, 117, 151, 156, 176, 291
Feudalism, decline of, 23, 35, 39, 56, 69, 139-40

Free goods, 69, 72, 118, 126-7, 136, 175, 212, 299
Futurism, 1-7, 20, 29, 39, 86, 158, 182, 199, 236, 238
Futurist methodology, 8, 11-12, 19, 21, 30, 39, 61-2, 68, 75, 86, 104, 106, 114, 135, 146, 159, 170-4, 181-2, 192, 199, 210-2, 228, 264-5
Government, growth of, 36, 42-3, 96-7, 125, 155, 178, 207; forms of 22-5, 35-7, 41, 66, 82, 124, 127-8, 131, 138, 156, 177, 184, 208, 215-6, 219, 251-2, 259, 265, 301
Government control, 36, 43, 98, 127, 132, 149-69, 175, 178-9, 207, 212, 215, 299
Government by experts, 22, 25, 82, 91, 208, 301
Health care, 16, 38, 76, 111, 118-20, 153, 175, 179, 202-3, 207, 259, 267, 290
Hours of labor, 35, 68, 70, 98-9, 102, 121, 147, 187, 267, 291, 293
Housekeeping, 76, 88-9, 151, 270
Immigration, 83, 149, 157, 164, 288
Income distribution, 18, 67, 119, 126, 166-7, 177, 207, 216-8, 293
Industrialization, 15, 36, 42, 63, 173, 195, 224
Initiative & referendum, 82, 259-60
Insurance, 17, 55, 136, 203, 295
Intellectual evolution, 10, 21-2, 30-2, 46, 52, 136
Intellectuals, 23, 138, 141, 201-3, 225, 229
Knowledge, growth of, 6, 13-4, 30-3, 54, 175, 201-2, 205, 241, 245-6
Knowledge industries, 202-4, 225, 255
Language, international, 77, 90, 93, 189, 277
Leisure, use of, 35, 90-2, 100, 103, 111, 121, 139, 147-8, 188, 234, 243
Life, length of, 16, 70, 93, 103, 110, 120
Managerial revolution, 63-4, 125-8, 146, 208, 211, 259
Marx, Karl, 31, 58, 61-73, 123, 126, 135, 139-42, 158-9, 173, 210-1
Mechanization, 63, 78, 90-1, 116, 151, 176, 195, 202, 246, 266, 270
Megalopoli, 87, 177, 186-7, 196, 225
Meritocracy, 25, 82, 180, 206, 223, 301
Money, 79, 96, 98, 127, 161, 192, 197, 270, 293, 297
Monopoly, 79, 160, 178-9, 295-6
Natural Resources, 99, 109, 117, 174-5, 194, 203, 214-5, 232, 234, 281
Nuclear bombs, 92, 183, 187, 198, 217, 278
Nuclear power, 108, 116, 147, 172, 187, 194-6, 247, 268
Philosophy, 11, 22, 290-34, 52-3, 107-9, 158, 173, 228, 279
Political evolution, 23, 35, 95-6, 75, 210, 215, 220
Pollution, 147, 178, 193-4, 214, 257, 266, 279
Population, 15, 49, 54, 89, 96, 117, 148, 180, 185, 193, 225, 233, 257, 266, 288
Post-industrial society, 63, 200-1
Professional class, growth of, 78, 88, 192-3, 196, 205

Progress, causes of, 30, 52, 54, 61, 123, 173; idea of, 6, 11, 19, 35, 126; Predictions of, 35, 92; rate of, 173-4, 181, 192-3, 205, 225-6, 234, 239, 255-6
Public ownership, 119, 124, 165-7, 178, 196-7, 213, 300
Rationalization, 136-7, 140, 159, 160, 226
Religion, 13-6, 22-3, 27, 31, 34, 47, 52, 82, 89, 102-3, 111, 154, 175, 184, 189-91, 206, 216, 222, 244, 250-1, 256, 262, 291, 293
Revolution, 37, 43-6, 66, 72-5, 85, 131, 141, 193, 219
Russia, 50, 73, 104, 120, 131, 144-6, 168, 184, 197, 231, 236, 242, 273, 303
Scale of production, 55, 119, 138, 150, 249, 255, 294
Scientific research, 11, 14, 22, 26, 34, 45-6, 106-7, 115, 153-4, 201-2, 206, 224, 228, 236
Servants, 48, 88, 176, 202, 234, 270
Service-industry growth, 64, 70, 88, 201-4, 225, 235, 243
Sex, 89, 97, 151, 154, 293
Social insurance, 17, 36, 43, 69, 81, 117, 136, 154, 167, 169, 197, 207, 293, 295
Social reform, 5-6, 19-21, 56-7, 135-6, 159-60, 207
Socialism, 25, 36, 42-3, 54, 57-8, 64, 67-71, 74-5, 91, 118, 123-6, 132-43, 165-7, 189, 218-9
Space colonies, 116, 233, 274-6, 279-84
Specialization, 26, 35-6, 250, 256, 290, 295
Standard of living, 98, 120, 195, 224, 232, 236, 269
Standardization, 122, 249, 298
Synthetic food, 110, 116, 149, 186
Taxation, 67, 119, 143, 145, 155, 160, 169, 176, 194, 300
Technological progress, 2, 13-5, 24-6, 52, 62, 77, 99, 107-16, 127, 147-55, 172, 185-7, 204-5, 214, 224, 231, 242, 256, 275, 290
Technology, spread of, 13, 24, 26, 52
Television, 77, 83, 115, 178, 197, 291
Transportation, 85-6, 107, 117, 147, 153-4, 186, 196, 271, 298
Trade unions, 36, 65, 119, 139, 150, 162-4, 169, 177
Unemployment, 70, 80, 90, 100, 108, 123, 127, 161, 195, 293
Urbanization, 81-2, 87, 110, 118, 148, 177, 186-7, 196, 225, 239, 250, 273
Wage rates, 45, 55, 64, 70, 100, 127, 160, 162, 176-7, 187, 228, 269, 293
Wars, 44, 54, 72, 92-3, 131, 160, 216-7, 274-9, 286
Welfare state, 43, 53, 69, 118, 159-60, 166-70, 197
Westernization, 23-4, 55, 121-2, 224-6, 236
World government, 18, 82, 93-4, 112, 130, 145, 157, 170, 180-90, 197, 217, 253, 277, 303

ABOUT THE AUTHOR

Born in Carthage, Missouri, in 1904, and raised largely in Pasadena, California, Burnham Putnam Beckwith was graduated from Stanford University with a B.A. in Philosophy in 1926. He spent the next two years at the Harvard Business School, and, after three more years of full-time graduate study, received a Ph.D. in economics from the University of Southern California in 1932. He held a post-doctoral research-training assistantship under Dr. Edward L. Thorndike at Teachers' College, Columbia University, from 1935 to 1937. He also taught economics at the University of Kansas, Queens College (NYC), and the University of Georgia before going to work for the War Production Board (D.C.) in 1941. From 1945 to 1948 he worked for the War Department in France (Biarritz American University) and in Germany (OMGUS, Berlin).

Since 1948 he has been an independant researcher and author, and has published a dozen books, most of which have described coming social trends and reforms. They include <u>The Next 500 Years, Scientific Predictions of Major Social Trends</u> (1967); <u>Government by Experts, The Next Stage in Political Evolution</u> (1972); <u>Liberal Socialism, The Welfare Economics of a Liberal Socialist Economy</u> (1974); <u>Free Goods, The Theory of Free or Communist Distribution</u> (1976); and <u>Radical Essays</u> (1981). He has also published several recent articles in <u>The Futurist</u> and <u>The World Future Society Bulletin</u>.